RETHINKING WOMEN'S COLLABORATIVE WRITING
Power, Difference, Property

Collaborative writing is not a new phenomenon, nor is it specific to a particular genre of writing. In *Rethinking Women's Collaborative Writing*, Lorraine York presents an eminently readable study of the history of collaborative writing and common critical reactions to it. Focusing on women, from Early Modern playwrights and poets to nineteenth-century novelists to contemporary writers and literary critics, York's survey exposes the long-standing prejudice against this form and encourages readings of these works that take into account the personalities of the collaborators and the power dynamics of their authorial relationships.

York explores writing by women in Britain, the United States, Italy, and France, illuminating the tensions in the collaborative process that grow out of important cultural, racial, and sexual differences between the authors. Current scholarship on collaborative writing is growing and *Rethinking Women's Collaborative Writing* presents a strong, thoughtful addition to the literature in the field.

Lorraine York is a professor of English at McMaster University.

D1430017

Lorraine York

RETHINKING WOMEN'S COLLABORATIVE WRITING
Power, Difference, Property

UNIVERSITY OF TORONTO PRESS
Toronto Buffalo London

© University of Toronto Press Incorporated 2002
Toronto Buffalo London
Printed in Canada

ISBN 0–8020–3623–6 (cloth)
ISBN 0–8020–8465–6 (paper)

Printed on acid-free paper

National Library of Canada Cataloguing in Publication Data

York, Lorraine M. (Lorraine Mary), 1958–
Rethinking women's collaborative writing : power, difference,
property

Includes bibliographical references and index.
ISBN 0-8020-3623-6 (bound)   ISBN 0-8020-8465-6 (pbk.)

1. Literature, Modern – Women authors – History and
criticism.   2. Authorship – Collaboration – History.   I. Title

PS8089.5.W6Y67 2002   809'.89287   C2001-903729-5
PR9188.Y67 2002

University of Toronto Press acknowledges the financial assistance to
its publishing program of the Canada Council for the Arts and the
Ontario Arts Council.

This book has been published with the help of a grant from the
Humanities and Social Sciences Federation of Canada, using funds
provided by the Social Sciences and Humanities Research Council
of Canada.

University of Toronto Press acknowledges the financial support for
its publishing activities of the Government of Canada through the
Book Publishing Industry Development Program (BPIDP).

If in this sleep I speak
it's with a voice no longer personal

(I want to say   *with voices*)

Adrienne Rich, *The Dream of a Common Language*

After all, when our lips speak together, as often as not,
they disagree.

Rebecca Pope, in conversation with her collaborator, Susan Leonardi

Contents

ACKNOWLEDGMENTS ix

1 Theorizing Contemporary Women's Collaborative Writing 3

2 'We Have Horrible Disagreements about "Moreovers"': Collaborative Theory and Criticism 38

3 Collaborative Predecessors 62

4 'The High Wire of Self and Other': Prose Collaborations 95

5 Being Alone Together: Collaborative Poetry 119

6 'It ... Shook Up My Easy Theories': Theatrical Collaboration 157

Epilogue 'Giving Each Other the Gears, We Are Still Engaged' 183

WORKS CITED 189
INDEX 199

Acknowledgments

I am fortunate to be surrounded by so many supportive colleagues, family members, and friends. My thanks, first of all, go to my partner Michael Ross, for encouragement, generosity, assistance with Italian translation, and creative (though invariably rejected) title suggestions, all offered with characteristic modesty and wit. I also appreciate your bringing Cora Kaplan's chapter to my attention. To my daughter Anna, thanks for being such a lot of fun to be around.

I am particularly blessed by creative and encouraging colleagues at McMaster University: the current chair of my department, Don Goellnicht, and my former chair, Brian John, have both been enormously supportive of my research. I thank colleague-friends Daniel Coleman and Ron Granofsky for being so good at both collegiality and friendship. Thanks to Joan Coldwell for making me aware of Carey Kaplan's and Ellen Cronan Rose's article on their collaboration when it first appeared in *Signs*. I thank the members of my 1999–2000 graduate seminar on women's collaborative writing. Although I had finished a draft of this book when I first met you, you'll see in my epilogue how much you taught me over the course of the year: Kristin Downey, David Jefferess, Tina Karwalajtys, Janna Nadler, Sonal Nalkur, Tara Nogler, Grace Pollock and Nicole Rosevere. You made Mondays a delight.

On research leave in England in 1994–5, where I did the initial research for and began to write this book, I benefited from the assistance of librarians at the University of London's Senate House

Library and at the British Library. Thank you to George Brandak and staff at the University of British Columbia Special Collections for your generous help. A special thank you to Ms. Traudel Sattler at the Milan Women's Bookstore, who agreed to meet and talk with me when I was in Milan in March 1995. I thank the Social Sciences and Humanities Research Council of Canada for supporting this project in the form of a Standard Research Grant.

Anonymous readers of the manuscript for the University of Toronto made very helpful suggestions from which I benefited, and I thank them for their collegiality. Thanks to Dr Miriam Skey for her careful copy-editing of the manuscript. My editor, Siobhan McMenemy, gave me incredibly detailed feedback on the manuscript and I warmly thank her for that and for all of her support and encouragement throughout this process.

RETHINKING WOMEN'S
COLLABORATIVE WRITING
Power, Difference, Property

1

Theorizing Contemporary Women's Collaborative Writing

Chloe liked Olivia. They shared a laboratory together.

Virginia Woolf, *A Room of One's Own*

Don't you remember the time I tried to hit you with my cowboy boots?

Maria Campbell to her collaborator, Linda Griffiths,
The Book of Jessica

In a 1993 issue of *Signs*, the collaborative literary critics Carey Kaplan and Ellen Cronan Rose wondered, 'Can there be a coherent theory of feminist collaboration?' (559). This book is a response to a reformulated version of Kaplan and Rose's question: 'Can there be a coherent theory of *women's* collaboration?' I have altered their useful question because, throughout *Rethinking Women's Collaborative Writing*, I will maintain that the act of collaborating on texts does not in itself determine a specific or consistent ideological stance, feminist or any other. As Wayne Koestenbaum reflected in *Double Talk* (1989), his book on late nineteenth- and early twentieth-century men's collaborations, 'Collaboration, itself neutral, can mean many things' (3). It is a theoretical point that I intend to take seriously in these pages. Although I am unwilling to postulate an originary, value-neutral act called collaboration – for I will theorize that all collaborations are, in some miniscule measure, challenges to the *status quo* at this particular historical moment in many countries and cultures – I am in agreement with the capacity of that germinally subversive collaboration to 'mean' many things, to augment its initial fund of subversiveness, or to write over it in a reactionary, back-tracking way. Consequently, I will theorize women's collaborations as ideological projects that harbour various ideological potentials, some more hierarchical, some more liberatory and subversive.

As women collaborators frequently point out, there is no one way to collaborate on a piece of art and, I would add, not simply one way to define collaboration. For the methodological purposes of this study, collaboration will mean any overt co-authorship or co-signature of a work of art. Obviously, some genres, like drama, are inherently more collaborative than others. In those cases, I focus on forms of women's collaboration which are more intensely or self-consciously collaborative than the usual division of labour suggested by the designations director, playwright, and actor. My choice to focus on overt co-signature does not stem, as does Koestenbaum's, from the sense that a 'text is most precisely and satisfying collaborative if it is composed by two writers who admit the act by placing both of their names on the title page' (2), though I can sympathize with that response. Still, I hesitate to rank the extensive field of collective artistry in order to identify one form of collaboration as more 'satisfying' (for whom? collaborators? readers? I think Koestenbaum suggests both). Besides, 'admit[ting] the act' is a historically and culturally mediated process that can, itself, take various forms. Two nineteenth-century British collaborators, Katharine Bradley and Edith Cooper, signed themselves 'Michael Field' on their numerous plays and collections of poetry, even though they 'admit[ted] the act' to numerous members of the literary community, because they figured, quite rightly as it turned out, that widespread knowledge of their double authorship would reduce interest in their works. But, of course, this eschewing of a double signature does not make their work any less precisely collaborative, though it does, admittedly, embed certain reading strategies potentially available to a reader of their works who is not privy to the secret.

Although definition is elusive, collaborative writers have struggled to define their art, and the tussle over finding apt metaphors for collective creativity is but one symptom of that struggle. Michael Field relied upon the metaphor of the mosaic to describe their partnership. More recently, women collaborators have mused over an array of other possible metaphors: sibling relationship, erotic bond, mixed salad, stew, operatic duets, and much else besides. But what I take as a cautionary note from this ongoing challenge to define collaborative writing is a valuable reminder that collaborative writing relationships (like all others) are not static, austerely classifiable objects. As the American academic collaborators Anne O'Meara and Nancy R. MacKenzie realized in the process of writing an article for a collection on women's academic collaborations, 'One of our most striking discoveries while attempting to describe our own collaborative research and writing process was that because of its dynamic nature, it tended to defy description' (218). In *Rethinking Women's Collaborative Writing* I will not be seeking to classify or rank collaborations as much as to observe their variable power dynamics and ideological positionings.

A particular comment from Hélène Cixous and Catherine Clément's collaborative 'Exchange' from *The Newly-Born Woman* sums up my own interest in the widely varying dynamics of collaboration, as well as my conviction that difference and disagreement strengthen rather than disable collaboration. Clément lists some of the differences between her 'discursive,' 'rhetorical' discourse and Cixous's theory-fiction, and she concludes: 'We see that there can be two women in the same space who are *differently* engaged, speaking of almost exactly the *same things*, investing in two or three different kinds of discourse and going from one to the other and then on to the spoken exchange' (136, emphasis Cixous and Clément's). Some years later, another collaborative pair, Canadians Daphne Marlatt and Betsy Warland, echo Cixous and Clément's influential text in their own poetic exchange, 'Subject to Change,' and, having weathered and negotiated their own collaborative differences, wryly proclaim: 'Giving each other the gears we are still engaged' (160). Marlatt and Warland invoke the colloquial, idiomatic expression for arguing, 'giving someone the gears,' as well as the metaphor of control suggested by the image of the gears of a car. Of course, giving a recalcitrant car the gears can be a grating, difficult operation, but it enables the car to start. Expressions of difference in these collaborations can be similarly grating and uncomfortable, but they also may allow the collaboration to run, to engage the gears of dialogue and exchange. So without denying or forgetting the very real sustenance and pleasure that collaborating on texts has given literary women, I will nevertheless resist idealizing those relationships as necessarily revolutionary, sisterly, or morally superior.

Although there have been recent movements in this direction of acknowledging difference amidst engagement in women's collective endeavours, for the most part I have found a strong tendency to celebrate women's collaborations unproblematically and idealistically. This tendency is particularly strong in North America, home of influential feminist theories that see women as more other-directed and caring, and thus more given to relational ethics and collaborative problem-solving, like those of Nancy Chodorow and Carol Gilligan. For instance, when Mary Belenky (one of the collective authors of the influential volume *Women's Ways of Knowing*) was asked in an interview why she thought women might be more comfortable with collaborative work arrangements, she immediately reached for 'Chodorow's powerful argument' about child caring being done primarily by women and establishing a relational ethic of caring, concluding that 'it provides a collaborative stance toward the world' (Ashton-Jones and Thomas 90). This maternalist line of reasoning about women's collaboration has proved surprisingly long-lived in a field of study that foregrounds the negotiative and the interactive. In her historical analysis of women's collaborative movements, Melodie Andrews argues that the collaborations of middle-class English women in the nineteenth century were enabled by the 'homosocial worlds of female friendship, which promoted some of the collective identity and gender solidarity imperative for subsequent collaborative endeavours' (19). It was, she emphasizes, an 'affirmative sense of community that nurtured feminist collaboration in the nineteenth and early twentieth centuries' (25). This idealistic brand of social history has filtered into analyses of women's literary and critical collaborations, particularly in America. As Mary Alm comments about academic women collaborative authors, 'Intimate collaborations do provide a "safe place" for thinking' (131), and she celebrates the synergistic 'formation of a collaborative mind and a collaborative voice' (132). If collaboration is a safe place of fusion, of affirmative union, and monovocality, then what has this theory to do with the notion of difference?

As I have suggested, there are collaborative writers and critics who are already starting to question this fusion theory of collaboration. However, many of those more sceptical voices still retain some degree of attachment to a celebratory, idealistic theory of women's collective acts. I emphasize, by contrast, the difficult negotiations of space (both of the page and of geographical spaces) in literary collaborations. In close connection with this idea, I also survey the persistence of the property ethic in collaborations that, according to fusion theory, effectively abolish questions of individual property. Like their Romantic predecessors, collaborators are relentlessly haunted by the question of property, the question that haunts Daphne Marlatt and Betsy Warland's collaboration *Two Women in a Birth* so forcefully that they figure it as an 'axe-split in the poem': 'where's mine?' (156, 159).

If women collaborators continue to be haunted by the question of property as they compose, then their works are even more strongly assailed by property questions once they enter into the marketplace. Critics and other readers feel a persistent need to 'de-collaborate' these works, to parse the collective text into the separate contributions of two or more individual authors. Often this desire is puzzling to collaborators of various historical periods; in spite of their own often unacknowledged property anxieties, they are frequently hard-put to imagine how their collective art could ever be surgically divided into 'mine' and 'hers.' As collaborative novelists, Joyce Elbrecht and Lydia Fakundiny voice what is a commonplace among collaborative writers,

After every sentence either of us wrote originally had been either deleted or reworked dozens of times by each of us (and, more rarely, both of us in concert), we lost all sense of who said what, when, and where – partly because which of us said it first became irrelevant once the 'it' became so transformed in the play of revision that it reflected back to us the unmistakable image of both of us working together. (256)

Rather than try to establish that this image of 'us working together' is denied or destroyed by the presence of property anxieties, I argue that collaborative work is, indeed, not easily divisible or parsable into its constituent parts. On the other hand, I do not use this metamorphic view of collaborative textuality as some sort of proof that women's collaborations dissipate or resist property desires altogether. Rather, the two conditions coexist, complexly, in women's collaborations, and so in theorizing them, I wish to deny neither the engagement nor the difference that are at work in women collaborators who are truly, in my view, differently engaged.

My area of concentration will be contemporary because poststructuralist reconfigurings of the author after 1968, after Barthes's 'The Death of the Author,' brought renewed theoretical and creative investigation into authorship as it was constructed in modernity. My methodological purpose is not to trace 'influences' as such of poststructuralist thinking on specific collaborative texts. Instead, the considerable currency of poststructuralist reformulations of authorship in artistic and academic circles – whether through the reading of theorists like Barthes, Derrida, and Foucault or through the admittedly often reductive trickle-down effect of phrases like 'the death of the author' – has provided me with a historical moment particularly conducive to experimentation with modes of authorship. In order to provide some historical context for this analysis, and to correct the frequent assumption that collaborative authorship or any author formation other than that of the single author has been a late twentieth-century poststructuralist or postmodern invention, I preface my study of contemporary women's collaborative prose, poetry, and drama with a chapter that treats the history of women's collaborative writing, with a special emphasis on the nineteenth century – a time when yet another watershed in authorship experimentation coincided with a higher level of opportunity and access for women writers.

Although my own theoretical approach to women's collaboration stresses the multiplicity of meanings that may attach themselves to collaboration, I recognize that the tendency to idealize women's collaboration has been an understandable reaction against the modern tendency to figure collaboration as monstrously subversive. In a way, the more contemporary idealizers have just taken the former terms of abuse for collaborative writing and have embraced them as positive strengths: the deplorably subversive has become the admirably subversive. To trace this process, it is useful to glance back at a modern fictional *locus classicus* of this association of collaboration with subversiveness: Henry James's 'Collaboration' (1893). In this story a Bavarian composer and a Parisian poet decide, against the wishes of virtually everyone except the narrator, to embark on an opera together. As E. Duncan Aswell notes in an article on 'James's Treatment of Artistic Collaboration,' this was just one of several stories that James wrote around 1881–2 that explored the prospect of artistic partnership, probably because James, at the time, was trying to attain success in the London theatrical world and may have even considered collaborating with a playwright. In 'Collaboration,' James plays on the other sense of 'collaboration,' of treasonable cooperation with an enemy, in order to examine and critique the boundaries constructed to keep artists and nationalities hermetically sealed and, consequently, mutually misunderstood and suspect. But as Aswell argues, despite this story's determined desire to be sympathetic to joint artistic endeavours, it betrays numerous anxieties and ambiguities about the nature and desirability of collaboration. Aswell concludes that because it was so 'difficult for James to idealize artistic unions,' 'his ironical treatments of artistic collaborations' (in works like 'Greville Fane' and 'The Real Thing') are much more convincing and dramatically powerful (186) and that 'James could never have viewed collaboration as a feasible or *healthy* artistic possibility' (181, emphasis mine).

This anxiety about the healthiness of collaboration holds the key to the dramatic shift I have mentioned, from deploring collaboration as degeneratively subversive to heralding it as revolutionary in its subversiveness. James's tale, I believe, is the site of hidden anxiety about homosexual collaboration, in a manner that is quite in keeping with Wayne Koestenbaum's study of male collaboration as an 'anxiously homosocial act' (3). James's men collaborate in a genre that Koestenbaum identifies as a 'touchstone of contemporary [i.e., fin-de-siècle] homosexual culture' (10) – opera. In so doing, they remove themselves from the women in the story who are the most virulently critical of their collaboration, ostensibly for its cross-national flavour. (As the narrator observes, the two men's collaboration 'represented for them abysses of shame and suffering' [428]; the matriarch of the story, Mme de Brindes, denounces it as 'a horror' [427].) Critics who have anxiously parsed or deplored women's collaborations may be homophobically reacting, like James's Mme de Brindes, against a form of textuality that they implicitly (or, sometimes, explicitly) figure as homosexual.

That women collaborators have been led to idealize their shared art can hardly be surprising, in the face of so much suspicion and, at times, open hostility. As Virginia Woolf argues in an anecdote from *A Room of One's Own* that is a gendered reversal of James's story, one woman joined to another in work and affection is another collaboration whose apparent novelty and subversiveness may inspire 'abysses of shame and suffering' among their contemporaries:

'Chloe liked Olivia' ... Do not start. Do not blush. Let us admit in the privacy of our own society that these things sometimes happen. Sometimes women do like women ... Now if Chloe likes Olivia and they share a laboratory, which of itself will make their friendship more varied and lasting because it will be less personal ... if Chloe likes Olivia and Mary Carmichael [the novelist] knows how to express it she will light a torch in that vast chamber where nobody has yet been. (126)

The unhealthy, shameful collaborative relationship has become, in reaction, an idealized lighting of torches. Many women collaborators have followed Woolf's tempting lead, characterizing their partnerships as founded in friendship, even though Woolf herself was characteristically somewhat divided on this subject of female friendship, here as elsewhere in her *oeuvre*, both hailing the closeness of Chloe and Olivia's 'liking' and cautioning that shared work will make a friendship 'less personal' and therefore stronger.

This power of artistic collaboration to reveal and unseat or reinscribe deeply held notions of the strange, queer, and natural produces conflicted responses in twentieth-century observers. In some cultural critics, the reaction is to put collaboration in its place, to relegate it to the margins of real authorship even though, as many theorists of authorship will attest, the single-author paradigm has been, historically, but one of many. Criticism of Early Modern textuality is a fascinating case in point. Mid-twentieth-century critics, like Samuel Schoenbaum, recognized the evidence of collaborative Elizabethan dramaturgy, but wished to harmonize it with prevailing assumptions about Early Modern authorship. In 'A Note on Dramatic Collaboration' in his 1966 book, *Internal Evidence and Elizabethan Dramatic Authorship*, Schoenbaum argues that there is a need for greater investigation of collaborative dramaturgy in the period, but he warns critics that 'while recognizing joint-authorship as a fact of Elizabethan theatrical life, we must guard against exaggerating its importance; many dramatists preferred to work singly as much as possible and increasingly they had the opportunity to do so (225).' This warning against exaggerating the importance of collaboration is oddly situated in this appendix, wedged between Schoenbaum's own observation that 'all the major dramatists' of the period collaborated (224) and his closing call for an entire book on the subject (226). Later in the century, Early Modern scholars, most notably Jeffrey Masten, would answer this call, producing, in his case, full-length studies of Renaissance collaboration, but the legacy of suspicion and caution regarding collaboration in 'the age of Shakespeare' would persist.

As Masten himself has argued, even by the middle of the seventeenth century literary collaboration became increasingly figured as 'odd.' By 1647, he notes, the collaboration of Francis Beaumont and John Fletcher was seen as a 'strange Production,' and 'by midcentury,' he concludes, 'They have become a distinctively odd couple' in the world of Early Modern theatre ('My Two

Dads' 282). So the characterization of types of textual production as odd or normal was extremely mutable and sensitive to historical and cultural change. Poet and critic Kenneth Koch makes the same point in his concluding note on the special 'Collaborations' issue of *Locus Solus*, the journal he co-edited with John Ashbery, Harry Mathews, and James Schuyler (1961), arguing that the effect of 'estrangement' that collaborative writing supposedly creates is a culturally and historically produced phenomenon: 'The act of collaborating on a literary work … jars the mind into strange new positions,' he begins, and he goes on to suggest that many artists, especially the surrealists believed that this strangeness would lead them 'to the unknown' (193), but Koch then reminds his (Western) readers that 'Japanese poets wrote together as naturally as Shelley wrote alone' (193).

Some readers were reluctant to grant such a fluid relation between normal and odd textuality when it came to collaborative authorship because they tended to view collaboration as an impure or contaminated form – an assumption shared by many textual critics and editors since the nineteenth century. As Charles H. Frey writes of Shakespeare, he 'is often treated as if he risked severely tainting his own labor by joining it to another's' (31). Schoenbaum refers to collaborations, lumped along with revisions after the fact, as 'categories of mixed writing' (224). Collaboration is clearly a textual miscegenation of a sort, and, standing above it is an assumed category of pure (individualized) writing. Accordingly, Schoenbaum argues that one aim of authorship assignment study is 'to establish the shares of the several authors in collaborations where some at least of the participants are known, as in the voluminous Beaumont and Fletcher corpus' (xv). So the textual critic sorts out the threads of the textual miscegenation, dividing the pure work of known (i.e., major) authors from that of the non-canonized rabble.

Those who feel particularly threatened by collaborative writing are, not surprisingly, the professed forgers of a stable canon. This explains why, in David Herd's words, 'almost without exception, critics treating collaboration take a swipe at [Harold] Bloom' (44). Canon-defenders like Bloom and other critics who inherit this tradition tend to characterize collaboration as 'weakness' as opposed to Bloomian strong (male) -poet *agon*. This is, of course, a further elaboration of the view of collaborative writing as dilution or miscegenation, and I would also link it to heterosexist figurings of male collaboration as queerly feminized. Bloom, speaking in New York to launch *The Western Canon* (1994), expressed great disdain for the 'sentimental' and 'absurd' 'feminist idea of women novelists as communal quiltmakers, taking in each other's seams' (Morrison 6). In fact, collaboration, whether by women or men, has often been figured as female passivity, sentimentality, and weakness. Jeffrey Masten detects this association of 'textual sharing with effeminacy' ('My Two Dads' 293) as early as the mid-seventeenth century, and Early Modern scholars of our own time seem to have inherited this tendency. Schoenbaum, for instance, implicitly figures dramatic collaboration thus when he observes that 'all the major dramatists of the period – if we accept Shakespeare's share in the revised *More* – wrote in collaboration at one time or another. Even the magnificently independent Jonson.' (224–5). Duncan Aswell, concluding his article on Henry James's view of collaboration, makes the same manly claim for his single author: 'He represented the creative artist throughout the rest of his career as a man resolutely self-reliant, certain of his goals and of his powers for achieving them, with no need of partners to complete his appointed work' (185). The Emersonian rhetoric tells the tale: for Aswell, James, like his artist-figures, was clearly no collaborative wimp. For that matter, some critics regard that most famous of literary partnerships, that of Wordsworth and Coleridge, as a similar union of the canonically strong and weak. Philip Sicker, for instance, in a markedly Bloomian article comparing the *Lyrical Ballads* with Nabokov's apparent portrait of his relationship with Edmund Wilson in *Pale Fire*, dramatizes the Wordsworth–Coleridge collaboration as a matter of a 'needy collaborator' (Coleridge) seeking 'self-validation through affiliation with a stronger artist' whom he characterizes as (to use Schoenbaum's words) 'magnificently independent' – and very male. Quoting Coleridge's description of Wordworth as one who 'of all the men I ever knew ... has the least femininity in his mind. He is all male,' Sicker concludes that Coleridge, like Nabokov's Kinbote, reveals a 'sexual insecurity and erotic attraction to a potently creative masculine ideal' (316). Coleridge becomes, in this view, the weak, feminized, unhealthily queer collaborator. Sicker even proposes this kind of analysis as a 'basis for defining essential collaborative difference' (316). Such persistent critical desire to find the real, strong, or gifted partner in a collaboration is born of the implicit denial of collaborative textuality. It is as though, in every collaborative writing relationship, critics who adhere to a normative single-author paradigm must somehow undertake an archaeological dig to unearth the single author from the rubble of miscegenated, monstrous, messy collaboration.

Uncomprehending critical reception is only one of the deterrents experienced by practitioners of collaborative art. For professional artists, there is the constant jeopardy of crucial government-sponsored grants. For theatrical collectives and performance artists, especially, pursuing collaborative authorship can mean courting financial ruin because of the prevalence of the single-author norm even in this most historically collective of art forms. The market exerts its power by insisting on a single, preferably recognizable, authorial name. George Landow, connecting the rise of print media and 'notions of intellectual property,' cites the example of Nancy Mitford's collaboration with her husband on *The High Cost of Death*: 'Only her name appears because the publisher urged that multiple authors would cut sales' (93). A publisher similarly urged Vladimir Nabokov and Edmund Wilson to publish their study of Russian literature under Wilson's then more recognizable name (Sicker 206). Although academic publishing appears to be more receptive of multiply authored titles, particularly in the sciences and social-sciences, co-authors of critical and theoretical works in the humanities have been subjected to negative treatment in university promotion and tenure processes. Doubtless, one reason for the low marketability of multiply authored works is the male, agonistic model of the artist outlined above, but another subliminal factor may well be the association of multiply authored works with a type of grass-roots political activism that many publishers might wish to avoid seeming to take seriously: the collective writing of pamphlets and manifestos. As Richard M. Coe has observed, 'The real social tendency is toward collective writing. This is especially true of progressive writings. A union leaflet is rarely the work of one person ... On the left, political writers often go out of their way to work collectively' (quoted in Ede and Lunsford n.p.). Of course, any such attempt to equate political ideology and collective writing practice is both theoretically problematic and empirically disprovable, but the association that Coe makes arguably functions within the ideological discourses of publishing, government granting bodies, and academia.

As I have suggested, in the light of such resistance, female collaborators have often and understandably been led to idealize and fetishize their shared art. But as this study will show, some women collaborators have found it necessary to perform a collective authorship (and a female community) that goes beyond Woolf's 'Chloe likes Olivia' idealization of female bonding in co-creation. Their texts, no matter how couched in idealistic terms, may also enact the possibility that Chloe disagrees with Olivia and can do so without reducing the artistic laboratory to acrimonious chaos and rubble.

Until the last few years, women's collaborative authorship has been as 'vast' an unlit 'chamber' as Virginia Woolf imagined for her Chloe and Olivia. Until the 1990s, works on collaboration in general (themselves few) tended to downplay the subject. The 1961 special issue of *Locus Solus* on collaborations that, as I have mentioned, has been hailed as the first anthology of collaboration, effectively silences women's collaborative art. It includes Japanese collaborative poetry in translation, verse letters by Donne and Goodyere, a selection from Coleridge and Southey's 'Joan of Arc,' and Eluard and Peret's 'Surrealist Proverbs,' but the only woman to be found in the special issue is Charlotte Kraus, and she is not even technically collaborating with another poet, let alone with another woman. For mysterious reasons, the (four male) editors include her poem 'News,' which wittily considers how poems by Marvell or Keats would sound as relayed by news reporters. Judging from the representations of collaborations in *Locus Solus*, it would seem that women do not really collaborate or, if they do, it is only in the sense of an ultimately respectful collaboration with strong, male predecessors. Even scholars who introduce texts co-created by women do not necessarily highlight their mode of collective production and its implications. Sandra M. Gilbert, for instance, introducing the English translation of Hélène Cixous and Catherine Clément's *La Jeune Née* (*The Newly-Born Woman*) (1986), refers briefly to 'this extended collaborative meditation' (x). This inevitable critical subordination of some aspects of the text might seem unsurprising, given Gilbert's considerable task, to situate Cixous and Clément – and French feminism – for an English-speaking readership, but it does seem odd, in the light of Gilbert's own position as a member of an equally renowned American team of feminist critical collaborators. Teresa de Lauretis has a similarly daunting task of locating the Milan Women's Bookstore Collective's text, translated into English as *Sexual Difference: A Theory of Social-Symbolic Practice* (1990), in the context of Italian feminism, a subject arguably less familiar to English readers than the more widely circulated French theories. She, too, foregrounds that necessary task and relegates to an endnote a brief mention of the practice of collaborative writing in Italy, 'no longer followed as strictly as it was in the 70s except by long-standing groups such as the Milan Libreria delle Donne' (Preface 20). The off-the-cuff comments have the effect of once again defamiliarizing collaboration, rendering it strange, abnormal.

When Wayne Koestenbaum set out, in the mid-1980s, to write his study of male collaboration from 1885 to 1922, he 'found no discussion of a group of doubly authored texts' (8). His own absorbing work on the erotics of male collaborations of the period is gender-specific, as is the work of Jeffrey Masten on Early Modern theatrical collaboration and David Herd's research on collaboration in the New York School poets; Koestenbaum argues that the collaborative work becomes psychoanalytically figured as the 'child' of the men's relationships. As several women collaborators, such as Susan Leonardi and Rebecca Pope, remark, such a thesis, while fascinating on its own terms, does not help them to account for the dynamics of female collaboration. As Leonardi and Pope point out, the corresponding theory would be one of collaborative maternalism, one that, as feminists and lesbians, they are unwilling to embrace. Nevertheless, in the last pages of his study, Koestenbaum does include a short section on women's collaborations of the period (Somerville and Ross, Michael Field, E.D. Gerrard, etc.), in which he describes women's collaboration as a similarly eroticized fin-de-siècle sanctuary for socially demonized homosexual desires and for anti-patriarchal resistance. Although his analysis is understandably brief and, as Pope and Leonardi argue, non-transferable in any simplistic way to women's collaborative acts, his notion of collaboration as an eroticized space has proven suggestive to me, as my discussion of several texts here will reveal. Still, Koestenbaum admits at the end of his book, 'I have, throughout this study, portrayed male sexuality as if it were an unambiguous, Arcadian balm' (177), and any corresponding notion of women's collaborative spaces as a feminized Eden is one that I want to avoid in *Rethinking Women's Collaborative Writing*.

Once collaboration became the object of greater scrutiny in the early 1990s, the male–female collaborative relationship tended to attract most attention, particularly those cases where a man received credit for what was, in actuality, a joint production and a silencing of women's creative labour. This tends to be true of Whitney Chadwick and Isabelle de Courtivron's collection of essays, *Significant Others: Creativity and Intimate Partnership* (1993). Male collaborators still tended to dominate an important book that appeared in 1990, Lisa Ede and Andrea Lunsford's (self-consciously) co-authored study of *Singular Texts / Plural Authors*. It focuses on a survey of collaborative work in the business world and on collaboration as a potentially valuable pedagogical practice in composition programs. As Ede and Lunsford acknowledge, most of the writing groups in the business world whom they surveyed were male. Still, they devote a few pages to the gender implications of collaborative writing (132–5) and they also analyse their own writing partnership. In their description of gendered collaboration, they invoke Bakhtin to formulate a 'dialogic' form of collaboration, one that would revise the effectively monologic, hierarchical style of collaboration that they find so widespread in business and the sciences. As with all gendered oppositions, it has its essentializing and fetishizing dangers, for Ede and Lunsford comment that because most of their study participants who talked about the more 'loosely structured' process-oriented dialogic collaboration happened to be women, and 'because it seemed so clearly "other," we think of this mode as predominantly female' (133). We seem to be back in an Edenic world where women, by definition, necessarily and essentially critique forms of power characterized as male. Writings on women's collaborations in North America will continue to feel the effects of this line of analysis for some time.

The 1990s saw greater attention being directed to women's collaborations, as Holly Laird notes in introducing a major contribution to this inquiry, the *Tulsa Studies in Women's Literature*'s special issues on collaborations: 'Around 1991 scholars in literary studies began to turn their attention to the question of collaboration in feminist scholarship and women's literature' (235). These two special issues (1994, 1995), along with Elizabeth G. Peck and JoAnna Stephens Mink's collection of essays *Common Ground: Feminist Collaboration in the Academy* (1998), helped to restore the balance. Some of the theorizings contained in these works are worth noting here, not least because they dramatize, to my mind, the persistent attraction of idealizations of women's collective work and a nascent distrust of such fusion theories. To begin, the very question of whether there is anything inherently female about women's collaborations, or whether there is a tradition of women working collaboratively is up for discussion in several of these articles. According to Peck and Mink, it was the first question that arose in their minds when they set about organizing their volume (1). On the whole, American theorists working on women's collaborations have tended to answer that question in the affirmative; in Peck and Mink's volume, for example, Carol J. Singley and Susan Elizabeth Sweeney maintain that the sort of intellectual, academic collaboration that they have engaged in over their careers is 'particularly feminist' (63), and they see themselves as taking part in an American feminist tradition of collective scholarship that reaches back to Susan B. Anthony and Elizabeth Cady Stanton. Stacey Schlau and Electa Arenal, writing in the second special issue of *Tulsa Studies*, agree: 'We situate ourselves, then, in a female tradition of collaboration' (47). Given the thoroughgoing critique of untheorized concepts of women's traditions in recent years, this claim for women's collaboration seems strangely outdated. Helen Cafferty and Jeanette Clausen, writing in the Peck and Mink volume, are a bit more hesitant to make this kind of claim, probably because they are aware of these critiques. They duly note that 'every collaboration, feminist or not, is uniquely shaped by the personal views and experiences of the participants,' but they feel drawn, nevertheless, to offer a taxonomy of sorts, to 'identify a range of qualities that characterize feminist collaboration' (81).

Other recent theorists and critics of women's collaborations have made similar attempts, and what is revealing about their work is the way in which a number of idealistic assumptions about women's collective work persist into the 1990s. Another collaborative pair of critics, Paula D. Nesbitt and Linda E. Thomas, base their theory of collaboration on a notion of 'authentic collaboration,' a collective working arrangement that is 'naturally egalitarian rather than mediated by vigilant awareness of status difference' (32). That is, they do not regard scholarship that maintains the dominance of a senior academic as authentically collaborative; neither does research that pays lip service to various perspectives without actually incorporating multiple voices qualify for collaborative authenticity. So on the academic level differences are to be levelled out, but in the same article, Nesbitt and Thomas characterize differences as feeding into the constructed egalitarianism that they propose for true collaborative relationships: 'Academic common ground is mutually negotiated and differences valued as a creative opportunity to explore shared human reality' (34). 'Common ground' – the phrase that, tellingly, serves as the title for the Peck and Mink volume in which Nesbitt and Thomas's article appears – is still the horizon, and difference is valued as a means of proving or establishing harmony. My own study will propose that collaborative difference may also form the basis of exploring the no-less-compelling condition of unshared human reality. True, Nesbitt and Thomas do acknowledge that what they erect as authentic collaboration is impossible, a horizon to work toward (for example, they cite the necessary listing of one of their names first in their own collaborative publications). In that case, it seems somewhat beside the point to construct a theory that does not correspond to a lived material experience of women's collaborations, however much one would like to construct ideals. In addition, that ideal is based upon a now widely questioned notion of what is natural to women; Nesbitt and Thomas cite Nikki Giovanni's lines to the effect that this type of collaboration is 'woman doing what a woman / does when she's natural' (32). Collaborative textuality plays havoc with conceptions of the natural and the normal, so to use the yardstick of women's nature to define it seems theoretically problematic.

At first glance, it would seem that the theories of Carol J. Singley and Susan Elizabeth Sweeney, also writing in the Peck and Mink volume, would provide a different reading of women's collaboration. In their article, 'In League with Each Other: The Theory and Practice of Feminist Collaboration,' they theorize that women's collaborations are characterized by a deep 'ambivalence about affiliation with another' (64) that they term 'anxious power' (66) – anxious because women's traditional affiliation in many societies has been through men. They also note that the 'tension between cooperation and competition is an important feminist issue that has yet to be fully addressed' (64). This kind of theorizing would seem to mark a departure from the natural egalitarianism and maternalist sociology of the previous work on women's collaborative relations, but the attraction of essentialist assumptions about women's nature persists in their work. Drawing on theorists like Chodorow and Gilligan, they construct an argument about women's affiliation being 'usually based on affiliation with others' (69), and so they are able to proclaim of their own working relationship (and other women's collaborations by extension), that it is a 'logical and productive solution to women's anxiety about authorship'(69), a sort of panacea for the Gilbert and Gubar *Madwoman in the Attic* theory of women's ambivalent relations to the 'pen.'

In recent years, the treatment of women's collaboration that has come closest to critiquing the idealism that I have seen at work in other theories is the conversation between Susan J. Leonardi and Rebecca A. Pope that I discuss in further depth in the next chapter. They seem very aware of the dominant ways of speaking about women's collective work and somewhat uneasy about them. As they note of the oft-cited conversational nature of women's collaborations, 'One of the problems with the conversation model is that conversation and dialogue, at least as they are practiced by "good girls," seem so often repressed by social convention. One shies away from serious disagreement ...'(267). Accordingly, they are explicitly critical of the fusion theory of women's relations: 'What I'm worried about is not that we will lose ourselves in some sort of psychic fusion, but that others might offer that fantasy as a model of women's collaboration as it's been offered as a model for lesbianism' (268). As my short stroll through theorizings of women's collaboration has shown, the danger that Leonardi and Pope place in the future has already come to pass; the fusion model or variations thereof has dominated the field, at least in North America. When Leonardi and Pope set about to describe what does characterize their own collaboration, they formulate a complex relation that comes closest to describing my own understanding of women collaborators being differently engaged: 'Our minds and interests come together when we write together. Your thoughts transform mine and vice versa, but we don't lose ourselves in the negotiations' (268).

My own approach to women's collaboration also differs from a number of previous treatments of the subject because of my focus on overt signature. Other covert forms of collective writing have been more plentifully discussed by critics under the generic banner of collaborative art. For example, there is what I would call implied collaboration, or what Elbrecht and Fakundiny call 'silent collaboration' (252), a variety of which is amply discussed by Jack Stillinger in his book *Multiple Authorship and the Myth of Solitary Genius* (1991): '*The joint, or composite, or collaborative production*

of literary works that we usually think of as written by a single author
(i, emphasis Stillinger's). That is, Stillinger is particularly interested in the ways in which interventions of editors or friends,
agents, and publishers in the writing or publication of a text make
a work that goes under the signature of a single author more
collaborative and social in nature than the published title pages ·
suggest. Stillinger's purpose is to provide a kind of rear-guard
action against the so-called 'death of the author' theorists, and
here he lumps together, in a cursory and problematic way, the
agendas of Roland Barthes and Michel Foucault because he feels
that '[r]eal multiple authors are more difficult to banish than
mythical single ones, and they are ... given the theological model,
more difficult to apotheosize or deify as an ideal for validity in
interpretation or textual purity' (24). The reasoning here is ques-
tionable, since Stillinger wants to reinstate the kinds of reading
strategies that actually form the object of critiques like those of
Barthes and Foucault: that is, the location of textual authority in a
notion of an author, whether that author is conceived of as single
or multiple. As Stillinger explains, he wishes to rescue 'the rel-
evance of the author in the interpretation, presentation, and evalu-
ation of a literary work' without having recourse to what he calls
the 'opposite extreme' of belief in authorial intention as an objective criterion of interpretation in the theories of E.D. Hirsch, Jr,
and P.D. Juhl (i). But how the mere fact of multiplicity would
make authorship somehow more resistant to poststructuralist critique remains somewhat mysterious. Stillinger's readings of textual intervention in Keats, Mill, Wordsworth, Coleridge, Eliot,
and others that form the bulk of the study could find their place
without too much difficulty amid fairly standard textual studies,
so the notion of authorship in itself is not radically altered thereby.
Stillinger basically wants to ensure that textual studies of editorial
intervention of various sorts need not be tossed out, like the
proverbial baby, with the tide of anti-authorial bathwater being
flung by poststructuralism.

   In spite of these methodological and theoretical flaws, Stillinger's
study is still valuable as a querying of single authorship as a
normative social and historical practice. As he suggests at one

point in his study, his notion of multiple authorship would prove congenial to the 'ongoing efforts of new and old historicists alike to connect literary works with the social, cultural, and material conditions in which they were produced' (183). Indeed, materialist theory has already conceptualized another form of implied collaboration that is valuable to my own study: a 'socialized ... authorship,' to quote Jerome McGann (8). Acknowledging textual intervention of the type that Stillinger studies as one example of a collective production of text, McGann takes the inquiry one step further: 'But the collaboration of the author with the institutions of publishing is an activity which cannot be adequately understood if we focus merely on the textual evidence of such cooperative processes. Because literary works are fundamentally social rather than personal or psychological products, they do not even acquire an artistic form of being until their engagement with an audience has been determined' (43–4). As a result, McGann calls for a materialist criticism of texts that would examine not only how many cooks are intervening in the textual broth, but also the 'conventions and enabling limits that are accepted by the prevailing institutions of literary production – conventions and limits which exist for the purpose of generating and supporting literary production' (48).

That said, however, McGann and Raymond Williams before him, who formulated a socialized authorship in *Marxism and Literature* (1977), tend to marginalize overt collaboration in their discussions, probably because they feel the imperative to go beyond the 'textual evidence,' and because textual study is, for them, so closely tied to underlying bourgeois assumptions of authorial individuality. But such a move clearly dehistoricizes overt collaborative authorship. McGann, for instance, touches on instances of overt multiple authorship in *A Critique of Modern Textual Criticism* (1983) when he refers to John Ashbery and James Schuyler's novel *A Nest of Ninnies*, but he quickly categorizes them as theoretically simplistic, even, implicitly, rather wacky: 'Examples like these highlight the problem of the nature of the critical concept of literary authority, but other sorts of case[s] are more useful for expressing the issues at more practical levels' (86). Williams makes a stronger statement about the relationship between overt collaboration and an implicit, socialized authorship, for he sees the former as an intellectual proving ground for the latter:

There is the relatively simple case of cultural creation by two or more individuals who are in active relations with each other, and whose work cannot be reduced to the mere sum of their separate individual contributions. This is so common in cultural history, in cases where it is clear that something new happens in the very process of conscious co-operation, that it does not seem to present any serious difficulties. But it is from just this realization of a relatively well-known experience that the second and more difficult sense of a collective subject is developed. This goes beyond conscious co-operation – collaboration – to effective social relations in which, even while individual projects are being pursued, what is being drawn on is trans-individual ... (195)

Williams's grasp of collaborative processes is impressive; would that many critics of overtly collaborative works took to heart his warning against reductive contribution-parsing. Still, Williams reproduces the same hierarchical division between the 'simple' example of overt collaboration and the 'more difficult' realization of socially collective authorship. More importantly, he tends to dehistoricize the more overt form of collaboration by characterizing socialized authorship as that which 'goes beyond' it and is 'trans-individual.' Yet, by his own characterization, so is overt collaboration between two or more individuals. Of course, what is needed is a materialist, historicist, theory of authorship that can grant to overt forms of collaboration the fluid, exchange-based historical and ideological processes that materialists have perceived at work elsewhere. That renewed social theory of collaboration is enabled by the work of Michel Foucault.

A thoroughly historicized treatment of collaborative art would also render the very distinction I have made here, between overt and covert forms of collaboration, fluid and mutable. For example, the development of hypertext or electronic textual systems at our own historical moment makes any such distinction problematic, at least within the discourse systems of hypertext. As George Landow argues in *Hypertext: The Convergence of Contemporary Critical Theory and Technology* (1992), 'Radical changes in textuality produce radical changes in the author figure derived from that textuality' (74).

Hypertext meshes overt and covert forms of collaborative creativity; as Landow phrases it, 'Within a hypertext environment all writing becomes collaborative, doubly so' (88), since a reader may co-create with an author by altering or responding to documents on the information highway and, especially, since writers compose in the 'presence of all writers "on the system"' (88), in a sort of technologically enforced intertextuality. In fact, the socialized authorship that materialist critics like McGann theorize finds an explicit model in hypertext for, as rhetoric instructor Carol Winkelman writes, 'Teachers and researchers are beginning to fathom how extensively our pedagogy must change as computers reaffirm our concepts of writing as social activity' (433). A materialist critic might question just how radical this electronic form of textuality is; doesn't hypertext merely draw attention to the social quality of text in general? I suspect that this is so, but the main significance of hypertext for my own project is its reminder that even co-signature, the feature of overt collaborative authorship that I have singled out as definitive for this study, is as mutable and historically situated as any other feature of writing. In *Rethinking Women's Collaborative Writing*, however, it is the arbitrarily chosen ground against which I discern other fluid and variable power relations in artistic collaboration.

More so than materialism, poststructuralism is the twentieth-century theoretical movement that has been most closely associated with rethinking the concept of authorship. Still, relating collaboration to poststructuralist theory has too often been a matter of theoretical extremes. Critics or writers either assume that collaborative textuality proves the clichéd 'death of the author,' or else they assume, as David Herd does in his study of collaboration and the avant-garde, that the 'poststructuralist idiom is ... fundamentally inappropriate to the collaborative situation' because 'in collaboration individuals do not disappear, they encounter one another' (45). Both extremes find their basis in very narrow and selective readings of poststructuralist theory. I maintain, on the other hand, that artistic collaboration, whether it predates or postdates Roland Barthes's 'The Death of the Author' (1968), Michel Foucault's 'What Is an Author?' (1969), or Jacques Derrida's *Of Grammatology* (1976), clearly belongs to the history of debates about authorship that, of course, did not originate with those theoretical texts. Poststructualist refigurings of those debates have, admittedly, created a discourse and a range of questions about authorship that have intensified intellectual investigations into the nature and functions of authorship. However, collaborative authorship does not act as a simple corollary to these widely varying poststructural theories of authorship. The signature of two or more authors does not, that is, signal the dispersal or 'death' of the author in any broad or simplistic sense. As Michel Foucault reminds us, at any rate, the author does not 'die' in the sense of 'dissipate'; instead, 'We should reexamine the empty space left by the author's disappearance; we should attentively observe, along its gaps and fault lines, its new demarcations, and the reapportionment of this void; we should await the fluid functions released by this disappearance' (121). I do not assume that artistic collaboration overthrows any totalized notion of the author. Instead, I argue that it enables the 'attentive' observation of 'new demarcations' of author functions, demarcations which are, as I have suggested, participants in a wide range of potential ideological discourses.

First, I need to be more precise about those issues involved in poststructuralist retheorizings of the author which prove most pertinent to my own theorizing of contemporary women's collaborative art. Many contemporary women collaborators see their work as a response to a particular construction (or constructions) of authorship, and so to argue, as Sean Burke has done, that this author construction 'never really existed in the first place,' that it is 'a metaphysical abstraction, a Platonic type, a fiction of the absolute' (*Death and Return* 27), may be quite true but slightly beside the point. Abstractions, types, and fictions are perceived to exist, and that is precisely the point; they take part in the signifying systems of a culture. Indeed, Foucault agrees that 'these aspects of an individual, which we designate as an author ... are projections, in terms always more or less psychological, of our ways of handling texts' (127).

A perfect illustration of Foucault's point is the projection of a unified, isolated author by the institutionalized discourse of textual criticism, its 'ways of handling texts.' Jerome McGann, who has described this construction at length, argues that standard bibliographical and editing practices rely on 'ideas about the nature of literary production and textual authority which so emphasize the autonomy of the isolated author as to distort our theoretical grasp of the "mode of existence of a literary work of art"' (8). This emphasis is, in McGann's view, so intense that he calls it a 'hypnotic fascination with the isolated author' (122). Jack Stillinger, who is, as an editor of Shelley and Keats, no stranger to bibliographical and editorial practice, agrees with McGann's assessment of the field, and adds that such a fetishizing of the autonomous, isolated author is particularly hostile to the brand of implied collaborative authorship that he formulates in *Multiple Authorship and the Myth of Solitary Genius*: 'The proponents of the [Greg-Bowers copy-text] system routinely view every alteration and revision by friends, relatives, copyists, editors, printers, publishers, and censors alike as impurity or contamination' (199). Overt collaboration, one can only surmise, would be, for classical textual criticism, a case of mutual, consensual contamination, a figuration that harkens back to the sexualized taboo against same-sex co-creation that I discerned in Henry James's tales of artistic collaboration.

For these sorts of reasons, more recent critics of collaborative texts have turned away from paleography and other traditional bibliographic methods as necessarily holding the answers to questions of authorship. Jeffrey Masten, for instance, working on the collaboratively produced plays of Early Modern England, departs from twentieth-century editing practices like those of the editors of Beaumont and Fletcher, who tend to 'separate the plays into singly authored acts, scenes, and lines' ('My Two Dads' 290). Instead, he poststructurally reconfigures the sorts of questions that have traditionally been asked about collaborative playwrights since the middle of the seventeenth century: who wrote what portions of text? Which collaborator's opinion has influenced the text more? In a mood closely approximating that of Michel Foucault at the end of 'What Is an Author,' when he reshapes the sorts of questions traditionally asked about authorship, Masten concludes, 'I do not favour bringing out the paleographical evidence as if it could answer these questions, or as if these are the right questions to be asking in the first place' ('Playwrighting: Authorship and Collaboration' 362). Such questions, for Masten, are anachronistic in that they normalize forms of subjectivity that 'are central to later Anglo-American cultural, literary and legal history' (362) and that may have little to do with Renaissance understandings of property, individuality, or textuality.

For materialists like McGann, this construction of the isolated, individuated author that is 'central to later Anglo-American cultural, literary and legal history' is a bourgeois discourse meant to write over the social formation of art. As Raymond Williams satirically renders it, in terms that may inspire memories of university period-survey courses, 'Against a "background" of shared facts, ideas, and influences, every individual (or in its more common bourgeois form, every *significant* individual) creates his quite separate work, to be subsequently compared with other separate lives and works' (196, emphasis Williams's). In this way, difference is transposed from history, society, culture onto the individual agent, in a psycho-ideological act of transference, and the author functions, in this case, as a means of social containment. As Michel Foucault noted, the 'author ... constitutes a principle of unity in writing where any unevenness of production is ascribed to changes caused by evolution, maturation, or outside influence' (128). For that matter, as novelist and poet Margaret Atwood muses, even the last item on Foucault's list routinely gets short shrift, for the writer in Western countries is often regarded 'as a kind of spider, spinning out his entire work from within. This view depends on a solipsism, the idea that we are all self-enclosed monads, with an inside and an outside, and that nothing from the outside ever gets in' (*Second Words* 342). This constellation of author projections – the individuated, unified and unifying, solitary spider-artist – is a potentially energizing one for women collaborators to react against, for it chimes in so readily with constructions of masculinity as non-rooted, gloriously and aloofly individuated. Such is the playfully subversive reactive energy that I find in a photograph of the late nineteenth-century Anglo-Irish collaborators Somerville and Ross (Edith Somerville and Violet Martin), pictured working together in an attic, that stereotypical haunt of the solitary male-gendered poet possessed by the frenzies of inspiration. This composition of two women occupying a space originally thought just barely big enough for one (man) alone is a leitmotif of contemporary women's collaborative art. The title of Daphne Marlatt and Betsy Warland's poem and subsequent collection, *Two Women in a Birth*, punningly proclaims what creativity can issue from this supposed overcrowding of the authorial space, the crowding of the solitary garret.

Other critical theorists – some poststructuralist, some not – have found a variety of ways to reconfigure this solitary, bourgeois writer, and some of these strategies inform my study of collaborative women's art. There is, for instance, the move to author-ize readers, to grant them a shared or even primary responsibility in the creation of texts. Some such formulations of reader theory arguably shift authority from author to reader in a way that does not truly reconfigure authority itself; the old solitary author has just moved house. This is why materialist versions of reader theory have conceptualized the reader not as a mirror-image of the bourgeois author, but as history itself. For example, Thomas Docherty argues in *On Modern Authority* (1987): 'The reader, the critical consciousness located in history, is the position which authorises or legitimizes the text or its reading. The author is the 'co-respondent' of this reader, and writes or transcribes the text in the face of its own critical reading ... the text is actually produced as 'always already read' *before* it has been written or 'legitimized' (10, emphasis Docherty's). In a sense, this position carries McGann's theory of socialized authorship one step further, since McGann, challenging textual critics and intentionalists, wryly observes that an 'author's work possesses autonomy only when it remains an unheard melody' (51). Docherty, moving up the horizon of *ecriture*, would deny even this tenuous foothold. A slightly different version of these co-respondent roles of author and reader is more pertinent to my study: Walter Benjamin's notion of 'The Author as Producer.' In that essay, Benjamin draws on the concept of collaboration to explain what happens in Brechtian theatre: '*An author who teaches writers nothing teaches no one.* What matters, therefore, is the exemplary character of production, which is able first to induce other producers to produce, and second to put an improved apparatus at their disposal. And this apparatus is better the more consumers it is able to turn into producers – that is, readers or spectators into collaborators' (233, emphasis Benjamin's). In some of the collaborative texts I discuss, especially the doubly authored ones, this play on the reader as producer and, to augment Benjamin, the producer as reader, is particularly marked. The back-and-forth, statement-response format of a number of those works highlights the reciprocity of those roles, an entwining that frustrates conventional desires to demarcate and rank writer and reader.

One poststructualist theory that touches on this reciprocity of writing is itself expressed in a collaborative text: Hélène Cixous and Catherine Clément's *La Jeune Née* (trans. *The Newly-Born Woman*). In 'Sorties' Cixous calls writing a 'ceaseless exchange of one with another ... A course that multiplies transformations by the thousands' (86). The third section of the book, a transcript of a conversation between Cixous and Clément, is, accordingly, entitled 'Exchange.' She is, in one sense, careful to steer clear of fetishizing writerly exchange, for she immediately notes that it 'is not done without danger, without pain, without loss' (86), but the dangers she notes are framed in mainly psychological rather than social or ideological terminology: 'of moments of self, of consciousness, of persons one has been, goes beyond, leaves' (86). Together, Cixous and Clément meditate on the risks involved in publishing an 'Exchange' section that might reify or simplify their positions: 'We would confront the risks of a dual discourse that does not proceed without reciprocal change, censorship or self-censorship' (135). In spite of this accounting of risk, there is an underlying assumption that writing the text together cuts through the Hegelianism that Cixous critiques in 'Sorties' to establish a recognition of difference that is itself arguably Edenic: 'One could, in fact, imagine that difference or inequality – if one understands by that noncoincidence, asymmetry – lead to desire without negativity, without one of the partners succumbing: we would recognize each other in a type of exchange in which each one would keep the *other* alive and different' (79, emphasis Cixous and Clément's). It would be easy to imagine a theory of women's collaborations that would proceed from these assumptions, but I am sceptical of a demarcation between 'desire without negativity' and the negative, male-gendered Hegelian variety. It seems another way of resolving instead of probing difference. An exchange theory of double authorship would need to account for power relations in a more complicated, less dualistic fashion.

The materialist notion of socialized authorship, which I have outlined above, highlights exchange but is wary of dualisms, preferring a model of fluid, historically mutable power relations. As Raymond Williams describes it, in terms that could serve as a critique of Cixous's notion of authorial exchange, 'This procedure can be summarized as a reciprocal discovery of the truly social in the individual, and the truly individual in the social. In the significant case of authorship it leads to dynamic senses of social formation, ... which have to be seen as in radical relationship without any categorical or procedural assumption of priorities' (197). Cixous's anti-Hegelian 'desire without negativity' is precisely the sort of 'categorical or procedural assumption of priorities' that jeopardizes a truly social model of exchange. Indeed, as Williams describes the fluidity that should characterize such an exchange, he sounds remarkably Foucauldian: 'This process of development [of an author] can be grasped as a complex of active relations, within which the emergence of an individual project, and the real history of other contemporary projects and of the developing forms and structures, are continuously and substantially interactive' (196).

Foucault, however, had already taken Williams's notion of fluid exchange in a slightly different direction, so as to retheorize the 'individual project' as performative. As he notes in 'What Is an

Author?' 'The "author-function" ... does not refer, purely and simply, to an actual individual insofar as it simultaneously gives rise to a variety of egos and to a series of subjective positions that individuals of any class may come to occupy' (130–1). This subject position theory would allow for an ideological reading of collaborative art that would not subordinate the overtly collaborative to the implied forms valorized by Williams and McGann, who socialize the latter at the cost of individualizing the former. It would, instead, acknowledge the subject positions of overt collaborators as performed, as thoroughly socialized sites of fluid and complex power exchanges. This is the strategy that I adopt in reading and theorizing contemporary women's collaborative art, for I agree with Cheryl Walker that a Foucauldian approach to authorship offers the most effective way for a feminist reader to negotiate what one critic has called 'the Scylla of essentialism and the Charybdis of deconstruction' (Hollis 117).

A number of critics have reacted to this perceived split between poststructuralism and agency by taking sides with one or the other, or by provisionally bracketing poststructuralist revisions of authorship and subjectivity, because they erroneously assume that the revision of the former equals the denial of the latter. Wayne Koestenbaum, for instance, distances himself from what he calls a 'gleefully poststructuralist path' and its 'spare axioms: (1) the Author is dead; (2) the Author is complex' – a characterization that he acknowledges is 'crudely sketched' (8). Nevertheless, that characterization serves as the basis for Koestenbaum's declaration that 'I follow a conventional method of close reading which applies biography to text, treats biography as text, and depends on the integrity of the author as more than a social construct or a fiction superimposed on intertextual anarchy' (9). But 'treat[ing] biography as text' is as 'gleefully poststructuralist' as one can get; Koestenbaum's identification of poststructuralism with the 'flight' of 'Roland Barthes and Helene Cixous' 'from the biographical, the concrete, and the literal' (9) is a reductive one, particularly since Barthes, rather than banishing biography, was arguing for it to be treated as one 'text' among many others. For that matter, Koestenbaum's absorbing thesis, that a 'collaborative text exhibits (shameful) symptoms of double authorship, despite the men's desire to make the work seem the product of one mind' (9), owes a great deal to poststructuralist understandings of authorship and textuality.

Koestenbaum's witty admission, at the close of his study, that he has 'quietly bowed to the cult of the individual genius, atomistic and apolitical' (177), needs to be set within the context of some ideological critics' suspicion of poststructuralist reconfigurations of authorship. It invites comparison with Nancy K. Miller's influential essay 'Changing the Subject: Authorship, Writing, and the Reader' (1986), in which she questioned what she saw as the poststructuralist tendency to empty out voice and subjectivity at the very time that North American feminism was warmly addressing or 'rediscovering' women's voices and concerns. What she sees as, initially, a productive alliance between feminism and poststructuralism (arguing that, after all, it was the old-style solitary 'Author' who kept women writers out of the canon) has become a restrictive pact that has 'repressed and inhibited discussion of any writing identity in favour of the (new) monolith of anonymous textuality' (104). Miller's way out of this situation is to shelve poststructuralist critiques of dominant concepts of subjectivity and authorship because, to quote the much-quoted passage from her article, the 'postmodernist decision that the Author is dead, and subjective agency along with him, does not necessarily work for women and prematurely forecloses the question of identity for them' (106). Although Miller seems to have steered clear of what she figures as the Charybdis of deconstruction, enter the Scylla of essentialism, against whom Miller now bumps most forcefully, for she claims: 'Because women have not had the same historical relation of identity to origin, institution, production that men have had, women have not, I think, (collectively) felt burdened by too much Self, Ego, Cogito, etc.' (106). So Miller relies on history to extricate her from the dilemma, but it is a history that is too untheorized, too static, too dualistic – and, yes, to invoke the bugaboo, too essentializing.

What Miller has attempted to do, in effect, is to reverse Derrida's bracketing of authorial names' designating power in *Of Gram-*

matology, where he declares: 'The names of authors or of doctrines have here no substantial value. They indicate neither identities nor 'causes ... The indicative value that I attribute to them is first the name of a problem ... Besides, this abstraction is partial and it remains, in my view, provisional' (99). But by setting aside poststructuralist authors and subjectivities for women, not provisionally but permanently, she has not so much named a problem as paved over one. For that matter, Derrida's use of provisional shorthand for the purposes of discussion is one thing, but provisional bracketing with a more long-range political strategy in mind is an ultimately more problematic act. So, sympathetic as I am to the political realities that move Gayatri Spivak, for example, to advocate a provisional postcolonial subjectivity, or Mariana Valverde to say that she would like for lesbians, no matter what they theorize about poststructuralist subjectivity, to act politically as subjects anyway, I think that both the postcolonial and the lesbian need to transform, not simply opt out of, poststructuralist accounts of authorship and subjectivity.

Postcolonial, feminist, gay and lesbian theories, in particular, have intervened in and transformed the field of poststructuralist thought in general, and the same is true of the specific question of authorship. Richard Dyer, writing on gay film, makes it very clear: 'If believing in authorship (in film) means believing that only one person makes a film, that that person is the director, that the film expresses his/her inner personality, that this can be understood apart from the industrial circumstances and semiotic codes within which it is made, then I have never believed in authorship' (187). At the same time, however, Dyer wants to distinguish this bourgeois, individualized authorship construct from other ways of constructing authorship. He argues, in terms that clearly derive from a Foucauldian subject-position theory, that 'one can have no concept of socially specific forms of cultural production without some notion of authorship, for what one is looking at are the circumstances in which counter-discourses are produced, in which those generally spoken of and for speak for themselves' (186–7). One can still discern the tug of a more expressivist theoretical strain here, in the framing of a group's act of 'speak[ing] for themselves,' but Dyer goes on to formulate a performative theory of gay film authorship that clearly indicates that this act of speech is not a totalized, collective one: 'Both authorship and being lesbian/gay become a kind of performance, something we all do but only with the terms, the discourses, available to us, and whose relationship to any imputed self doing the performing cannot be taken as read' (187–8).

There is a similar tug of discourses at the end of Nancy K. Miller's essay. Indeed, she prefigures what became, in the 1990s, an influential range of performative theories when she advises that the 'possibility of future feminist intervention requires an ironic manipulation of the semiotics of performance and production' (116). Unlike Dyer, though, she does not fully connect the performative, and its Foucauldian underpinnings, with the political agency that she seeks. As a result, the tug of collectivist speech pulls the conclusion of the essay back to a less mediated theory of expressivism, and Miller calls for a definition of a 'female writing subject ... that acknowledges ... the (perhaps permanent) internal split that makes a collective identity or integrity only a horizon, but a necessary one' (116–17).

For feminist theory, such a split is neither necessary nor permanent. Cheryl Walker comes to this conclusion after rereading Barthes and Foucault alongside Miller's essay and other feminist statements on authorship in her article 'Feminist Literary Criticism and the Author' (1990). She sees Barthes's manifesto 'The Death of the Author' as occupying a position far more extreme than that of Foucault's 'What Is an Author?' because Barthes argues that texts should 'be construed as fields of discourse without *any* boundaries (authorial or otherwise) to limit the free play of the signifier' (552, emphasis Walker's). Steven Knapp and Walter Benn Michaels in 'Against Theory,' in Walker's view, represent the opposite extreme, since they recognize authorial intention as the only valid criterion for interpretation. Surveying these diametrically opposed theories, Walker observes: 'What we are often seeking as feminists, it seems, is a third position' (555). She recognizes Nancy Miller's desire to find this elusive third path between poststructuralist critique of authoritarian authorship and (some) feminists' recourse to 'Woman' as knowable subject, but she trenchantly critiques Miller's *cogito*-deficiency theory of women's subjectivities: 'Identity formation may have different structural patterns for women, but these are irrelevant to the question of whether women can, under such poststructural theories of textuality, operate as the authors of their own works' (557). In response, Walker formulates her own 'third position,' a 'politics of author recognition' (553) that she feels has the potential to break down this perceived split between poststructuralism and agency: 'What we need, instead of a theory of the death of the author, is a new concept of authorship that does not naively assert that the writer is an originating genius, creating aesthetic objects outside of history, but does not diminish the importance of difference and agency in the responses of women writers to historical formations' (560). So, in effect, Walker maintains that numerous sources of interpretation, for example, biography (to cite the particular object of Barthes's and Foucault's anti-authorial critique), should not be seen as unmentionable in literary criticism, but neither can they be seen as determinative. As she elaborates, 'Though there is no presence behind a text, there is an infinite number of presences, or traces, in a given text' (569). Walker finds herself, as a Foucauldian, drawn to these 'presences' not as immutable realities or signs of textual plenitude, but as complex and perhaps even contradictory signals of social conditions that call for deeper scrutiny.

In *Rethinking Women's Collaborative Writing*, I have followed Walker's lead in steering clear of the 'horizon' of 'collective' female experience or identity that Miller found so 'necessary' to posit in the light of poststructuralist critiques of subjectivity, preferring to see in contemporary women's collaborative texts 'traces' of many varying, sometimes contradictory, ideological positionings and placements. Like her theoretical model, Foucault, and like critics such as Jeffrey Masten, I hope to alter some of the common (Foucault called them 'tiresome') questions asked about authorship: 'Who is the real author? Have we proof of his authenticity and originality? What has he revealed of his most profound self in his language?' Instead, in reading the power dynamics of women's

collaborations in poetry, prose, theatre and criticism, I will pose
the sorts of new questions that Foucault foresaw:

> 'What are the modes of existence of this discourse?'
> 'Where does it come from; how is it circulated; who controls it?'
> 'What placements are determined for possible subjects?'
> 'Who can fulfill these diverse functions of the subject?' (138)

The discourse that is contemporary women's collaborative writing
has many, many placements: ways of expressing not only the
moments of harmony and fusion that many of its critics have
discovered, but also the differences, property issues, and negotiations of power that I find when I read these texts. When I come to
the supposedly cramped and overcrowded quarters of two or more
women authors 'in a birth,' I find, instead of an easy harmony, the
much more absorbing cultural spectacle of women who are differently engaged.

2

'We Have Horrible Disagreements about "Moreovers"': Collaborative Theory and Criticism

When the collaborative critics Sandra Gilbert and Susan Gubar were asked in an interview with Laura Shapiro whether their writing styles were similar, Gubar immediately responded, 'Oh, not at all. We have horrible disagreements about "moreovers"' (60). Gilbert and Gubar are, of course, the authors of well-known works of literary criticism such as *The Madwoman in the Attic* and *No Man's Land: The Place of the Woman Writer in the Twentieth Century*. Although this chapter will emphasize the tensions, power differentials, and even the 'horrible disagreements' that occur in the process of collaborating on works of critical theory and literary criticism – dynamics that operate both at and far deeper than the level of the occasional disagreement about grammar – I will not forget the sustenance that women intellectuals like Gilbert and Gubar have found in collaborative groups and pairs. In fact, critical collaborative groups occupy spaces (sometimes several simultaneously) on a continuum that one might call the fusion/differentiation scale, ranging from the theoretical belief in the submersion of individual concerns in the collective, to an explicit analysis of the individual power differentials in collaboration or, even, an anxious reinscription of the individual contributions to collaborative work. And although I sometimes characterize the belief in critical fusion as theoretically naive, I also recognize the powerful forces at work assailing the integrity of women's collaborations, forces that understandably call forth a defensive emphasis on unity and harmony.

It is often said that academic collaboration is a commonplace in the maths and sciences, and that scholars in the humanities and social sciences would do well to emulate this tradition. True, multiple authorship is the norm in most scientific and mathematical fields. As Anne B. Piternik discovered, 'In the life sciences, 15 of the most-cited articles [in 1997] were single-author articles; the average number of authors was close to 6, and the highest number was 22' ('Author! Author!' 80). But any assumption that research and publication in the sciences and maths are less hierarchical because of this emphasis on shared authorship is mistaken; as many commentators have pointed out, the listing of multiple authors forms a territorial pecking-order. Linda and Michael Hutcheon, a literary theorist and physician respectively, knew from the first that their collaboration did not fit the pattern of scientific collaboration that Michael Hutcheon was familiar with, with its 'clear authority pattern':

The head of a lab (the senior author – listed last in a scientific article's attributions) usually generates the idea (and the grant money); the 'first author' may be a student or postgraduate fellow and will likely have both done the experiment and physically written the paper; the others listed as coauthors of the article will usually have contributed expertise in some specific area of the work. (62)

Primary authorship, then, is determined not necessarily by who writes the paper but (usually) by the relative amount and importance of the research contributed to the project. There are stories aplenty of researchers challenging their place in the hierarchical listing of authors and of debates over methods of attributing scientific authorship. At times, even researchers who did not contribute research to the present project have been listed as co-authors, either because their previous research enabled the discoveries made in the project or, more rarely and controversially, because they were thought to be impressive 'names' to have on one's paper on a particular subject – a practice that respected North American scientific journals have recently denounced. So it would seem that the sciences do not offer women in the humanities and social sciences any sort of clear-cut or attractive collaborative model.

In fact, one of the strongest forces discouraging North American or English scholarly collaboration in the humanities is institutional apathy or even hostility, in spite of the respect accorded high-profile collaborators like Gilbert and Gubar. Pairs or groups of critical collaborators bear repeated witness to the apathy or active discouragement that their collaborations receive in scholarly institutions such as the university, through negative tenure or promotion considerations. As Elizabeth G. Peck and JoAnna Stephens Mink acknowledge in the introduction to their book *Common Ground: Feminist Collaboration in the Academy*, they decided to limit the number of collaborative ventures they contributed to because the 'reception on the part of university administrators who evaluate for promotion and tenure decisions was a factor when we made individual decisions about when and how to invest our academic energies. We were acutely aware of the tradition of rewarding individual scholarship and knew that collaboration was a risky business indeed' (2). Several of the contributors to their volume reiterate their language of risk, telling their own or others' stories of the costs of working together (Nesbitt and Thomas 32; Singley and Sweeney 73), of being asked by 'T & P committees to make Solomonic decisions about how to cut up their collaboratively produced scholarship' (Alm 136). In reaction to this set of circumstances, I argue, Anglo-American women critics and theorists are the likeliest to idealize their collaborations and, consequently, to play down their disagreements and divergences. Even when those disagreements are explicitly acknowledged, collaborators often subscribe, theoretically, to a theory of critical unity or, at least, consensus.

To say that this is the inherent condition of women's academic collaborations, however, would be a misstatement based on an enormous cultural generalization. To counteract this tendency, I begin with an analysis of academic collaborations in two cultures where collective intellectual writing has had a long and distinguished history: in France and, especially, Italy. These collaborations not only set their more contradiction-ridden Anglo-American cousins in cultural perspective, they may also help to convince Anglo-American collaborators in the academy that their collective projects need not be based on a theory of collective writing as the fusion of several voices into one seamless author-critic.

Since the early to mid-1980s, Anglo-American feminists have had access to one of the most influential of these collaborations, that of Hélène Cixous and Catherine Clément. To be sure, this is not a collaboration that could easily be resolved into a partnership-of-equals paradigm; there is no doubt that Cixous is the star of the intelligentsia and Clément does tend, in works like *The Newly-Born Woman*, to play a second-fiddle (if an impressively articulate and thoughtful one). My academic, readerly sense of this was borne out in a more circumstantial form when I visited the Paris Librairie des femmes in the course of researching this book. Everyone was rushing about, hand on head, preparing for a special event to take place at the Librairie that evening at which Cixous was to be the guest of honour. The star system of French academia was palpably in evidence.

Nevertheless, the collaboration between Cixous and Clément has strongly influenced the work of other collaborators, most notably that of Canadians Daphne Marlatt and Betsy Warland who were strongly influenced by the French feminisms of the 1980s. Cixous and Clément are, in fact, the primary influence on their collective writing. There is, for instance, the same use of interpolated statements that you find in Cixous and Clément's *The Newly-Born Woman* (e.g., 'Maid in the family' [150]; 'Can one put desire to sleep?' [157], emphasis Cixous and Clément's). In *The Newly-Born Woman*, Cixous contributes a 'creative' text – a poem based on Freud's 'Dora' case study that immediately calls to mind the poetry of Marlatt and Warland in its cadences and textual spacings:

not Mummy   put me to sleep –   some gold for Dora

DADDY-   MUMMY-   DORA-

Mr. K.   only for Mrs. K.-   only for Daddy-   not Mrs. K. (148)

Beyond being stylistically influential, however, the partnership of Cixous and Clément involved a negotiation of space and of difference that a number of their Anglo-American admirers of the mid-80s tended to play down in the midst of the idealistic celebration of their textual union. The text 'A Woman Mistress' from the 'Exchange' section of *The Newly-Born Woman* immediately strikes this chord of difference and individual discourse:

> C: Let's start out with the difference between our discourses. Yours is a writing halfway between theory and fiction. Whereas my discourse is, or tries to be, more demonstrative and discursive, following the most traditional method of rhetorical demonstration. That doesn't bother me; I accept that method ... We see that there can be two women in the same space who are *differently* engaged ... (136, emphasis Cixous and Clément's)

Here is the paradigm of two collaborators inhabiting one conventionally singular author position, 'two women in a birth' as Marlatt and Warland phrase it, without ceding to a fusion theory of collectivity. This provides a space for intellectual disagreements to occur and be recorded without creating the impression that the collaboration is a failure. Cixous responds to Clément at one point, 'I can't go along with you there' (139), clearing the way for collaborators like Marlatt and Warland to have similar collaborative exchanges: 'It wasn't that way for me ...' (108).

Cixous and Clément also set the tone for many subsequent collaborations when they identify the risks involved in this model of collaboration without fusion, disagreement placed on the page rather than ironed out in pre-writing discussions. The first word of their short introductory note on the 'Exchange' section (in English translation) is a revealing '[i]ncautiously.' They explain that the differences that are implicitly present in the rest of the collection need to be made apparent, but that doing so involves confronting the 'risks of a dual discourse that does not proceed without reciprocal change, censorship or self-censorship' (135). This is remarkably clear-eyed for a collaboration that has tended to be celebrated as a landmark in collaborative mutuality. In addition, the 'oral format,' they write, tends to reinscribe differences in a hasty and thus risky way: 'Some of our positions hardened immediately. They were also exaggerated by the oral form, which rushes and simplifies concepts. Divergences became entrenched and investments marked. ... So we have not "written" but have let through, trans-scribed clashes and collisions' (135). This is the decision that Marlatt and Warland also arrive at in their collaboration when they decide to 'trans-scribe' sometimes tense discussions of the collaborative process and its painful personal repercussions: 'well, i feel intimidated by it now / *i feel intimidated by you – you were writing everything down*' (163; emphasis Marlatt and Warland's). In both instances, the risks are personal, relational, and psychological, as befits the psychoanalytically informed French feminism at work, not the sorts of institutional risks that many American critical collaborators will perceive in their acts of collective writing.

The firmly established collaboration among members of the Milan Women's Bookstore Collective, on the other hand, betrays a sense of security and authority that is characteristic of the writings of collectives in Italy. There is a long-standing tradition of collective political writings in Italy, largely because of the fairly integrated leftist political presence or tradition in many Italian centres. Paola Bono and Sandra Kemp argue in their introduction to *Italian Feminist Thought* that there are

two crucial characteristics of Italian 'feminism': first, the presence all over Italy of many groups (with frequently more than one group in the same city), the attempt to create nationwide networks, and the pluralism of the groups, the conflict and dialogue between them; and second, the importance of politics for Italian feminism, reflecting the strongly political character of Italian society in general. (2)

In Italian collaborative feminist texts, I would argue, we see the two strands interacting, the legacy of vital political publishing by collectives infusing and informing the work of women's groups spread around the country. As Bono and Kemp note for their non-European audiences, 'Collaboration and teamwork are the practice of many Italian feminists, and quite a few of the publications listed in our bibliography have collective authors' (5). So collective writing was a natural way for Italian feminists to proceed – a valuable corrective to North American assumptions that critical writing, whether of a political or academic nature, is naturally or normally undertaken by individuals.

These collaborative writings are readily available in Italy and they address a wide variety of subject matters and audiences. When I visited the Milan Women's Bookstore, I was shown a range of collectively produced texts; there seemed to be an inexhaustible supply. There was, to start, the Milan Collective's own publication *Sottosopra* which is, as Paola Bono and Sandra Kemp note, published occasionally, 'whenever (and only if) they [collective members] feel they have come to articulate satisfactorily a position they wish to circulate and discuss' (413). The copies that I saw in Milan were printed also in German and French, but none in English – proof, I felt, of the lack of exchange between Anglo-American and Italian feminisms. There is also the productive and high-profile 'Diotima' group, whose *Il pensiero della differenza sessuale* (1987) is co-authored by twelve Italian women, among them noted Italian feminists like Adriana Cavarero and Luisa Muraro. Teachers, I discovered, are notably active in collective publishing, and they adopt an explicitly political vein that would surprise their North American colleagues, used as they are to more implicitly political educationist writings. A group calling itself 'Gruppo insegnanti di Milano' (Teachers' Group of Milan), for instance, published a volume on teaching, *Liberta femminile nel '600* (Women's Freedom of the Sixteenth Century), that opens with a piece called 'Il piacere di pensare insieme' (The Pleasure of Thinking Together). There, the five members comment: 'Infatti, quando lo scambio funziona, pensare insieme e un piacere, discutere un'appassionante attivita, cercare e un'avventura' (7; 'In fact, when the exchange works, thinking together is a pleasure, discussing is an impassioned activity, and inquiry is an adventure'). Another teachers'collective, *Gruppo pedagogia della differenze sessuale*, published a book, *Educare nella differenza* (Teaching Difference), and there are many more, evidence of a vital, ongoing tradition of collective pedagogical writing. But I concentrate on a theoretical text that is more readily available in English translation, the only

Italian feminist text that has received wide distribution in North America: the Milan Women's Bookstore Collective's work *Sexual Difference: A Theory of Social-Symbolic Practice* (1987), published in English by Indiana University Press in 1990 and introduced by the well-known Italo-American theorist Teresa de Lauretis.

In spite of the widespread use of collective writing strategies in Italy, de Lauretis actually plays down the practice in her introductory remarks on the volume. In a footnote, she observes that 'collective authorship ... [is] a practice no longer followed as strictly as it was in the 70s except by long-standing groups such as the Milan Libreria delle Donne' (20), but this comment seems belied by the active workings of groups of various kinds: teachers, philosophers, activists. Perhaps the workings are no longer as strictly collective, and members may collaborate with group members and sign pieces individually, but the collective writing practice in Italy has by no means gone by the boards.

In the writings of a number of these groups, there is a strong sense of a common subject – a trademark of political writings or *manifesti*, though these writings, it should be stressed, go beyond the manifesto in extended analysis and complexity. Take, for example, the opening of the manifesto of the Milan 'Demau' (short for demystification of authority) group active in the 70s: 'The group bases itself in essence on the following programmatic points ...' (Bono and Kemp 34). How, then, did (and do) these groups handle difference, divergent opinions? The example of the Milan Women's Bookstore Collective offers a fascinating case study. In *Sexual Difference* we hear of many occasions when the group had to handle tensions and disagreements. At times there were cultural differences, specifically between French and Italian perspectives, that arose in group operations. The Collective notes that the Italian women tended to be influenced by American feminist concepts of sisterhood and were surprised to see the French women taking 'note of the sexual component in all of its manifestations, including that of power'(50). In addition, the group had continuing trouble with the concept and practice of leadership in the collective (97, 49). In fact, the group had to work very hard to acknowledge the presence of aggression and conflict in a group that, conventionally speaking, should have been one of cooperation and mutuality (53), and they had to accept that political stances did not line up unproblematically in accordance with sex. The example of the latter issue is the group's discussion of legalized abortion. There was, initially, the assumption that women in the group would, somehow, unite seamlessly over this issue – a difficult scene to imagine in terms of the influence of the Roman Catholic church in Italy. One whole meeting, in fact, focused on the very problem of the relationship of the individual and the collectivity (55). And at another meeting, the realization that, to quote the group, 'We are not all equal here' (110) erupted with the eclat of a thunderclap. 'A regime of pretense had ended,' the group recalled of its dramatic disillusionment (111).

Eventually, the group worked out a way of seeing strength in the differences that arose in the course of drawing up a collective document. As they wrote, 'Suspending all judgment [of women by other women], as early feminism desired, is not liberating'(142). And, in their most widely cited theoretical construct, 'entrustment,' the Milan Women's Bookstore Collective devised a paradigm that, in my view, grows out of their experiences of negotiating their own collective statements, though the group itself does not make this connection explicit. 'Entrustment' is the term that the group devised to describe a relationship between two women that recognizes its power differential. In this sense 'entrustment' aptly describes my own critical project in analysing theories and practices of women's collectivity, bearing witness both to the power of women's connectedness and to the inevitability of power differentials and politics in those connections. This was not a terminus or final resting point for the group, however: such is not the nature of processes of power negotiation and entrustment. As I was told when I visited the bookstore, some members of the community were displeased by the publication of *Sexual Difference*, arguing that the collective statement issued in their name did not necessarily represent *them* (Sattler). However painfully and provisionally, the Milan Women's Bookstore Collective was able to work their way to a theoretical understanding of women's collectivity largely,

I believe, because they had the confidence born of a long tradition of collective writing. As I will argue in the next few pages, American collective criticism is still struggling with this process, this long journey toward entrustment.

Sandra Gilbert and Susan Gubar are the best-known North American collaborative literary critics: they numbered among *Ms* magazine's 'women of the year' for 1985 and their books, particularly their *Norton Anthology of Women's Literature*, have gained canonical status in the North American academy. 'Gilbert and Gubar' has become a familiar campus literary shorthand. But this writing relationship, regarded widely as a notable collaborative success and the exception that proves the disastrous collaborative rule, is marked by many ideological and strategic tensions and anxieties.

I am not referring to Gilbert and Gubar's personal relationship here, even though, like many North American critical collaborators, their shared work grows out of a pre-existing friendship. As Gilbert and Gubar recalled in an interview, they met as new faculty hired at the University of Indiana – getting on an elevator, to invoke, if circumstantially, my motif of two women sharing a space. Actually, this fact of friendship is of more than circumstantial interest; North American collaborators tend to see their collaborations as correlates or extensions of friendship. This is a telling sign of how they tend to encode critical collaboration as mutuality rather than adopting a more strictly professional demeanour as the Italian feminist groups do. Of course, friendship as a concept often does suggest comfort with acknowledging difference and disagreement, but all too often, in North American collaborations, such complexities are overshadowed by the need to present a unified front. Holly Laird refers to these kinds of writing relationships as 'coalition collaborations,' wherein 'women acknowledge their differences both in the immediacy of trying to write together and in their retrospective meditations, yet their more conscious aims and desires are to bridge those differences and to achieve solidarity with each other' ('Preface' 15). And yet I am tempted to believe that in many coalition collaborations, the acknowledgment of difference is often cursory or quickly erased

by the overarching objective of harmony. As editorial collaborators Helen Cafferty and Jeanette Clausen frankly admitted, '[o]ur
success in arriving at a consensus on most points of disagreement
may have blinded us to how long and hard we had to work to
reach that consensus' (Peck and Mink 90).

For all of the mutuality signalled by the partnership of Gilbert
and Gubar, this collaboration is also the site of a marked anxiety
about individual property ethics. In their introduction to *The
Madwoman in the Attic*, they carefully parcel out their individual
contributions, and, furthermore, they suggest that this practice is
the norm in collaborative projects:

> Like most collaborators, we have divided our esponsibilities: Sandra
> Gilbert drafted the section on 'Milton's Daughters,' the essays on *The
> Professor* and *Jane Eyre*, and the chapters on the 'Aesthetics of Renuncia-
> tion' and on Emily Dickinson; Susan Gubar drafted the section on Jane
> Austen, the essays on *Shirley* and *Villette*, and the two chapters about
> George Eliot; and each of us has drafted portions of the introductory
> exploration of a feminist poetics. We have continually exchanged and
> discussed our drafts, however, so that we feel that our book represents
> not just a dialogue but a consensus.' (xiii)

Consensus it may be, but the process is decidedly individualistic,
and it was based on individual taste. As Gubar recalls in conversation, 'It was clear that the poets were for Sandra. She's a poet and
she was getting the poets. Austen I had always loved, so I got Jane
Austen' (Shapiro 60). More recently, Gilbert and Gubar have
moved away from this critical placing of bids toward a more
integrative collaborative practice. When they set to work on the
No Man's Land volumes, they discussed, formulated notes, and
wrote together. As they explain in an interview, they now tend to
sit together with notebooks, draft together, discuss, and write
'every word together' (Shapiro 60). That doesn't mean that they
now subscribe to an unproblematically corporate view of writing,
however. When the interviewer then asked in a nervously North
American fashion, 'Do you ever feel you're losing your separate intellectual identities?' the team did not for a minute consider

that they would ever do so. What I particularly enjoy about their response, in fact, is its negotiative collective nature: 'Gilbert: I think we have separate ideas. Don't you think so? Gubar: Yes, I think we do' (60). As Susan Gubar goes on to point out, they still present papers and write articles under their separate names. What interests me above all in this anecdote, however, is the interviewer's anxiously fearful approach to collaboration as the loss of prized American individuality.

Of course, Gilbert and Gubar originally wrote together in a relatively atomistic way not only because they were feeling their way toward a collective writing that is, unlike in Europe, decidedly counter-trend. The material conditions of academic life in American post-secondary institutions were also influential. They began work on *Madwoman*, 'exactly when Sandra went to Davis [University of California], and we were physically separated by miles and miles of the continent' (60). The American academy's tenure system, with its seemingly never-ending, gruelling period of apprenticeship and indentured academic labour, was certainly part of the material influences on the form that their early collaboration could take. 'And that's when it began,' Gilbert recalls, 'the phone bills and the mail, the planes' (60). This is a situation replicated in the working lives of other North American academic collaborators. As Gilbert and Gubar's collaborative partnership prospered and they each gained tenure and academic acclaim, and as their young families (another material consideration) grew older, it became easier for them to afford the luxury of working together, notebooks at the ready, in the same room, even though their lives continued to be centred in separate American cities.

What happens when the notebooks' observations don't tally? when difference creeps into the partnership that is 'Gilbert and Gubar'? In interviews, Gilbert and Gubar talk about their process of working through interpretations of literary works through discussion, in order to arrive at a consensus, 'our position on such-and-such' (Gubar, in Shapiro 61). As I've already mentioned, though, these two collaborators don't agree on a number of basic questions of taste, of liking one author rather than another. That is hardly surprising, but it is exactly the sort of difference that they

had to come to terms with in order to produce, even in individualistic ways, criticism on a range of writers. Sandra Gilbert, remem-
bering the dividing line on George Eliot (whom she didn't like;
Gubar did), reflected 'Interestingly, that's where our differences
were productive, because we knew we were going to have to sit
down and work out a mutually agreeable stance toward the problem of George Eliot' (Shapiro 60). The rhetoric is strikingly
legalistic: in this working out of the case of George Eliot, presumably there is also a legal process of compromise, of give-and-take,
that places this collaboration more on the consensus-building,
meet-in-the-middle model of collective authorship – an attempt,
in short, to merge two critics into one voice.

What I think happens in this particular model of collaborative
process is that difference is displaced in a number of ways. First of
all, when they are interviewed, Gilbert and Gubar save their
strongest, most conflictual rhetoric for matters of style rather than
intellectual substance – hence the battles royal over 'moreovers.'
'There are a lot of disagreements,' says Gubar (after refusing to say
who's on what side of the 'however' debate), 'but usually we feel
that they go somewhere, they make the prose more interesting'
(Shapiro 60). There's precious little insight offered into how the
disagreements proceed on matters of interpretation and ideology,
however. This difference is displaced onto the compositional aspect of the collaboration.

Another site of displacement for Gilbert and Gubar is their
work on women's patterns of affiliation. In their essay, 'Forward
into the Past: The Complex Female Affiliation Complex,' they
attempt to balance examples of twentieth-century women writers'
admiring references to their female foremothers with the indisputable record of their sometimes barbed criticisms of women writers
of the past (a quick survey of Virginia Woolf's prose alone could
provide an entire catalogue of these). What Gilbert and Gubar
arrive at is a 'paradigm of ambivalent affiliation, a construct which
dramatizes women's intertwined attitudes of anxiety and exuber-
ance about (female) creativity' (243). What I find absorbing about
this thesis, apart from any question of its validity, is its mode of
(co)production. Using women's writerly relationships across dec-

ades and centuries, Gilbert and Gubar examine what the Milan group would call entrustment: a relationship between women that takes account of their differential power (and, I would add, their differences of opinion). But they do not, in their collective writing lives, turn the lens of this analysis onto their own complex act of female affiliation. The correlation remains displaced and implicit, hidden between the co-written lines.

Another American collaborative team of critics, Carey Kaplan and Ellen Cronan Rose, have explicitly and closely surveyed the workings of their collaboration. But their self-analysis serves as a reminder that explicit commentary, in and of itself, does not imply a dissection of differences and a critique of power differentials. This collaboration strikes a celebratory tone much of the time, though that celebration is riddled with tensions and, at times, contradictions that tell us much about the pressures involved when two women collaborate in the American academy.

Like Gilbert and Gubar, Kaplan and Rose locate the origins of their collaboration in friendship. They open their article 'Strange Bedfellows: Feminist Collaboration' with the observation: 'Work and friendship. From our first encounter, we have been unable to distinguish between the two' (547). They met at a Margaret Drabble conference and quickly established a close friendship: 'We looked forward to meeting at subsequent conferences for dinner or a drink and to gossip about our lives' (547). In their co-published work – two edited collections and a book on *The Canon and the Common Reader* (1990) – they repeat these references, usually in introductions, to the inseparability of their work and their friendship. In the preface to *The Canon and the Common Reader*, for instance, they remember that they continued their conversations about Drabble and Lessing 'over years of drinks, dinners, and a continuing correspondence' (xiii). More recently, in their writings on the subject of their collaboration, Kaplan and Rose have made the decision to call their collaboration a lesbian one, even though only one of the pair is a lesbian woman and the other identifies as celibate. This is problematic enough, and Kaplan and Rose indicate that they are aware of the critiques of such loosely metaphorical uses of the term lesbian and their power to erase the historical and present lived experience of a woman loving another woman. However, my own interest in their decision to label the collaboration a lesbian one has to do with its status as a further gesture toward intertwining the concepts of friendship and work in a way that tends to place a great deal of pressure on the collaborators to demonstrate mutuality and harmony. Relating friendship and work does not inherently have to do this; another working of the relationship could figure entrustment, subject positioning, and an analysis of difference. The way Kaplan and Rose formulate the dynamic of their relationship, however, exacerbates the tension between an idealistic urge to celebrate harmony and a recognition of disagreement and difference.

A rhetoric of unity pervades their piece 'Strange Bedfellows: Feminist Collaboration.' They claim, for example: 'Our intellectual, ideological, and political convictions dovetail as smoothly as our writing styles,' and they refer to the 'shared assumptions' that their three published books reflect (548). To say that works have shared assumptions seems fair enough, but to say that all one's ideologies match up and weave themselves together seems a high expectation to uphold, theoretically and in practice. Even more sweepingly, Kaplan and Rose state: 'We are both feminists and the same kind of feminists' (548). Again, that may be so to a degree, and in terms of broad categories of subject positions and opinions on major issues, but it seems a bit inattentive to nuance. No wonder that they see a close examination of their collaborative practice as threatening, dangerous to the unity that they have posited: 'The collaborative "we" is unified, yet we have agreed to deconstruct that unity for the purposes of this essay – although this self-reflexive project threatens to render us speechless' (548). Clearly, they see speech as a plenitude, a property that can only grow (or can best grow) out of a condition of harmony and consensus.

From my perspective, the collaborative relationship of Kaplan and Rose does not need to be deconstructed, for it is, to use the terminology they choose, always already in that condition of endless tension. Kaplan and Rose appropriate the language of literary deconstruction that was prominent in the North American literary academic at that time in order to find a safe space for their collaborative unity: ' "We" emerges from the space between our individual, different voices, its meaning elusive, dispersed, always deferred, never unitary' (549). But they have not really taken the deconstructive paradigm to heart. If the 'we' is never unitary, then what of the claim just a page earlier that the '"we" is unified'? Is it 'never unitary' just for the purposes of academic discussion?

Kaplan and Rose do go on to admit differences and disagreements, but they see their collaboration as a conscious decision to transcend them, as one of Laird's 'coalition collaborations.' Again, this is a theoretical crux, considering the earlier deconstructive move that would render any transcendent move impossible, phantasmal: 'There are between us tensions, bifurcations, complexities, and ambivalences that we choose to ignore or elide for the purposes of our work and because of our profound, admittedly idealistic, personally transformative political beliefs' (553). Can the agency of a collaborative 'we' choose to ignore difference?

I have been very critical of the claims made by Kaplan and Rose of their collaboration, but I should point out that there is a material consideration that accounts fully and understandably for this tension between idealism and difference, a tension that North American collaborative writers share in varying degrees and fashions. It is, again, the pressure-filled American academy, with its lack of respect for collaboration in the humanities and its relentless emphasis upon the individual scholar and her productivity. At various points in their texts Kaplan and Rose bear witness to its presence in their professional and personal lives. 'For example,' they acknowledge, 'one of us has reason to believe that grants and release time are not readily granted her by her institution because all her recent projects have been cowritten' (556). At the same time, there is a certain amount of internalization of the prevailing construct of the single critical author that this institution seeks to foster: 'The other [collaborator], carrying a four-course teaching load each semester, worries about losing her separate intellectual identity because she has time only for collaborative projects' (556).

Some of this anxiety about 'who speaks' or publishes gets

encoded in Kaplan and Rose's handling of the persistent stylistic question that attaches itself to scholarly collaborations: which pronouns to use? Unlike Gilbert and Gubar, who use a 'we' to signal a consensus position that grows out of discussion, Kaplan and Rose alternate between a 'we' and the use of their names 'Carey' and 'Ellen.' This is the stylistic marker of the oscillation between collectivity and individuality that characterizes this collaboration. Kaplan and Rose use the 'we' to signal the shared assumptions of which they write and the 'Carey' and 'Ellen' to signal difference, divergence (that they figure as transcended in the 'we'). For example, when they direct attention to their working-style (rather than ideological) differences, the proper names appear: 'Carey must accept Ellen's relentless efficiency, Ellen must trust Carey's unpredictable bursts of energy' (556). Still, Carey Kaplan and Ellen Rose are adamant that '"[s]he" and "I" metamorphose into "we:"' (549).

The next pair of collaborative critics that I've singled out (of many) for analysis is a special case in that their self-conscious work on their collaboration isn't just a subsidiary commentary on their non-self-conscious collaborative criticism: it is part and parcel of that critical project. Lisa Ede and Andrea Lunsford are the co-authors of one of the studies that have informed and helpfully preceded this one: *Singular Texts / Plural Authors* (1990). But they appear here as practictioners rather than students of the collaborative act. Although much of their work on collaborative writing practices in the business and pedagogical worlds necessarily pays attention to the role of dynamics and difference, there is still a tendency on their parts to adopt a stance of defensive idealization of their collaboration. Like Gilbert and Gubar and Kaplan and Rose, they open their writings with a statement about their work growing in an organic way out of their friendship: 'We wrote together as an extension and an enrichment of our long friendship' (ix). Instead of the incompletely theorized deconstructive posture that Kaplan and Rose strike to resolve the contradictions between an idealized writing friendship and a negotiative process, Ede and Lunsford tend more toward a Bakhtinian model. Like Kaplan and Rose, they are using theoretical tools that were at hand for North American literary critics in the late 1980s, since Bakhtin was very much *au courant* at that time: 'In the process of making each of us present to the other, of hearing our "selves" echoed back and forth, of constituting and reconstituting, forming transforming, and reforming voices to speak our texts, we came ineluctably to hear within ourselves a large polyphonic chorus rather than just a duet' (ix). This is another strategy for clearing a theoretical space from whence a 'we' can speak, but speak variously, with difference. It seems easier postulated than enacted, but Ede and Lunsford make intriguing efforts to engage this polyphony. Between chapters they insert sections called 'Intertexts,' which consist of quotations regarding collaboration registered without commentary. Another stylistic strategy that they draw on has to do with the inevitable question of how to list co-authors, usually ending in the conventional practice of alphabetical listing. Although Ede and Lunsford cannot escape that practice in the cataloguing of their book, they and the book designers use the title page to draw attention to the institutional dictates of author-naming. Lining the top and the bottom of that page are their names, scrolled out one after (or before) another, with no spaces between, thus:

A E D E A N D R E A L U N S F O R D L I S A E D E A N D
R E A L U N S F O R D L I S A.

If this formation looks a bit like a wall as well as an interwoven fabric, there is ample reason for the defensive posturing. Like the other American collaborators I've examined here, Ede and Lunsford have their own institutional horror stories to tell, and they do so in more detail than the other collaborators I've surveyed:

We began collaborating in spite of concerned warnings of friends and colleagues, including those of Edward P.J. Corbett, the person in whose honor we first wrote collaboratively. We knew that our collaboration represented a challenge to traditional research conventions in the humanities. Andrea's colleagues (at the University of British Columbia) said so when they declined to consider any of her coauthored or coedited works as part of a review for promotion. Lisa's colleagues (at Oregon State University) said so when, as part of her tenure review, they supportively but exhaustively discussed how best to approach the problem of her coauthored works. (ix–x)

Ede and Lunsford do not let the matter rest here, in the preface; they continue in the next chapter to emphasize the institutional discouragement that they received, and they link that discouragement to ignorance of what the Milan teachers group called 'the pleasures of working together':

Some in our field cautioned us, for instance, that we would never receive favourable tenure decisions or promotions if we insisted on publishing coauthored articles. Even those who did not caution us about the dangerous consequences of our habit professed amazement at our ability to write together, questioning us in detail as though we had just returned from a strange new country. (6)

Co-authorship is here figured as both institutional and interpersonal danger or risk, and the prizes accorded by the institutions of post-secondary education connote safety and acceptance by one's peers. It seems as though it is in contemporary criticism and theory, rather than in creative endeavours, that we see the persistence of the nineteenth-century problem of outsiders prying into the 'unnatural' closeted workings of collaborations like Edith Somerville and Violet Martin's. The institutions are different, but the incomprehension and disapproval sound uncomfortably alike.

So far, I have sketched a rather stark dichotomy between naive and fearful North American collaborative criticism and the worldly, non-idealistic European variety. This is not quite the whole story; some collaborators are caught up in the tensions between the two models. This is dramatized in a story told by the American expatriate literary critic and theorist Cora Kaplan about her involvement with a particularly well-known British women's writing group, the Marxist-Feminist Literature Collective, from 1976 to 1979. It started, like the nineteenth-century literary clubs that Anne Ruggles Gere has researched in the United States, as a reading club. Its members embodied various differences, of age, institutional entitlement (both faculty and students), and ideological perspectives, even though the group, as its name suggests, retained a strong central commitment to an analysis of literature that 'took account of both class and gender' (62). But rather than talking unproblematically about 'shared assumptions' like Kaplan and Rose, or 'mutually agreeable stances' like Gilbert and Gubar, Kaplan immediately muddies the apparent group focus: 'some of us believed that we could also integrate psychoanalytic theory with both [Marxism and feminism], but we were aware from the beginning of the considerable difficulties of such syntheses, and our discussions continued to raise new problems' (62). So far this does sound more Continental, closer by far to the Milan Women's Bookstore's process of negotiating theoretical perspectives than to the uneasily 'friendly' North American collaborations.

For all that the group was operating on arguably more Continental bases, its British critical audience apparently was as uncomfortable with its workings as the North American academy has been with their collaborative critics. As Kaplan recalls, the group presented its well-known paper, 'Women's Writing: *Jane Eyre, Aurora Leigh*,' to the Essex Conference on the Sociology of Literature in 1977. Given the event and its locale, a meeting of socialist critics at an institution known for fostering social and specifically Marxist approaches to literature and history, one might expect an openly sympathetic response, but Kaplan reports:

Ten of us appeared at the conference and we gave the paper a dramatic performance, all of us reading parts of it out, ten women on the platform. Even at a conference of socialist literary critics, our presentation and the paper itself caused a mild sensation. Very few of the men at the conference had any experience of collective writing of an intellectual as opposed to an agit-prop, political kind, and I suspect that we were challenging more than a male Marxist hegemony of criticism and theory but, equally important, the 'individualist' notion of criticism as the work of single intellects, something that Marxist critical practice as opposed to theory had not really confronted. (62–3)

So the political alignment of critics on the left was set astray by the workings of the variables of gender and theories of authorship. At the same conference, when chairing a discussion between Terry Eagleton and Frank Kermode, Kaplan was struck by how, despite their theoretical and political disagreements, both seemed to subscribe to a notion of the critic as a single author. Ironically, the British academy seems still attached to the 'Man of Letters' or oracular model of critical authorship, so aptly represented by the figure of F. R. Leavis, whose influence on the British academy Eagleton has so trenchantly decried. The source of institutional discomfort differs from the North American model, but it remains discomfort nevertheless.

Lest I seem to suggest otherwise, I should point out that even Kaplan gets caught up in the tension between idealism and difference that I've observed in several North American collaborations, but she is aware of the workings of both sensations, and of the need to negotiate them. She does not scruple to identify the Marxist-Feminist Literature Collective as a source of critical inspiration: 'For me,' she writes, 'that group was absolutely formative for my work' (63). It consolidated her interest in nineteenth-century women's texts and it removed any traces of the 'fear of theory as an alien and impenetrable discourse' that she identifies with members of her academic generation. Both areas are, indeed, foundational for Kaplan, as a well-known theoretically informed socialist-feminist critic of nineteenth-century literature. But she does not use that transformative aspect of the collaboration as a reason to defend it against charges of dissension or disunity. Rather, she sees those forces as equally and simultaneously formative. The group, for example, had discussions about the extent to which 'it was appropriate to use our collective work to aid our careers which were at very different stages' (63), a remarkably sophisticated and mature question for a critical collective to pose to itself. And Kaplan's observation that the collective was subversive in its inclusion of both faculty and students does not preclude her clear-eyed assessment of why this association of differently empowered members of an institution was less politically riven: 'This was made easier because we were not students and teachers at the same institutions' (63). Finally, Kaplan does not claim that the issue of private intellectual property can be transcended or temporarily put in mothballs during collaboration: 'We learned a great deal about the contradictions and difficulties of working collectively in a field that prized the individual and original insight above any other, learning how hard it was to "let go" of a private property in ideas and language. We did not entirely let go' (63). With that keen perception, rather than denial, of contradiction, and the refusal to chart a journey of critical transcendence of individual academic property ethic, Kaplan's perspective on collaborative criticism has much to offer analyses of other collaborators' works.

Another phenomenon in collaborative critical writing that also troubles my broad division between North American and European attitudes is the reaction of more recent North American writing partners against coalition collaborations. However indebted they are to pioneering academic pairs like Gilbert and Gubar, some of them have begun to define their collaborative practices and objectives differently. In their discussion in the first *Tulsa Studies* special issue on collaboration, Susan Leonardi reminds her collaborator Rebecca Pope, 'I learned my first collaborative manners at the seminar table of Sandra Gilbert and Susan Gubar' (269). Still, Leonardi and Pope, in their own collaborations on literature and cultural studies, have turned away from 'coalition collaboration' that Gilbert and Gubar and so many of their admirers have forged. Of all the North American collaborators I survey, they seem most eager to explore issues of power within their own working relationship. From the beginning of this discussion, their own relative academic roles are foregrounded; Pope reminds her collaborator and readers that, unlike Leonardi, she does not have tenure, and both she and Leonardi are aware of the risks of collaborative endeavour. In fact, they quote the passage from Ede and Lunsford about their tenure and promotion difficulties that I have quoted above.

For all that the prevailing academic climate places them on the defensive, however, they do not find shelter in a theory of undifferentiated agreement and harmony, for, as Pope jokingly rewrites Irigaray, 'After all, when our lips speak together, as often as not, they disagree' (262). They also seem aware of the ways in which prevailing North American feminist theories of working together may silence difference, perhaps because of these institutional pressures on academic women to 'behave': 'One of the problems with the conversation model is that conversation and dialogue, at least as they are practiced by "good girls" seem so often repressed by social convention. One shies away from serious disagreement, one doesn't interrupt, one doesn't too obviously stake out one's territory, one tries not to digress. One never, ever screams' (267). As a result, Leonardi and Pope are explicitly wary of any fusion theory of collaboration, and they are theoretically aware of the ways in which such a theory would be implicated in figurings of lesbian relationship. As Pope comments, 'But what I'm worried about is not that we will lose ourselves in some sort of psychic fusion, but that others might offer that fantasy as a model of women's collaboration as it's been offered as a model for lesbianism' (268). In this respect, their theoretical interests approach very closely my own; as Pope elaborates, they may transform each other's thoughts in the process of their collaboration, but they don't lose themselves in that process either. In fact, Leonardi offers the wry rejoinder that perhaps they write about divas, the subject of their collaboratively produced cultural studies project, 'to defuse our own prima donna tendencies' (268). In their witty, theoretically sophisticated understanding of collaboration, Leonardi and Pope may struggle with the same institutional and cultural pressures that have tempted other North American collaborators to embrace fusion theories or 'coalition collaborations,' but they opt, instead, for a collaboration in which women need be neither solely prima donna nor patient Griselda.

As I mentioned at the beginning of this chapter, collaborative groups can occupy many spaces, sometimes simultaneously, on the spectrum that runs from fusion to difference. But overwhelmingly, North American collaborators continue to have the most difficulty being accepted as doing respectable scholarly work. There are many more groups I could cite, for I have been struck by the similarity of their accounts of institutional apathy or punitiveness. The collective that wrote *Feminist Scholarship: Kindling in the Groves of Academe* sum up my discoveries most succinctly:

'Scholarship is ordinarily an individualized endeavour, especially in the field treated here [i.e., humanities and social sciences]. The academic frameworks for recognition, reward, and promotion presuppose this, but, even more important, so do our own habits of thought and work' (DuBois et al. viii). In differing measures, this is what I have found in North American critical collaborations: a combination of institutional pressures and internalizations of conventional theories of critical authorship. The Author whose death Roland Barthes was conventionally said to have heralded is alive and well and seeking tenure and promotion at a university.

3

Collaborative Predecessors

Introducing his book on men's fin-de-siècle collaborations, Wayne Koestenbaum notes that an 'entire other book could discuss the history of female (and lesbian) collaboration' (13). *Rethinking Women's Collaborative Writing* is not that other book, for my aim is less to produce a history than to analyse the power dynamics and ideological polyvalence of contemporary women's collaborations. Still, a historical framework for my analyses of contemporary women's collaborations is essential if we are to understand those collaborations not as aberrations, as the isolated brainchildren of the twentieth-century avant-garde. They are, instead, products of a number of historical moments when writers felt the impulse to challenge the modern construction of the singular author and its dominance of the cultural field or, earlier, to work with paradigms of authorship that pre-date that modern construction. This need for historical assessment is all the more pressing because the existing critical accounts of collaborative authorship tend to focus on men or, more frequently, on male-female literary associations, many of which do not involve overt collaboration. Often, those literary relationships are closer to influence than to co-composition, like that of Dorothy and William Wordsworth. Studies of male-female collaboration also tend to heterosexualize these writing partnerships. In the collection of critical essays edited by Chadwick and de Courtivron, *Significant Others: Creativity and Intimate Partnership* (1993), a volume whose title announces a fundamental sexual-creative link, only one of the thirteen essays focuses on a female creative pair: Virginia Woolf and Vita Sackville-West. In the pages that follow I seek to redress this imbalance and to consider the historical precedents for women's collective writing.

Here, as elsewhere, the writing partnerships that I examine are those that involve overt collaboration; for that reason, celebrated literary partnerships between women that one might otherwise expect to see accounted for here are absent. An interesting case in point is that of the Bronte sisters. As Edward Chitham remarked: 'The Brontes' literary activity was initially communal, much of it associated with plays' (32). The Brontes' early experience of a common eighteenth- and nineteenth-century middle-class English pastime, the private theatricals that Jane Austen described (and decried) in *Mansfield Park* some decades earlier, developed into the extended collective play of the Gondal sagas. As early as 1933, Fannie Ratchford, writing about *The Brontes' Web of Childhood*, maintained that the 'younger Bronte girls were not so close in their literary work as were Charlotte and Branwell' (259), and more recent criticism of the young Brontes tends to bear her out. As Christine Alexander notes in the introduction to her *Edition of the Early Writings of Charlotte Bronte*, it is true that Emily and Anne took the occasion of Charlotte's brief absence in 1834 to redirect aspects of the Gondal saga. Apparently the two younger sisters felt that Branwell and Charlotte had assumed control of the writing and had demoted their characters to secondary roles. Still, Alexander maintains that the closest collaborators were the elder brother and sister; she calls 1833–5 a 'period of intense partnership between Charlotte and Branwell Bronte' (xiii). Even so, this intensity did not take the form of overt collaboration in the sense that I define it; according to Alexander, Charlotte and Branwell 'wrote increasingly about each other's characters and assumed a knowledge about each other's latest productions' and they 'cooperated on the basic outline of the plot but pursued their own interests' (xiv). If that was as intense as the early Bronte collaborations got, then clearly the sisters' collaborations, like that of Branwell and Charlotte, would appear to belong more to the wider sense of implicit collaboration that I identify in my introductory chapter.

So too does the later creative relationship between Gertrude Stein and Alice B. Toklas. Although many of their friends and associates wondered whether Alice hadn't taken a greater hand in composing *The Autobiography of Alice B. Toklas* than the volume declared, Alice denied co-authorship of *The Autobiography* to the end of her life. And, as Toklas's biographer Linda Simon points out, 'Though Alice denied many things which were subsequently found to be true, there is no evidence that she wrote her own autobiography in 1932' (150). If Alice Toklas didn't write in this explicit sense, she did, of course, have enormous creative input into Stein's work, as many critics have evidenced. Those critics remain divided, however, as to the power dynamics of that relationship, debating whether Toklas could be considered literary collaborator or glorified amanuensis-wife. James S. Williams, for instance, notes that the authorship of *The Autobiography* is 'far from clear' but adds: 'The Stein-Toklas marriage illustrates ... how collaboration can easily degenerate into the rhetoric of collusion' (577). Either way – celebrated as avant-garde experimentation with authorship or criticized as power-laden collusion – this collaboration is implicit rather than an act of co-signature in the precise way I want to study.

Although I pay close attention to the closeting of women's collaboration in the preceding century, it does not follow that I read the history of women's (or men's) collaborations as a progressive enlightenment, ranging from dark secrecy to the broad light of disclosure, any more than I believe in an evolution from normative singular authorship to new collaborative freedoms in the twentieth century. In fact, the contemporary collaborations that I analyse negotiate cultural space, territorial and privacy issues that are not divorced from the challenges of their nineteenth-century predecessors. Many of those issues are, simply, reconfigured.

In terms of historicizing collaboration, then, I agree with a number of theorists of collective writing that the Western Romantic individual artist or the individualist cult of Shakespeare, say, were closer to aberrations in the history of writing practices than transhistorical norms. As Sean Burke writes, 'What distinguishes premodern conceptions of authorship is their assumption that discourse is primarily an affair of public rather than private consciousness' (*Authorship* xviii). Martha Woodmansee, who has written cogently on authorship issues in relation to copyright law, would go further; not only does she claim that research suggests that the 'author in this modern sense [i.e., "an individual who is the sole creator of unique 'works'"] is a relatively recent invention, but that it does not closely reflect contemporary writing practices. Indeed,' she adds, 'on inspection, it is not clear that this notion ever coincided closely with the practice of writing' (Woodmansee and Jaszi 15).

Although authorship has always already been public, as Woodmansee and others such as collaborative critics Lisa Ede and Andrea Lunsford have argued (in *Singular Texts / Plural Authors*), at certain historical moments, this dominant practice, this primary, public Western discourse, yielded to a more visible, or at least popular, image of private authorship. The Renaissance was a time of widespread public collaborative activity, particularly in the theatre, though conditions of dramatic production and the conventions of public life made it very difficult for women to participate in that burgeoning collaborative creativity. As G.E. Bentley noted in his study, *The Profession of Dramatist in Shakespeare's Time*, almost half of the plays written in this period reflected the work of more than one dramatist. Bentley argues that title pages of the time tended to 'simplify the actual circumstances of composition' (quoted in Masten 'Playwrighting' 364). Another Early Modern drama scholar, Neil Carson, has used records of payment of playwrights of the period to show that collaboration was both a frequent and a 'casual' practice, and that 'there is relatively little evidence to suggest that one writer [in these loosely-formed alliances] acted as the guiding spirit or co-ordinator' (22). Still, Donald E. Pease, like Jeffrey Masten, sees within that rich field of collective production the seeds of the individual, private author figure, significantly moving up Michel Foucault's historical calculations of its emergence by a couple of centuries. Pease has suggested that the increasingly individuated late-modern author should be understood in the context of the so-called Early Modern 'new men,' cultural agents (significantly masculinized by Renaissance historians) who leashed and distributed the cultural power created by explorers' observations of the New World. For Pease, this distribution caused a crisis in representation and culture, since new phenomena and experiences ruptured the more medieval notion of authorship as a chainlike reliance on the authority of previous authors' texts. Those authoritative texts of the past could not hope to offer precedent for representing the New World. Pease maintains that, indeed, these new authors 'exploited the discontinuity between the things in the New World and the words in the ancient books to claim for their words an unprecedented cultural power' (266). In this respect they were not unlike others 'who exploited this dissociation between worlds: explorers, merchants, colonists ...' (266).

There are aspects of Pease's theory that I would question. For example, it relies upon a conceptualization of new experience, unrepresentable by recourse to precedent. As a result, it overdramatizes the New World's power to break open Old World modes of representation. Still, the theory is valuable for suggesting that authorship itself is always culturally and historically in play. It matters little whether one accepts with Foucault the fact of the emergence of the single author around the end of the eighteenth or the beginning of the nineteenth centuries, or whether one traces it, following Pease and Masten, back to the Renaissance. Such emphasis on periodization is less to the point than the recognition that notions of authorship may not necessarily evolve so much as they compete, in widely varying and ever mutating versions and combinations. As Donald K. Hedrick, writing about Bentley's estimates of the frequency of collaboration, points out, 'What we can infer is not the existence of some procedural norm, but the existence of a system in which modes of production are themselves in competition for privilege. Authorship competing with collaboration was the Elizabethan theatrical situation' (51), one which he sees dramatized in Shakespeare's *The Two Noble Kinsmen*.

Although much of the best-known work on Early Modern collaboration addresses drama, there is also evidence of other sorts of collaborative texts during this period. Seventeenth-century poetry scholars John O'Neill and Claudia A. Limbert have identified two versions of a 'feminist antimarital satire,' 'Advice to Virgins,' that they believe is the work of the seventeenth-century poet known as 'The Matchless Orinda,' Katherine Phillips, and a later collaborator who may have picked up the poem after Phillips's death and revised it. Of course, such a collaboration does not fall under the terms of this study, since, as O'Neill and Limbert note, the 'co-creators are not working consciously together' (492). They suggest the term 'composite authorship' to describe this form of collective writing, and they argue that it was very common in the seventeenth century, perhaps because of the casual practice of private circulation of texts among close circles of friends. What is important for my purposes, however, is the evidence of a richness and diversity of collective writing practices in Early Modern non-dramatic literature. Another, more explicit form of collective textual production was popular in France at this time. Leonard Hinds, writing about the circle of Madame de Scudery, argues that she and her literary group used collectively produced fictions to pronounce upon political matters of the day, alternating from the pronouns 'je,' 'nous,' and the ambiguous 'on'; as Hinds argues, such 'malleable manifestations of authorship' (500) opened up 'a new subjective space for authorship and for contestatory, political pronouncements' (493).

The eighteenth century, as we know from the more canonized forms of literary collaboration – that of Addison and Steele, for instance – was another time of vigorous literary cooperation. Still, critics of that period seem to have only very recently begun to assess the impact of these widespread collective writing practices. In a 1987 article in *Essays in Criticism*, Dustin Griffin notes that although 'literary collaboration is surprisingly common in Restoration and eighteenth century England ... [w]e have not often paid attention to this phenomenon, except as editors (concerned to establish a writer's canon) and biographers (concerned to chart a writer's literary career)' (1). There is, to cite but one example, Thomas M. Curley's 1983 article on the collaboration between Samuel Johnson and Sir Robert Chambers on *A Course of Lectures on the English Law* (1766–70), which offers the perhaps unsurprising observation that 'Johnson preferred to counsel rather than to listen during the collaboration' [95]. The article appears as part of an inquiry into Johnson's career in a volume entitled *The Unknown Samuel Johnson*. In his preliminary study of the implications of collective authorship in the eighteenth century, Griffin makes no mention of any women collaborators; the article concerns itself entirely with the canonized male authors of the period: Pope, Dryden, Johnson, Swift. We know, however, that women writers like Sarah Fielding and Anna Letitia Barbauld wrote fiction collaboratively. In his article on Barbauld, Daniel E. White argues that she used collaborative production of texts within a family circle to disseminate the ideals of the eighteenth-century middle-class Dissenting community:

Reason, science, free enquiry, abstract philosophical speculation, theological disputation, religious liberty, personal self-denial, and a middle-class commercialist ethos would be tempered, made warmer and more beautiful through familial collaboration and poetic techniques of sensibility that would together associate the masculinist features of nonconformity with the intimate plenitude of the home and the domestic relationships within its walls. (515)

As with Madame de Scudery, collaboration of women and their acquaintances or family members could be made to serve political ends, at times when political discourse was considered the domain of men and, increasingly, of individual men in particular. Then, as now, however, those political ends could be strikingly various.

The Romantic period was one that, as Michel Foucault maintained, forged a link between ownership, copyright rules, and literary activity, and in so doing it arguably helped to produce the social imperative, in the West, for an individuated author to assume additional authority as the owner of a text. This period of greater emphasis on legal ownership of text coincided, of course, with the decades of the late eighteenth and nineteenth centuries during which women of the middle and upper classes gained greater access to publication as well as limited access to legal action and empowerment. It is because of this historical coincidence, I believe, that the influential collaborations among women that I explore in this chapter are drawn from the late nineteenth century. Noting the incidence of male collaboration during this period, Wayne Koestenbaum attributes it to the closeting of homosexual desire, citing the Labouchere Amendment of 1885 England which, until its repeal in 1967, rendered homosexuality punishable by law (2–3). My own analysis of the two most prominent literary collaborations by women in this period, that of Michael Field (Katherine Bradley and Edith Cooper) and Somerville and Ross (Edith Somerville and Violet Martin), suggests at several points some of this anxious closeting of same-sex desire. At the same time, however, I would locate this collaborative activity by women in the historical context of a complementary resistance to Romanticism's construction of the author as particular male types: Byronic wanderer, possessed visionary, calm meditative gentleman musing amidst nature. I read these nineteenth-century collaborations as expressions of the interventions of women into an increasingly legalistic and atomizing discourse of authorship. Jeffrey Masten argues, along similar lines, that in the middle of the seventeenth century, the 'earlier, homoerotic discourse of collaboration' that 'insisted upon the indifferentiation of style and subjectivities' was being 'regendered,' replaced by a heterosexual model of companionate-marriage collaboration in which patriarchal ownership of text was scrupulously differentiated 'by sex' ('My Two Dads' 300–1). In this increasingly legalistic and heterosexualized arena of authorship, women's literary collaboration was one cultural site where a wide range of same-sex relationships could be coded and closeted, even as they were, if anxiously, expressed and embodied.

Extending Donald Pease's historicist approach, I would also be tempted to see the ascendence of the ideology of the individuated author in nineteenth-century Europe as similarly caught up in imperial projects and designs, in this case various nation states' accumulations of a string of colonies. Martha Woodmansee sees the rise of textual property concerns in the German states at the end of the eighteenth century and beginning of the nineteenth as a reaction, in part, to the textual piracy that was previously the norm in the German literary world. I would add that it was also a response to a growing anxiety about state properties. The arguments of philosophers such as Fichte for regarding an author's text as property came at a time when European nations also sought rationalizations for extending and consolidating their colonial holdings, particularly in Africa. As postcolonial analysis has repeatedly shown, these justifications often made strategic use of the metaphor of ownership of the colony through words or language. As Foucault notes, in this same period, the author 'was accepted into the social order of property which governs our culture' (125), and one area of European culture that was aggressively governed by the order of property was imperialism. This link between authorship as it was formulated in the nineteenth century and imperialism continues to haunt contemporary collaborations, for collaborators often figure themselves as decolonizing agents.

Because these nineteenth-century spatial and territorial issues do not melt away in a postcolonial age, I do not simply recount the biographical and bibliographical facts of earlier female collaborations as though they were distant case histories. Instead, I investigate the negotiations of cultural space that occur when women collaborators must operate in a century in which genius, for whatever socio-historical reasons, was deemed not only male but singular. In this sense, I take very seriously Michel Foucault's celebrated spatial metaphor for authorship as, paradoxically, the 'empty space left by the author's disappearance,' a space that is, in true Foucauldian style, 'reapportion[ed]' (121) over time rather than emptied of its cultural currency.

A particularly claustrophobic example of closeted nineteenth-century collaboration was that of Katherine Bradley and Edith Cooper, an aunt and niece team born into a thriving Birmingham middle-class mercantile family. The two women signed themselves 'Michael Field' on the twenty-six plays and eight collections of poems they wrote from the 1880s until their deaths, just a few months apart, in 1913. In 1878, when Katherine was 32 and Edith was 16, they departed for Bristol to study classics and philosophy, where they impressed observers as unconventional

'New Women' aesthetes (Moriarty 122–3). It was at this point in their lives that they decided to live and write together. Their first joint work, *Bellerophon* (1881), was published under the androgynous pseudonyms Arran and Isla Leigh and two years later they published a poetic play inspired by Greek legend, *Callirrhoe and Fair Rosamund* under the decidedly masculine name 'Michael Field.' During the 1880s, only a small circle of associates knew the secret of the collaboration; it was not generally known to the public until 1893, when Katherine and Edith's play *A Question of Memory* was produced – disastrously – for the London stage and the two authors attended the premiere performance.

It was, however, the very first work published under the nom de plume Michael Field, *Callirrhoe and Fair Rosamund*, that attracted the attention of the elderly and influential Robert Browning, and he became the first prominent literary figure to be let into the secret. Katherine and Edith quickly forged a close and influential friendship with the rather frail elder poet, now in the last years of his life. He, in turn, promoted their work, proclaiming to Arthur Symons, for instance, that he had found a 'new poet,' while keeping the secret of their dual, female identity (Field, *Works and Days*). The public promotion of an author veiled in secrecy proved to be a rather complicated affair, one uncannily appropriate to the author of the manifold secrecies of *The Ring and the Book*. Browning invited Katherine and Edith to his house many times, for the social dinners for which the elder Browning was well known. There, they met a number of the literary luminaries of the day, all of whom, for the time, were ignorant that these two rather unassuming women were the 'new poet' much vaunted by their host and, on one occasion at least, currently under discussion at the dinner table.

Apparently Browning found their collaboration analogous to his own fondly remembered literary partnership. As he wrote to them early on, when Katherine had particularly requested his secrecy, 'I wanted to say (I remember) that you may depend on your secret – as to the divided authorship, and the rest – being kept by me – who am very unnecessarily apprised that the difference in age between such relatives need not be considerable'

(*Works and Days* 5). (Elizabeth Barrett was six years older than
he – hardly a significant difference but, in light of the conventions
of the day, certainly atypical.) We also know that they extensively
compared their writing partnerships in a further conversation.
Browning told the aunt and niece that he and Elizabeth had never
discussed their individual works until they were finished. Picking
up a volume of Euripides that had belonged to Elizabeth, Robert
noted: 'She would join my name to hers in all the books that
belonged to her, she would have nothing of her own – it was very
pretty of her' (*Works and Days* 15). And yet, of course, Elizabeth
evidently did have something of her own, artistically. When
Katherine asked whether he approved of writing together, Browning said he did, 'if you are two sympathetic souls' (15). He went
on to lament his own recent personal and literary loneliness: his
distance from his son, and even from his sister Sarianna, who, he
sadly reflected, had not yet read his newest poem. Such confession
drew from Katherine, in her journal entry for that day, sympathy
and a keen appreciation for her own shared creativity: 'I give
thanks for my Persian [nickname for Edith]: those two poets, man
and wife, wrote alone; each wrote, but did not bless or quicken
one another at their work; we are closer married' (*Works and Days*
16). Katherine was undoubtedly hasty in her characterization of
the Brownings' marriage as one of literary segregation, as scholars
of that literary couple will aver, but there is an important distinction to be made between the Brownings' implicit collaboration,
which more closely resembled literary influence, and the explicit
collaboration of Katherine Bradley and Edith Cooper.

Ironically, though, for all the explicit nature of their actual
working relations, the collaboration had to remain socially implicit and hidden, a condition that arguably both fostered and
hushed Katherine's and Edith's creativity. In the 1880s portion of
the Michael Field correspondence held in the British Library,
there are repeated solicitations for secrecy and corresponding promises by correspondents not to reveal the secret of the collaboration.
Alexander Laing wrote in solemn tones in 1887, 'P.P.S. The secret
of authorship which you have confided to me I hold perfectly
sacred' (BL Add. 45851); Edmund Stedman, editor of *The Victo-*

rian Poets, wrote to assure the poets: 'As you wished, I respected your incognita in "The Victorian Poets" and I do so now,' though he seemed to be under the impression that Michael Field was one singular reticent author rather than two (his letter bears the salutation 'To Michael Field = Dear Madam') (12 August 1888; Add. 45851). As Katherine wrote to the man who would become their close confidant, J.M. Gray, in 1886: 'My request is that you will do your utmost to conceal the dual authorship & in fact will treat me as chivalrously as you would the Pretender, were he in hiding' (Add. 45853). Katherine was adept at playing on the gendered and ethnic predispositions of her correspondent; in effect, she calls upon Gray, as a gentleman and as a Scot, to honour the secret.

One of the forms of creativity that this hothouse atmosphere fostered was the devising of secret codes, a linguistic creativity that I would describe as anxiously humorous. As the editors of the slim selection from their voluminous journals, T. and D.C. Sturge Moore, observed in 1933: 'They were prolific in nicknames, for themselves and others; but as the years went by Katherine became Michael, and Edith, Field or Henry; this last by Michael, either drawn out to Hennery or shortened to Henny' (xvi). As nicknames often do, these gave rise to many a rueful joke or turn of phrase. J.M. Gray opened a letter from 1890, 'How fare ye? – dearest of double poets?' and even Katherine was not above a painful pun, referring in an 1889 letter to herself as 'the elder – shall we say the fallow field' (BL Add. 45853).

Predictably, this name game led to considerable pronomial anxiety on the part of early correspondents. Reading through that correspondence I was amused to see the variations concocted by uneasy letter writers, some of whom knew more of the secret than others. J.M. Gray, for instance, relayed to Katherine and Edith their supporter, Robert Browning's greetings: 'He knew at once whom I meant, & said very pleasant things of Michael's work – *very* – & told me to take to him "to both of him", he said, his best wishes and kindest messages' (31 January, 1888; Add. 45853, emphasis Gray's). Gray, in an unconsciously revealing stroke, inserted Browning's jest, 'to both of him' in a marginal addendum, a veritable sign of the quiet marginality of this pronomially irregular relationship. In another letter, Gray inscribes a heraldic shield, 'For Michael Field her very own selves' (7 October 1890; Add. 45853). Even Katherine was not immune to pronoun difficulties in her attempts to represent 'Michael Field'; to Gray she writes, 'He – I – or we – send the 3 other poems we shd. like printed' (13 October 1886; Add 45853). Although the pronoun game gave the participants some sense of hidden, playful pleasure, I also read it as a sign of cultural anxiety, a joke which at least partly relies on a sense of two women collaboratively writing as an authorial circus trick.

Another telling sign of the depth of the textual closet in which Michael Field felt themselves and the spatial complexities it engendered was the intense concern with what I call parsing the collaboration, separating out the strands of individual authorship and ownership of the work. Even in a relationship as relatively private as this one was before 1893, inquiring minds wanted to force the collaboration into a single-author model. When Edith Cooper sent *Callirrhoe and Fair Rosamund* to Robert Browning, describing it as 'partly mine,' he replied to this very first missive with the inevitable question of ownership: 'Dear Miss Cooper, I should be glad to know – since it is *you* whom I address and must thank – how much of the book that is "partly yours" is indeed your own part' (*Works and Days* 2, emphasis Browning's). As Jeffrey Masten has shown, this desire to isolate the individual author within a collaboration finds its roots in Early Modern transformations of notions of textuality. Citing a couplet written by an early editor of Beaumont and Fletcher, 'And the Presse which both thus amongst us sends / Sends us one Poet in a paire of friends,' he notes that the editor is, 'in a sense, mystifying collaboration into the author-function' ('My Two Dads' 289), as Browning would do two centuries later to another pair of collaborative friends. Eventually, Browning came to treat the collaboration with respect and took Edith and Katherine's advice not to become too fixated on the property ethic of its workings. Still, as more literati were let into the secret, the question was repeated *ad nauseam*. Katherine rather wearily recounts a meeting with George Meredith to Edith: 'He asks which one of us "does the Males?" ... "Who did Bothwell?" comes next' (*Works and Days* 82). George Moore inquired, with comic (perhaps dark) understatement, 'Who does the love scenes? – they are so good. You get such words in them' (*Works and Days* 201). Eventually, of course, Michael Field became impatient with this desire to portion out the collaboration; writing to Havelock Ellis, who had made the well-worn inquiry, 'Michael' reprimanded, 'As to our work, let no man think he can put asunder what God has joined' (quoted in Faderman 210) – heady words addressed to the writer who pronounced so roundly on earthly unions.

Twentieth-century bibliographical and editorial practices have been particularly susceptible to this fixation on parsing collaboration, because of what Jerome McGann calls their fascination with the singular author. Although only a small portion of Michael Field's work has been published or reissued, this holds true for the editorial projects that have been completed. Mary Sturgeon, in her 1923 edition of their selected poems, seems to feel compelled to point out, in occasional, anxious footnotes, the traces of single authorship that she can discern in the collective works. 'The following poems,' she writes, for instance, 'are from *Poems of Adoration*, which book was, save for one or two pieces, entirely written by Edith Cooper' (Field, *Selection* 120), or 'The remaining poems, except the very last, are from *Mystic Trees*, a companion volume to *Poems of Adoration*, but written as predominantly by Katherine Bradley as that [i.e., the latter] had been by her "fellow"' (130). A similar editorial anxiety manifests itself in T. and D.C. Sturge Moore's selections from the journal, *Works and Days*, published in 1933. The manuscript copies of these journals, held in the British Library, show both hands clearly at work; one writer will jot down some sentences, followed by the other author, but the authorship of the entries is not assiduously noted or guarded. There is a palpable sense of these pages as fully shared that transcends the mere question of the holder of the pen for, as Holly Laird, like Jeffrey Masten, reminds critics of collaborative texts, manuscript evidence may be 'misleading since a change in handwriting may not in fact indicate a change in authorship' ('Preface'

13) In the Michael Field manuscripts, it is true that one writer may make additions to the other's entry, finding space on a facing page, if need be. On one occasion, for instance, Edith makes her differing perception clear by adding, with an arrow, the following comment to one of Katherine's criticisms of the room that served as their study: 'But I have taken to the little place' (Friday, 6 March 1891; Add. 46779). At these times, the Sturge Moores, like Sturgeon, have recourse to anxious footnotes, in an attempt to parcel out the authorship of a shared journal space. At times, however, I can sense their editorial practice, schooled in the ideology of the single author, creaking under the strain of a collective text that resists an easy equation of handwriting and authorship. For one particularly dialogic entry from 4 July 1888, the editors supply the following footnote: 'There are entries by both Edith and Katherine. They have been mingled to give a consecutive narrative; where necessary the writer of a particular phrase or paragraph is indicated' (*Works and Days* 20–1). This anxiety, this necessity, is, I sense, all the more pressing in editing a genre that is so firmly entrenched in assumptions about the singularity of authorial inspiration and meditation: the journal.

I raise the issue of the readerly parsing of collaboration – what Jeffrey Masten calls the 'individuation model of collaboration' in scholarly editing ('Playwrighting' 374) – because it is a major part of the spatial dynamic of women's collaborative work, from Michael Field's day to the present. Even in a 1993 study of 'creativity and intimate partnership,' *Significant Others*, the editors, Whitney Chadwick and Isabelle de Courtivron, ironically hold to this singular model of artistic production, in their highlighting of the parsing process: 'Investigating notions of collaboration ... offers one way that we can move toward untangling the ... singular achievement from the collaborative process' (9). Authorship itself is not significantly retheorized or rethought in this view of collaboration; once again, the shared collaborative space must be territorialized so that the individual authors can remain intact. This view, of course, is replicated in and is reproduced by legal sanctions governing authorship. As Peter Jaszi notes, copyright law does not adequately come to terms with artistic collaborations of various sorts; he denounces 'law's insistence on formally disaggregating collaborative productions, rather than categorizing them as "joint works"' (52). As literary critics, we have more often than not done the same. As Charles H. Frey notes of the critical and editorial handling of Shakespeare's *The Two Noble Kinsmen*, 'most of the scholarly energy, if not total human energy, devoted to this play has been concerned with separating out the respective contributions of the collaborators' ('Collaborating' 31). This continues to hold true of critical treatments of women's collaborations, even though many of these contemporary collaborators have gone on record to say, like the collaborative critics Carey Kaplan and Ellen Cronan Rose: 'At the end of several hours we are scrolling through something neither of us would or could have written alone and honestly cannot say which word "came from" Carey, which idea "came from" Ellen' ('Strange Bedfellows' 549). I very much suspect that Michael Field would have said the same of their journals, plays, and poems.

As Kaplan and Rose's comment suggests, the sharing of the collaborative page is a complex dynamic of collective and individual praxis. When Michael Field sought to describe that dynamic, they frequently did so by recourse to spatial and visual metaphors that were organic and corporeal. They did not, significantly, adopt the more economic metaphors of some of their correspondents. Of these, J.M. Gray, for instance, was particularly fond of the economic and legal metaphor; on 7 October 1891, he inquired after Edith: 'Well and how *is* the younger member of the literary firm – a firm now so famous?' In the same letter, he devises an heraldic shield for the poets: 'For Michael Field her very own selves from J.M.G.' (BL Add. 45853), drawing once more on Browning's verbal jest about 'both of him.' Eschewing both law and heraldry, Katherine and Edith refer, time after time, to their partnership as an organic incorporation, the merging of two bodies rather than two economic or family powers. To Gray, on 9 June 1889, Katherine signs herself Michael, adding 'And by Michael I mean the whole of him – poet within poet' (BL Add. 45853). When bodily separated, the poets saw themselves as incomplete texts; as Edith writes in the journal in July 1892: '[S]he [Katherine] is in Oxford – I am here a fragment' (BL Add. 46780). This understanding of the collaboration as bodily incorporation is particularly striking in a letter that Katherine writes to Gray from Dresden in September of 1891; describing a particularly serious illness that befell Edith on this journey, Katherine writes: 'They tried to rend Michael in twain, & he [has] preserved his integrity through the blessed swiftness of a young German doctor' (Add. 45854). Five years earlier, Katherine had jokingly written to Gray that his memoir of a departed friend was so fine, that 'you must undertake the obituary notice of Michael; – it is quite cheering and worth a dual death, to think of being noticed in such a charitable, human, friendly, way' (Add. 45853). Even death, it would seem, that most conventionally isolating of human experiences, was collectively imagined by this 'poet within poet.'

The garden, as a collective organic production, was another appealing way for Katherine and Edith to imagine their poetic incorporation. As Katherine, signing herself 'Michael' wrote to J.M. Gray in 1889, 'I weed Edith's garden she mine; then examining each other's withering heaps we exclaim – "Well, you might have spared that" – or, "that weak twining thing had yet a grace" – but the presiding horticulturalist is ruthless, & it is borne away to the barrow' (9 June; Add. 45953). Each poet is here envisioned as occupying territory, but that very territory is reworked, cultivated, and thereby shared with the other. Power is by no means denied; there is a 'presiding horticulturalist' who presumably wins the debate of the moment, whatever it may be, but Michael Field tellingly emphasize the function rather than the personal occupant of that function (to draw on a Foucauldian distinction about authorship). Still, the pressure of the demand to disentangle the collaboration was intense, and at times Michael Field were invariably touched by its discourse. When Edith did reply to Browning's early question about artistic ownership, she did so in a mixture of communitarian and individualistic discourses:

Some of the scenes of our play are like mosaic-work – the mingled, various product of our two brains ... [She then goes on to acknowledge 'ownership' of various scenes.] I think that if our contributions were disentangled and one subtracted from the other, the amount would be almost even. This happy union of two in work and aspiration is sheltered and expressed by 'Michael Field.' Please regard him as the author. (*Works and Days* 3)

Michael Field could and would speak the mathematical, territorial discourse of authorship if they needed to. Still, I read much more of the social will to please and justify in Edith's mathematical rationale to Browning and more of the heartfelt in her invocation of the 'mingled' and 'various' mosaic work, a metaphor that both inscribes and deconstructs personal artistic territory (the tessera cannot conceptually exist independent of the concept of mosaic.). The manuscript examples of their journals do, indeed, reveal the justice of Edith's metaphor. There is usually a main author of entries, but then, as I have mentioned, the other poet enters comments or emendations on the facing page (BL Add. 46777). One long poem that appears in their journal shows both hands at work on separate stanzas (though this may be Michael Field's preferred method of fair copying), and on one page they each try a version of the same stanza (Add. 46777). As Edith describes their inspiration for the closing lines of *Otho* (1891), in a phrase that significantly mutualizes the Promethean discourse of artistic inspiration, 'Our brains struck fire each from each' (Add. 46779).

As this reworking of standard Romantic discourses of creativity pointedly reveals, the anxiety involved in describing the collaborative space is intricately tied up with nineteenth-century and earlier understandings of genius. Christine Battersby, in *Gender and Genius*, painstakingly traces the notion of masculine genius through several centuries of aesthetic philosophy, but she does not specifically focus on the nexus of masculinity and solitude. And yet, for philosophers critically interested in creativity as social production, the concept of genius is troublesome at worst, negligible at best. As Pierre Macherey brusquely observes in 'Creation and Production,' 'All considerations of genius, of the subjectivity of the artist, of his soul, are *on principle* uninteresting' (232, emphasis Macherey's). But they were not only interesting to late Victorians;

they were all-absorbing. When Robert Browning wrote to Edith to inquire about the status of her authorship of *Callirrhoe and Fair Rosamund*, he did so because he naturally associated what he took to be the presence of genius in that work with the textual presence of one strong poet, and he needed to be satisfied on this point. He posed the question and immediately explained: 'It is long since I have been so thoroughly impressed by indubitable poetic *genius*, a word I consider while I write, only to repeat it, "genius"' (*Works and Days* 2, emphasis Browning's).

Just as Michael Field, in a touching move, carefully tipped the predominantly vicious reviews of *A Question of Memory* into their journal, I think they internalized some of the underlying assumptions about genius and the solitary poet circulating in Victorian culture. In the journals, for instance, they tend to speak of inspiration as individual and revision as collective and interactive. One 1888 entry by Edith reads: 'This has waked my Muse. She is with me, I have sung' (BL Add. 46777), and another entry by Edith, written five years later, makes the pairing of isolation and inspiration explicit: 'While my Love [Katherine] was away I lived beneath the sunny showers of the most complete inspiration I have had for years' (Add. 46781). These would seem to be strange recurrences to dominant discourses of authorship in a partnership that figures itself as incorporated, as a merging of 'poet within poet.' But I think they both had recourse to and chafed under these assumptions, just as generations of English poets before and after them chafed under the long, solitary shadow of Shakespeare, even as they may have praised or emulated the Bard. And so, in what is probably their best-known poem, 'Prologue,' Shakespeare figures both as reference and as pressure point:

> It was deep April, and the morn
> Shakespeare was born;
> The world was on us, pressing sore;
> My Love and I took hands and swore,
> Against the world, to be
> Poets and lovers ever more. (Field, *Selection* 18)

As Jeffrey Masten remarks in his article on Beaumont and Fletcher: 'In a scholarly field dominated by the singular figure of Shakespeare, it is easily forgotten that collaboration was the Renaissance English theatre's dominant mode of textual production' ('Beaumont and Fletcher' 363). How fitting that these two poets, one of whom described their work to Robert Browning as working 'together in the manner of Beaumont and Fletcher' (*Works and Days* 4), should have felt similarly overshadowed by this avatar of singular genius.

Only when Edith and Katherine were secret collaborators could they be together on the page in the sort of 'fellowship' (to quote Katherine's last poem, written in Edith's memory) sheltered from dominant constructions of genius. Only then, when they were publicly presentable as a single male poet could they gain access to honest criticism, they felt. When they feared that Robert Browning was letting the secret of their dual authorship slip out, they upbraided him with this very rationale: 'We must be free as dramatists to work out in the open air of nature – exposed to her viscissitudes, witnessing her terrors: we cannot be stifled in drawing-room conventionalities ... you are robbing us of real criticism, such as man gives man' (*Works and Days* 6–7). This fear was one that preyed upon Katherine and Edith; in a poem published in the posthumous volume *Dedicated*, they explore it, as they explored so many other carefully coded issues, through classical mythology. In 'Caenis Caeneus,' the sea-god Neptune hears the girl Caenis's prayer to participate more fully in public life and determines that the only way to accomplish this desire will be to transform her into a man:

> But he will grant this maiden's hope,
> And let her reach, as she would choose,
> Her goal of wellnigh impious scope,
> She shall be changed – a very change be wrought,
> And she become a man in form and thought. (44)

As a male, Caeneus is free to taste of bodily, sensual experience and to mingle freely with others, a liberty clearly denied to respectable Victorian womanhood:

A stranger, on the grass he laughed.
And ate with them at close of day,
And of their liberal vintage quaffed. (46)

Michael Field clearly see this classically inspired gender-bending as a harbinger of the liberation of Victorian women; Caenis/ Caeneus is killed when he intervenes in the Centaurs' rape of women. In this poem I see a highly worked and encoded meditation on the poetic collaboration that transformed Katherine Bradley and Edith Cooper into Michael Field, a male poet entitled to 'real criticism, such as man gives man' in the public thoroughfares. When this collaborative relationship struck up against public utterance, in the form of the London performance of *A Question of Memory* in 1893, Caeneus was transformed back into Caenis, and the possibility of Edith and Katherine ever gaining access to 'real criticism' was dashed forever. This performance, which in the preceding months was attended by many negotiations, second thoughts, and worries on the part of both poets, signified for Katherine and Edith an anxious transversal of the private and public spaces of their collaboration. And indeed, if the critic from *Winters Weekly Magazine* of 11 November 1893 is to be believed, the transformation from serious critical consideration to condescension took place immediately after the curtain fell. The mixture of hisses and applause died away to pure applause when 'two graceful young ladies' stood up, revealing themselves as Michael Field (though this critic, typically, uses this narrative to demonstrate the courtesy of English manhood at its best) (BL Add. 45852). As Edith recorded her response to this painful evening of revelation and disgrace: 'I felt suddenly as if I stood in a clearing where there was no humanity – where I was a mortal alone' (*Works and Days* 182). Michael Field was rent 'in twain,' not by death but by disclosure.

This public show of generous condescension to the two 'lady' playwrights was quickly taken up by the press, and the loss of serious critical estimation, which Katherine and Edith had so feared, was now a reality. The *DY Chronicle* reviewer called them 'members of the fair sex who chose as a *nom de plume* Michael

Field'; the *Dramatic Review* similarly highlighted sex first, accomplishment second: 'the ladies who style themselves "Michael Field"' (BL Add. 45842), and the *Glasgow Herald* identified them as 'two clever ladies who prefer to disguise their identity under the name of "Michael Field"' (Add. 45852). Typically, these notices, which Katherine and Edith tipped into their journal, would invoke the adjective 'clever,' added to the designation of their sex, and then dismiss their work. *The Pall Mall Gazette* sniffed derisively, 'It [*A Question of Memory*] is a drama written by ladies for ladies.' *People* was cruel in its explicit linking of sex and (lack of) serious critical comment: 'two ladies whose identity is veiled, but scarcely hidden, under the pseudonym of Michael Field. The courtesy due to the sex of this feminine combination restrains the critic from speaking in such downright terms of this crude and inartistic work as it not only deserves, but provokes.' And *The Speaker*'s review sounds like Katherine and Edith's fears embodied; the reviewer makes it clear that 'ladies' have no knowledge of the thoroughfares of theatrical (read public) life: 'A couple of ladies, who know nothing of the practical requirements of the theatre, who stand outside the current of dramatic evolution, have attempted to write a play; that is all' (Add. 45852). To think that Katherine and Edith painstakingly tipped these reviews into their journal, that space of collaborative play, is a sad thought indeed. The secret space of collaboration, where creative fellowship could thrive, had become a publicly devastated paradise lost. Sadly but fittingly, the rest of Michael Field's dramatic production consisted of closet dramas.

But was the closet drama a form of mourning and suppression for Michael Field? On the most concrete level, the two women felt virtually driven away from the public stage, silenced, in Katherine's words, because they had 'many things to say that the world will not tolerate from a woman's lips' (*Works and Days* 6). Still, David J. Moriarty argues in his 1986 article, '"Michael Field" (Edith Cooper and Katherine Bradley) and Their Male Critics,' those closet dramas may have been a space in which to create more freely precisely because of the limited readership of the volumes (they were privately printed in small numbers). 'After their real identities were known,' claims Moriarty, 'their work took on a more complex, less traditional, more innovative tenor' (133). Moriarty is thinking formally here, since, earlier in his article, he notes the challenges to social conventions presented in the earlier drama: the love scene between two women in *Canute the Great* (1887), for instance (124). Nevertheless, he figures the two women in their later years as bitterly disillusioned (130) and, oddly, limited by their own regard for each other which, aestheticized, led them to become prisoners in a kind of Tennysonian Palace of Art. I am not convinced that this inverse relationship between social and formal innovation or challenge exists in the works of Michael Field, nor am I ready to concede that a closeted collaboration betrays nothing more than the pain of forced concealment. As evidence of both the creativity and the concealment of closeted collaboration, I offer a closing example: a poem written by Katherine in response to Edith's death, shortly before her own death in 1913, 'Fellowship' (originally called 'Fading' in the journals). The poem opens with an acknowledgment of the closeting of their desire:

> In the old accents I will sing, my Glory, my Delight,
> In the old accents, tipped with flame, before we knew the right,
> True way of singing with reserve. (Sturgeon 142)

In the 1933 selected poems, this 'reserve' is kept to the end; Katherine ends with a tribute to this special literary and personal relationship:

> Now, faded from their sight,
> We cling and joy. It was thy intercession gave me right,
> My Fellow, to this fellowship. My Glory my Delight! (Field,
>   *Selections* 142)

In the journal, the last line ends, 'My Henry [Edith] my Delight!' But lest one assume that naming could occur only in the closet, the line was, for reasons that still remain unexplained to me, picked up in the American edition of *Underneath the Bough*, a much-revised collection of love poems. And so, 'speaking out' of their claustrophobia, Michael Field, riven in twain by hostile reviewers and literati, were, in Katherine's words, once more 'Full Michael.'

The Anglo-Irish collaborators, Edith Oenone Somerville and Violet Martin (pseud. Martin Ross) operated in a much more public space than did Michael Field. They published their first novel, *An Irish Cousin* (thereafter affectionately christened by the authors 'the shocker' because of some of its sensationalist elements) in 1889. Buoyed up by some positive reviews, they went on to assemble light-hearted travel writings (*Through Connemara in a Governess Cart* 1892; *In the Vine Country* 1893) before they achieved a measure of public success with their novel *The Real Charlotte* in 1894 and, to a greater degree, with *Some Experiences of an Irish R.M.* in 1899. The farcical fox-hunting stories in the latter volume created a public demand for more of this material, and Somerville and Ross obliged, until Martin's death in 1915 ... and beyond, according to Somerville, who claimed to have continued this close collaboration with her cousin's spirit beyond the grave via seance. So, by comparison with the contemporaneous Michael Field, this collaboration inhabited a most public-seeming space (Edith Somerville was even honoured with a D. Litt. from Dublin University in 1922, though her attempts to have the university authorities confer the honorary degree on the deceased Violet Martin as well received a rather chilly bureaucratic response). One would think therefore that the anxieties of public and private space would not be as pressing, and certainly the pressure to represent the collaboration as a single writing genius would be negligible. But such is not the case. Because of the public venues in which this collaboration thrived, however, the pressure to represent singular authorship came mainly from Somerville and Ross's critics – of the late nineteenth century, the early twentieth century, and even today. The anxiety of collaborative space is transferred to the public sphere. One of the pair's most fervent expressions of faith in the collaborative process, Martin's avowal to Somerville 'To write with you doubles the triumph and enjoyment, having first halved the trouble and anxiety' (quoted in Cronin 21), is itself a response to criticism levelled by a reader, that 'though I think the book [*The Irish Cousin*] a success, and cannot pick out the fastenings of the two hands, I yet think the next novel ought to be by *one* of them' (quoted in Cronin 20, emphasis Cronin's).

In the matter of the very names they chose to publish under, I discern both an increased openness to publicity and a persistent secrecy. Of course, Edith Somerville used her own surname, even though both of the cousins' families were opposed to the idea, mainly because they felt it was beneath the families' dignity to have their names associated with trade (Lewis, ed. 143). As a result of that pressure, their first novel was published under the masculine pseudonyms 'Geilles Herring and Martin Ross.' This bowing to family pressures irked Edith, who remarked to Violet in an early letter: 'I can't send it [an early short story] off until you say what signature you want. Is it our names – or what? You once said you wanted Martin Somerville – *I* think our good names' (Lewis, ed. 129). Though Edith got her own way next time and thereafter, signing her own 'good name' Somerville, Violet Martin continued to prefer the demi-secrecy of Martin Ross, and rumours continued to circulate for a while as to their gender. As with so many other issues of space in this collaboration, the apparent greater openness and publicity belie the persistence of the anxieties about public and private space that Michael Field knew so well.

Space is, indeed, a major issue in the collaboration of Someville and Ross, in several senses. On the most material level, Edith and Violet had to fight their families most determinedly for working space, even though, as Gifford Lewis has argued, it was the family's tradition of working collectively on creative productions such as plays and masques that arguably fostered the cousins' projects (32). As their nephew, the Chaucer scholar Nevill Coghill recalled: 'They would sit in the studio, or in a Railway carriage or wherever it might be' (Lewis, ed. 145). 'It might be' almost anywhere for, as Edith recalled, they 'were hunted from place to place like the Vaudois, seeking in vain a cave wherein we could hold our services unmolested' (quoted in Robinson 86). The families, as Anglo-Irish old families, had certain expectations of the young women's participation in visiting and entertaining, and writing together in the collaborative cave certainly did not count for many service points; to quote Edith's account once again, 'When not actually reviled, we were treated with much the same disapproving sufferance that is shown to an outside dog that sneaks into the house on a wet day' (quoted in Collis 45).

When they were not being curbed, like canine offenders, by their families, they were physically separated by some miles, Edith at 'Drishane' in West Cork, and Martin at 'Ross' near Galway, until 1900, when Martin moved to Drishane. This is a condition shared by many contemporary collaborators; Andrea Lunsford and Lisa Ede conclude their *Singular Texts / Plural Authors* with a contemporary transoceanic scene of collaboration: 'Lisa is on a consulting trip in the east and Andrea is in her office, feet up, gathering notes for one more marathon telephone conversation' (143). 'Like other long-distance collaborators,' write Carey Kaplan and Ellen Cronan Rose, 'we usually work physically separated from each other, exchanging and editing each other's drafts by mail or modem' (549). But in a time with no telephone, fax, or computer, the mail had to suffice for Somerville and Ross. As the editor of their selected letters, Gifford Lewis, observes: 'Manuscripts oscillated between Drishane and Ross for six months or so before clean-copying and the journey eastwards to their publishers in London' (xxii). As Edith plaintively wrote to Martin: 'I wish you were here, or I was there – it would save much time and trouble' (Lewis, ed. 103).

Though Edith and Violet had difficulties with the geographical frustrations of writing between 'here' and 'there,' they developed creative strategies for sharing the space of the page that bounced back and forth across counties. Like Michael Field, they would write on one (in this case, the right-hand) side of an exercise book, with revisions entered either above the original words or on the left-hand page (Robinson 42–3). More so than Michael Field, though, they evolved a shared writing strategy that openly acknowledged the role of conflict in their deliberations. One of Edith's favoured terms of criticism was 'puke,' for instance (Lewis, ed. 65). In their letters, they almost seem to anticipate the prospect of a good editorial battle with some appetite; as Edith bellicosely commented, 'I know you must loathe my sticking in these putrid things [love scenes!] and then fighting for them ... Please goodness we will have many a tooth and naily fight next month – but don't let us combat by post; it is too wearing' (63). Wearing it certainly was, to negotiate the spaces of the page across the spaces of geography, but the letters reveal a remarkable ability to share detailed criticism of passages, right down to the adjectives and possessives. I was particularly impressed by these women's ability to be frank with each other; as Edith writes to Martin on one occasion, 'What struck me when I read it first, was a certain tightness and want of the ideas being expanded. It read too strong. Like over-strong tea' (Lewis, ed. 101), to fall upon that most stereotypical of Irish images. But we also have on record accounts of their working relationship that suggest that this frank exchange was part of a larger process of consensus-building. As Nevill Coghill explained, 'They talked their stories and their characters and their every sentence into being. As soon as anything was agreed it was written down and not a word was written down without agreement' (Lewis, ed. 145). In her later memoir, *Irish Memories*, his aunt Edith corroborated this account: 'Our work was done conversationally. One or other – not infrequently both simultaneously – would state a proposition. This would be argued, combated [*sic*] perhaps, approved or modified; it would then be written down by the (wholly fortuitous) holder of the pen, would be scratched out, scribbled in again' (quoted in Collis 45).

Edith's parenthetical claim '(wholly fortuitous)' is a reaction to the public pressures operating on the collaborative textual space shared conversationally by Somerville and Ross: what she would call, time and time again, the old question of who-holds-the-pen. Because of the heightened publicity surrounding this collaboration, there was a similarly heightened desire on the part of the public to parse or disentangle the collaboration, to force these two unruly collaborators into the conceptual mould of individual creativity and genius. It was a desire that, of course, was familiar to the contemporary writing pair Michael Field, and it seems to have particularly irked Edith Somerville. As she reported to Violet, editors 'attacked me to know whc [*sic*] of us wrote which parts – by chapters or how – the usual old thing' (Lewis, ed. 243). On another occasion, she was similarly attacked by a reader after the publication of *The Real Charlotte*: "'And is it you that do the story & Miss Martin the" &c &c for some time' (Lewis, ed. 207). After enduring several years of this kind of dissection, with critics vying with each other to discern separate authorship of particular passages in their novels and stories, Edith finally vented her anger: 'Already various journalists have been tearing at me to write, to give them data for articles, anything, to try and make money out of what is to me a sacred thing ... how abhorrent is to me all the senseless curiosity as to "which held the pen"' (quoted in Robinson 47).

Senseless curiosity seems to have had a rather long shelf life, since virtually all of the authors of extended criticism on Somerville and Ross exhibit its effects. The published criticism is full of repeated attempts to parse the collaboration and, in effect, to reformat it in terms of individuated authorship. Gifford Lewis, for instance, confidently asserts that 'We can track the two personalities in their manuscripts' and, soon after, she makes the claim for Edith as the 'major partner in their writing' (70, 72), as though she needed, first, to parse the collaboration in order to resuscitate the major, singular author from its shards. Novelist-critic Molly Keane, introducing both Lewis's edition of the selected letters and the Hogarth Press's reissue of *The Real Charlotte*, strives to articulate a division of labour: Martin 'held the rapier pen,' Edith 'had the stronger force of invention' (*The Real Charlotte* ix); Edith was the 'more emotional writer of the two,' Martin the 'remorseless censor' (Lewis, ed. xviii). Maurice Collis devotes a disproportionate amount of his biography of Somerville and Ross to the same sort of disentangling exercise, attempting to deduce the (single) authorship of passages and chapters on the basis of evidence such as the stylistic markers of their individual letters. Such an obsession with de-collaborating Somerville and Ross ultimately leads him to adopt an oddly mathematical sense of collaboration: he asks of Edith's writing life after Violet's death, 'Could the survivor carry on? There was only half as much talent available' (182). John Cronin, in his 1972 volume on *Somerville and Ross*, plays the same find-the-suture game, even though he reminds readers: 'Any successful literary collaboration is by its very nature greater than the sum of its parts' (22). Still, he proceeds to do sums, and it becomes clear that the two women's collaboration poses a particularly difficult long-division problem for him as an evaluative critic: how does one apportion praise or criticism when one is dealing with a 'closely knit partnership, one member of which outlived the other by a whole generation' (100)? Hilary Robinson marvels at the 'lack of fastenings' (39) in the collaborative prose, but she then proceeds to worry the seams that she does perceive (39–40). Even Violet Powell, who, near the beginning of *The Irish Cousins* (1970), likens Somerville and Ross's collaboration to the woven 'shot-silk, where the colour changes but the texture remains constant' (17), part way through that study, calls *Some Irish Yesteryears* a 'valuable book for disentangling the threads of Somerville and Ross' (84). Critics of this collaborative team, it seems, can only apprehend the woven authorship by picking at its threads, trained as they are to associate their own critical enterprise with the *oeuvre* of an individual writer. Far better the response recorded by Edith Somerville at a seance, when she asked the spirit of Violet Martin about the possibilities of collaboration beyond the grave: 'I shouldn't know which were my own thoughts and which yours,' to which the disembodied Violet replied with a prescient touch of the Foucauldian: 'That would not matter' (Collis 181). ('What matter who's speaking,' Foucault concludes his 'What Is an Author?' [138].)

This anxiety on the part of critics and readers, to determine 'who's speaking' is, as with the case of Michael Field, caught up with their cultural constructions of genius, but I think it is just as entangled with social anxiety about lesbian desire. Critics of Somerville and Ross, like Gifford Lewis, Violet Powell, and Hilary Robinson, in homophobic passage after passage, 'defend' Somerville and Ross against claims in Maurice Collis's 1968 biography that the two women were lovers. Powell, for instance, informs us that Edith was not lesbian because she 'was not ill at ease with men' (142). And Hilary Robinson hastily assures us that though their love for each other was paramount, it 'never transgressed the bounds set by Christianity' (19). But the homophobia prize definitely goes to Gifford Lewis, who never seems content to let the matter rest in *Somerville and Ross: The World of the Irish R.M.* (1985). In a bizarre turn of logic, she maintains that Somerville and Ross couldn't be lesbian because their observations of men and of the relations between men and women are 'chillingly accurate' (12). Later, she quotes a number of Edith's and Violet's teasing retorts to each other, and concludes, on grounds that remain mystifying, 'This is not the language of a Sapphic sexual love' (201). When Edith and the departed Violet decide not to care 'which were my own thoughts and which yours,' they intellectually enact an aspect of mutuality that is fully eroticized in many contemporary women's collaborations. Compare, for example, this conclusion of an erotic passage from Suniti Namjoshi and Gillian Hanscombe's 1986 collection, *Flesh and Paper*: 'And sometimes there was the wondering about who was who' (22). In terms of nineteenth-century English authorship, critics then and now have wished to disentangle the legs and arms of these collaborations, for the spectacle of two women 'holding the pen' may have suggested all too easily the notion that they might hold each other too.

Though the late nineteenth century was a time of vigorous collaborative activity, the earlier years of the twentieth century were by no means a quiet interlude before a poststructuralist resurgence. Traditionally, of course, scholars of Modernism have constructed a redoubtable pantheon of individual literary figures as a means of narrating this movement – Joyce, Eliot, Yeats, Woolf, Lawrence – but more recent scholarship has uncovered the simultaneous existence of other modernisms at work. The plentiful scholarship on Modern women writers' networks is particularly relevant to the operations of collaborative writers during this period. Many of these collaborations, like the celebrated Stein-Toklas literary relationship, were implicit, but there were also explicit writing partnerships during these years, like the Australian partnership of 'M. Barnard Eldershaw' (pen name for Marjorie Barnard and Flora Eldershaw) and the collaboration of expatriate British writers Vernon Lee and Kit Anstruther-Thomson.

The work that Maryanne Dever has done on M. Barnard

Eldershaw yields a picture of two Modern collaborators who faced many of the same challenges that their nineteenth-century predecessors did. Between the 1920s and the late 1940s, these two women, Marjorie Barnard, a librarian, and Flora Eldershaw, a teacher, wrote five novels and a number of non-fictional prose works (Dever 65). They had to confront the same sort of public scrutiny about their collaboration that Somerville and Ross did: the never-ending question of who was the real writer or genius of the collaboration. At the time, commentators suspected that Barnard, the better-known writer, was the animating force behind the partnership, very much as critics of Somerville and Ross tended to paint Violet Martin as the Wordsworthian genuine genius, and Edith Somerville as the less-talented Coleridgean hanger-on. A complicating factor, in this case, was the habit that Barnard developed in later years, after Eldershaw's death, of recollecting their collaboration in terms that tended to showcase her own role in the collaboration (Dever 68). That tendency to privilege one member of the writing team has not dissipated over time; Maryanne Dever has revealed: 'When I commenced work on this collaboration [in the 1990s], it was argued to me that my task was simply one of establishing who was the *real* author' (66). Her reaction to the pressure to parse the collaboration is very much in line with my own, and with the work of Early Modern scholars like Jeffrey Masten who have questioned the primacy of paleography in dealing with collaborative texts: 'But how is it possible,' she asks, 'to reconstruct from the evidence on the page the precise conditions of composition?' (67). As with Somerville and Ross and Michael Field, M. Barnard Eldershaw was more drawn to metaphors of incorporation (like Field's mosaic) that frustrate any such atomizing desire. As Barnard once commented: 'It comforts me to empty my little vial into her fountain and see it lifted' (quoted in Dever 69).

Barnard and Eldershaw, again like Somerville and Ross, were also subjected to critical voyeurism on the subject of their sexual orientation. As Dever tartly comments: 'Prurient interest in the sexual behind the textual has certainly been a popular response to the Barnard-Eldershaw union' (70). But she resists the sort of detection work that critics of Somerville and Ross have engaged in, either claiming M. Barnard Eldershaw for a lesbian tradition or homophobically 'defending' them against 'charges' of lesbianism for, as she rightly notes, such questions 'lock the critic into a voyeuristic search for the kind of evidence seldom required to "prove" the assumed heterosexuality of other writers' (71).

In the case of Vernon Lee and Kit Anstruther-Thomson, there would seem to have been little need for such voyeuristic speculations, since they openly lived together as lovers, friends, and co-authors for a period of twelve years and remained close friends until Anstruther-Thomson's death in 1921. Lee and Anstruther-Thomson collaborated on non-fictional works, particularly treatises on aesthetics, beginning with the publication of an article on 'Beauty and Ugliness' in 1897 and culminating in the 1912 publication of their work *Beauty and Ugliness and Other Studies in Psychological Aesthetics*. But for all the apparent openness surrounding their writing and personal relationships, the public and scholarly reception of their work revealed a strong prejudice against their collaboration. As Phyllis F. Mannocchi writes, adopting Lillian Faderman's controversial notion of romantic friendship: 'Their friends' severe criticisms of Vernon and Kit's work also derived from a failure to acknowledge the possibility of an intellectual collaboration between two women who were romantic friends' (140). According to Mannocchi, friends and associates of Lee and Anstruther-Thomson may have been supportive of their personal relationship, but they dismissed their professional relationship because they assumed it was built on 'personal motives' (140). As a result, Lee and Anstruther-Thomson felt that their work was not taken seriously, that it was belittled and isolated. Matters only got worse when art historian (and their neighbour in Florence) Bernard Berenson accused them of plagiarizing his ideas in their first article 'Beauty and Ugliness' (Mannocchi 138). So, for all the apparent openness of this artistic collaboration and worldliness of the Modern expatriate community, the issues of public disapprobation and neglect that plagued Michael Field were replayed in a more Modern, cosmopolitan key.

This excursion into earlier collaborations between women serves the purposes I mentioned at the outset: to combat the notions of collaboration as textual aberration or product of the twentieth-century avant-garde and as a narrative of progression from secrecy to openness and freedom. It also reveals the persistence of critical attitudes toward women's collaboration as a monstrous, unnatural bond that needs to be severed, so as to rescue from its shards the evidence of an individual author – the sort of pact between homophobia and editing practice that I mused over in my introductory chapter. But equally important, this historical excursion has reminded me how various are the political ends which collaborative textuality can serve, from Somerville and Ross's gentrified fox-hunting farces in *Some Experiences of an Irish R.M.*, to the Sapphic feminism of Michael Field. As my next chapter on contemporary prose works will show most dramatically, the ideological spectrum covered by women's contemporary collaborations is no less sweeping.

4

'The High Wire of Self and Other': Prose Collaborations

At first glance, contemporary prose collaborations by women seem far removed from the closeted anxiety of their nineteenth-century predecessors: photographs of smiling collaborative teams grace the back covers of these books. But as I have suggested, I resist drawing a progressive trajectory from nineteenth-century collaborative closeting to twentieth-century full disclosure because I believe that many of the issues of privacy and publicity, property, and space continue to haunt contemporary works, both the prose works I examine here and the poetry I examine in the next chapter. They persist, evolve, and infuse themselves into a wide variety of cultural discourses and social exchanges.

Collectively written prose embodies exactly that: a wide variety of cultural discourses and social exchanges. As Lisa Ede and Andrea Lunsford point out, business and technical writing – a major portion of writing in contemporary society – is fundamentally collaborative, though we do not tend to dignify or pay much critical attention to such forms of writing. Closer to those forms of writing called literary, there are, of course, the many instances of autobiographical prose, from memoirs deemed classic by certain critical traditions, to popular ghost-written paperback tell-all autobiographies that garner a good part of the book-buying dollar today. Throughout this full spectrum of autobiographical writing, collaboration is, again, a marked presence. Closer to the academic side of the spectrum, Albert E. Stone, for instance, has paid close attention to the role of collaborative practices in contemporary

African-American autobiography, though, as Carol Boyce Davies has argued, Stone has tended to valorize the subject of an autobiographical study (for example, Alex Haley's *The Autobiography of Malcolm X*) and to deemphasize the conditions of its joint production (4). On the other hand, scholars who study the transference of oral history to the page by the workings of an intermediary of some sort (an editor, ghost-writer, etc) are intensely aware of the power exchanges that animate the very processes of collective storytelling. As Carol Boyce Davies notes in her study of 'Collaboration and the Ordering Imperative in Life Story Production': 'Affiliations or disjunctions of gender, class, nationality, language, and shared politics seem to be the primary facilitators of, or interferences in, the collaborative life story telling process' (12).

Although what Boyce Davies says about the capacities of these affiliations and disjunctions to influence the collaborative process holds true for many of the texts I examine in this study, collective oral histories are not the main subject of my study, nor are the many ghost-written popular autobiographies that deserve closer academic attention than they have received. As I have explained, overt collaborations in which two or more authors sign themselves as co-creators are my focus because they throw the crisis of the single author into high relief, but they, in turn, need to be seen against the backdrop of the formidable variety of collective forms of writing in contemporary societies and throughout literary history. Only then will they cease to be read and reviewed as freaks of authorial nature.

Having said that, however, the two North American examples of contemporary collaborative writing by women that I have chosen to focus on could not, it seems, be more disparate. Canadian novelists Carol Shields and Blanche Howard's 1991 novel *A Celibate Season* is an epistolary account of a middle-class husband and wife's ten-month separation while she pursues a legal position on a crown commission studying women and poverty and he, an unemployed architect, becomes the primary caregiver for their two teenagers. The epistolary exchange charts the rough waters that the couple face during this separation, and the crisis point is curiously, even farcically, bourgeois: the wife comes home for a brief visit to find that her *sanctum sanctorum*, her North Vancouver home, has been desecrated, violated by her husband's surprise addition of a solarium. A Martha Stewart–like middle-class WASP domestic sanctity hangs over the entire work, and it is no surprise to discover that, secret extra-marital flings aside, heterosexual marriage emerges triumphant, if a trifle battered about the edges, by the end of the novel. Nothing could be further from the dynamics of my other text under study, Americans Sandra Butler and Barbara Rosenblum's *Cancer in Two Voices* (also published in 1991), so much so that it seems a study in gross discrepancy to bring the two works together for purposes of discussion. Butler and Rosenblum's collaboration is a moving account of Barbara Rosenblum's battle with breast cancer – a battle that she lost at the age of 44. The text comprises journal entries, longer meditational chapters, and occasional letters from Barbara to her friends. And although the journal mourns her loss fiercely, it also, writes Sandra Butler, is a celebratory testimony to the sustaining love that the two women found in each other: 'But this is also the history of our loving ...' (n.p.), a history made visible in a way that Michael Field and Somerville and Ross could not do in their collaborations, their world. Bringing these two disjunctive texts together underscores the theoretical point with which I opened this book: that collaboration, 'itself neutral, can mean many things' (Koestenbaum 3), can serve many ideological masters. In particular, it acts as a corrective to the impression I may have created in my preceding chapter that collaboration necessarily or inherently embodies a challenge to heteronormative assumptions. It certainly has the power to do so, and that is a power that lesbian collaborators may explore to the fullest. But collaboration can also reinstate heteronormative and other conservative positions. In terms of sexual politics, the collaborative spectrum runs, metaphorically speaking, from Butler and Rosenblum's San Francisco to Shields and Howard's North Vancouver.

A study of Shields and Howard's novel usefully challenges another easy assumption about collaborative writing: that contemporary collaborations self-consciously exploit their conditions of joint production, the text often bearing explicit meditations on the joint creativity that has brought it into being. But in spite of its dualistic epistolary format, *A Celibate Season* retains the air of the unself-conscious collaboration that aims at an appearance of authorial seamlessness, like Somerville and Ross's stories and novels, for instance. Of course, this is likely to be the case in fictional prose of the non-postmodernist type, where collaborators are working with narrators and personae, rather than in autobiographical prose or in lyric poetry. And so the disjunctions and divisions that are explored, along with the mutuality, in many contemporary collaborations are displaced onto the two main characters of this novel, Jocelyn (nicknamed Jock) and her husband Chas, and their marital stresses and strengths. The mode of collaborative composition appears, on the surface, to be similarly individualized, with Shields being responsible for the letters written by the husband Chas and Howard taking the part of his wife Jock. Even this initial division of labour found its origins in individual career aspirations: 'Carol wanted to write the male part,' notes Howard (74). Shields herself has talked about the attractions, for her, of writing from a male point of view, partly because she was 'tired of being called a women's writer' (Anderson 141). It's a perspective that she explored in an earlier novel, *Happenstance* (1980) and, more recently, in *Larry's Party* (1997). So individual career profiles and aspirations were at work in this collaboration from the beginning, but the collaboration is more complex than this simple parsing of labour would suggest. Holly Laird's warning about deducing authorship of earlier collaborative texts from superficial characteristics such as manuscript handwriting is just as applicable to this contemporary pair of writers.

In spite of the apparent conservatism of this novel (in collaborative format as well as subject matter), it seems predictable that Shields, the better-known writer of the two, should have engaged in an authorial experiment. The novel that she had just completed, *Swann: A Mystery* (1987) is an extended satire on the ways in which critical voices create an image of an author in terms of their own solipsistic, selfish meaning systems. (Shields would explore similar ground briefly in *The Stone Diaries* when she has a number of family members and friends write segments 'explaining' and diagnosing the life of the central character, Daisy Goodwill Flett, in ways that are transparently egocentric and self-interested.) As Brian Johnson argues in his article, 'Necessary Illusions: Foucault's Author Function in Carol Shields's *Swann*,' in terms that clearly mesh with this study's central concerns: 'The relentless search for the dead woman "behind" the work firmly locates the disappearance of the author as the text's central mystery and suggests ways in which Shields's novel addresses the debate about authority in contemporary criticism, inaugurated by Roland Barthes's 1968 eulogy for the author' (56). Ultimately, Johnson intimates, *Swann's* stance on the author is conservative, suggesting 'that Barthes's total eradication of the author is too severe,' but it nevertheless 'suggests ways in which a new theory of authorship must somehow accommodate the issues of power and appropriation that are intimately linked to Swann herself throughout the novel' (59). Clearly, these would be the author functions, the new questions about authority and power in texts that Foucault proposes at the end of his essay 'What Is an Author?' If Johnson is right, as I think he is, that Shields, at least, was already in the process of philosophically decentring authorial power, she would have been theoretically primed to enter into a collaborative writing relationship that, on a basic level if not a deep ideological one, redistributes but does not dissipate authorial power. From letters that Shields and Howard exchanged, we know that the collaborative venture that they embarked upon was likely inspired by Shields's reading of a women's collaborative text. As Howard wrote to Shields as early as 13 September 1983, when the two friends were just beginning to consider collaborating, 'I'm sure it was you who urged me to read Between Friends, by Gillian Hanscombe, wasn't it? In any case, I'm just starting it, and as you no doubt know it is in the same format as we've discussed, letters between two friends' (Howard archive, Box 2, file 6). We also know that Shields has had a long-standing interest in women working together; as she commented to Marjorie Anderson in an interview, apropos her play *Thirteen Hands*:

I want to present this notion I have of what goes on in small groups of people, how groups feed us and sustain us and in a way become an alternative to the family which has failed us to a certain extent in our society. I wanted to show how those stereotypical, 'blue-rinsed' women are thinking individuals, worthy individuals, and how they often feel brilliantly alive in those moments when they come together with other people. (144–5)

Given the fact that Shields's own resolve to write and publish gained impetus from an insensitive creative writing professor's remark to her about blue-rinsed women and their illusions about their creative powers, it seems appropriate that Shields should participate in a writing partnership in which, as Raymond Williams has said of collaboration, the creative whole is greater than the sum of its parts.

But am I not doing exactly what I have criticized so roundly in other critics' approaches to collaborative texts: separating out the strong (and in this case, canonized and Pulitzer-prize-winning Bloomian) writer from the collaborative rabble? What of Blanche Howard's decision to enter into collaboration with Carol Shields? Howard, the author of three previous novels, has tended to characterize the collaboration in somewhat similar terms, as something of a favour done her by her younger but more successful colleague. In a piece called 'Collaborating with Carol' she frankly admits that

Carol's reputation, when we started the novel, was burgeoning, whereas mine had languished after my three novels were published. I jumped at her suggestion that we do a novel together, recognizing her generosity in wishing to spend time on a work that might very well not further her career, and indeed might use up valuable time more beneficially spent elsewhere. (71–2)

So Howard types collaboration as a generous break from the exigencies of building an individual career as an author, a sort of pre-Barthesian holiday. This self-deprecating note is one that Howard sounds repeatedly in the letters that she wrote to Shields during the composition of *A Celibate Season*; typically Shields tends to be much more sanguine about the eventual acceptance of the novel. On 10 May 1985, just after Methuen had rejected the manuscript, Howard dejectedly wrote to Shields, 'Insofar as our strategy is concerned, I don't have a great deal of faith in myself but have a great deal in you, since you have been much more successful than I.' As they picked themselves up and began to rewrite the novel during the next year, Howard's deference to her more successful colleague persisted. On 22 July 1986, she wrote, 'I feel ever so much better about my part of the ending – I think yours was great as it was – you have a much surer touch than I on the first go-around.' As the revisions reached a late stage, and the two writers debated how to handle a particularly tricky episode in which a co-worker of Jock's announces that she has fallen in love with her, Howard deferred once more to what she saw as Shields's greater expertise: 'Please do anything you think will work – I have more faith in your judgment re structure than in mine' (Howard archives, Box 2, file 6). No matter how amicable this writing partnership was, the unequal power relations that Howard openly felt, and that Shields may have silently sensed, cannot be denied.

Significantly, responses to the book and its very marketing tend to reinforce this sense of the Shields–Howard collaboration as a short excursion of a major author in the company of a friend. Jeffrey Canton reviews it in *Paragraph* along with Shields's *The Republic of Love*, opening his review with a sentence that leaves no doubt as to its authorial focal point: 'Love is certainly in the air for novelist Carol Shields' (32). (The only review that did justice to the collaborative format was, not surprisingly, a wittily collaborative, epistolary review written by an academic pair geographically separated, like Jock and Chas, because of the demands of their work, David Ingham and Kathleen Barnett.) The book itself, published by Coteau, breaks with the usual alphabetical listing of multiple authors and lists Shields as the first author. Inside the jacket, Coteau reprints separate blurbs about Shields's and Howard's previous books. Shields's appear first and in a rather embarrassing profusion, with blurbs from Alice Munro, Margaret Atwood, the

Globe and Mail, the *Times Literary Supplement,* the *New York Times* drowning out a handful of review blurbs for Howard's novels drawn from the *Toronto Sun, Chatelaine, Western Living,* and the *Brantford Expositor.* No doubt here about which collaborator holds the big Canadian canonization arsenal at her disposal. It probably does not help, either, that Shields has written domestic fiction whereas Howard has written the more popular-culture form of the suspense novel. Even now, the novel is, surprisingly, still in print, in spite of mainly negative reviews – one in particular, in the influential *Globe and Mail* – and its own troubled publication history. According to Howard, it 'racked up nine rejections,' and was 'temporarily abandoned' before they sent it to Coteau (76). In fact it has recently been reprinted, along with earlier Carol Shields novels, as part of the whole-scale remarketing of her work in the light of her critical and popular success with *The Stone Diaries* (1993). Institutionally speaking, from inception to republication, this collective novel has been, ironically, a testament to the continuing power of the individual author paradigm.

Still, what of the actual experience and process of writing the novel collaboratively? Although I have shown how unequal Blanche Howard felt the distribution of literary talent to be, and though the very format of the novel suggests an individualistic division of labour, the manuscript copy of the novel, as well as the letters that Shields and Howard exchanged during its composition, show that the two collaborators were not inhabiting entirely separate artistic spheres. True, they had the isolating effect of geographical distances to deal with, as did their nineteenth-century predecessors Edith Somerville and Violet Martin, and like them, they relied primarily upon the postal system to vitiate them. Until the mid-to-late 1980s, when both women traded in their typewriters for computers, they would painstakingly type out drafts of letters by their characters Jock and Chas, xerox them, and send them back and forth between Vancouver, where Howard was living, and Winnipeg, Shields's home at that time. As middle-class women, they faced social expectations and obstacles that were also surprisingly similar to those encountered by Somerville and Ross a century ago. Howard, for instance, writes on several occasions of the need to entertain group after group of guests, or to give dinner parties, an expected part of her role as a wife of a Canadian member of parliament. Those entertaining activities, along with the accounting jobs that she continued to take on as a chartered accountant in her sixties, necessarily took time away from her work on the manuscript (13 September 1983; 19 June 1986, Howard archives, Box 2, file 6).

When they did find time to work on the manuscript, they would scrupulously read each other's drafts, make marginal notes about word choice, logic, sequencing, and send the letter or letters back, with a covering letter summarizing and elaborating upon the changes that they felt were necessary. The collaborator receiving the marked-up copy would then make changes in the margins, sometimes adding comments on the comments, and then would incorporate any changes she saw fit to make in the light of the suggestions. There was, then, give-and-take in all portions of the novel. One interesting example that the manuscript reveals involves the scene early in the novel where Chas, newly alone in the house, begins to write poetry for a course in Creative Communications that he decides to take while Jock is away. In an early draft of the letter that Shields sent to Howard, Chas recounts, 'I also composed, as I sat there, the opening lines of my second poem for Creative Communications, and to my surprise and happiness, the words sprang into my head without the least urging or agonizing' (Howard archive, Box 8, file 2). In this early version, Chas merely describes the act of writing that poem, but because Blanche Howard asked, in the margins, 'Will we get to read these? [i.e., poems],' Shields was moved to compose, and include, the opening lines of that poem. Or, in the letter where Chas describes their daughter Mia getting her first menstrual period while her mother is away, Shields initially has their teenage son Greg suddenly offer to go to the local convenience store to pick up sanitary pads. Once again, Howard probes with a question perhaps based upon her assumptions about, or experience of, teenaged boys: 'Would Greg really go?' (Howard archive, Box 8, file 2). In revision, Shields has Greg make his offer only after a moment of somewhat awkward silence. She retains his offer, however, since she presumably wishes to create the impression of Greg as a good kid, which will subtly undermine Chas's growing suspicions that he is in some sort of trouble, perhaps dealing drugs. So although Carol Shields and Blanche Howard may have occupied positions of unequal power in the literary world, and although they were working in a compartmentalized-seeming format, this collaborative project was, from beginning to end, a product of exchange and negotiation.

Not too surprisingly, then, in spite of its heavily individualized production and circulation, *A Celibate Season*, like the collaboration that brought it into being, engages in some of the complex dynamics of exchange frequently seen in contemporary collaborative texts. The statement-response format that is so prominent in other works such as Namjoshi and Hanscombe's *Flesh and Paper* is necessarily a part of this epistolary novel. Indeed, the epistolary novel, now largely out of favour, as Howard notes (73), has collaborative meaning, multiple centres of authorship at its very heart and in its history. In a very concrete rendering of Benjamin's notion of the producer as reader and the reader as producer, authors of letters in epistolary novels are simultaneously readers of letters, and, as in the English prototypical epistolary novels, Richardson's *Pamela* and *Clarissa*, much is made of those moments where reader and writer change places, connect, miss each other, and interact in a variety of ways that signal the inherent instability of the act of writing. For example, in Jock's and Chas's exchange of letters, the not-said, the lack of response to a stimulus, is often as important and troubling as the said, the response. When Chas faxes to Jock the news of the publication of his first poem, and she responds with a letter that makes no mention of this exciting news, Chas reads this absence as a troubling sign of the state of their marriage: 'Dear Jock, Question: did you or did you not get my fax telling you about the acceptance of my poem in the *Capilano Review*? I am unwilling to, I *can't* believe that you could have received this news and failed to respond to it. Respond, hell! – not even a comment'(125, emphasis Shields and Howard's). Tellingly, the urgency of the message sent by the author is technologically rendered in that most presence-laden of writerly formats, the fax. Not to respond to this hyper-present letter, this facsimile, is truly to confer absence on its author, its originator.

Authorship does not remain as philosophically transparent a presence in *A Celibate Season* as this example of the facsimile-original relationship seemingly implies. Authorship as a function that confers presence is destabilized at the end of the novel, when collaborators Howard and Shields bring on board the well-worn epistolary device of the unsent letter. Both Jock and Chas write and then destroy letters after they have indulged in some extra-marital sexual consolation. And although reviewers were right to protest the awkwardness of both of these letters and flings landing, like one wandering shoe after another, with wearying predictability, it is also true that the unsent letters destabilize what the novel has seemed to be saying about the communication between these two people and, implicitly, about authorship itself as a firm and transparent function of relaying meaning as a facsimile of thought and intention. If, then, as I have commented, heterosexual marriage emerges triumphant, though tattered, at the end of Shield and Howard's novel, with Chas's closing, Tennysonian invocation, 'Onward!' (191), perhaps we as readers who have been privy to the unsent letters will be likely to forecast rougher waters ahead for our bourgeois couple. Marriage, like authorship, has been subtly destabilized even as it has been, finally, reaffirmed.

Of course, marriage, like collaboration, has conventionally been figured as two people inhabiting one unified space, and some collaborators, like Michael Field, have readily reached for this metaphor when seeking to describe their writing partnerships, in spite of the sexually exclusionary nature of the metaphor. In *A Celibate Season*, however, that conventional view of marriage as the sharing of one space by two is destabilized by the celibacy invoked in the title. This destabilizing celibacy is, in many ways, a metaphor for the novel's collaborative conditions of production by two geographically separated but mutually engaged letter-writing individuals. Not surprisingly, then, this novel, like so many other collaborations, is obsessed with space. *A Celibate Season* opens with a volley of remarks from the two correspondents about the awkwardness of the new spaces they are inhabiting. It is as though they have experienced a reversal of marriage's negotiations of space. As Jock writes in her first paragraph, 'But here I am, huddled on one of their [Chateau Laurier's] oversize beds, feeling as though I were drifting around the Strait of Georgia in our leaky old dinghy' (1). She cannot let this perception of empty spaces rest; calling up the image of the Sahara in a metaphor, she adds, 'which, incidentally, the dimensions of this room are beginning to remind me of' (1). She continues: 'I'd have felt less bereft if the room had been little, with, instead of two big double beds, one modest, cell-like single covered with chaste white cotton' (1). From the doubled-yet-single space of conventional marriage to the clichéd nun's cell of chastity, Jock finds her spaces expanded, though as a locus of complaint, the Chateau Laurier isn't too bad a situation. Later, when she relocates to a bed-sitter, she finds, conversely, that the spaces are claustrophobically small: the bedroom is the 'smallest in the Western world,' boasting a 'whole twelve inches of clearance' between bed and dresser and a 'tiny' closet, 'small' livingroom-kitchen and 'tiny' park outside (17). She saves, however, a 'double bed' in the hopes that Chas will visit and, presumably, fill up the spaces that she senses constitute a marriage. In this Three-Bears-like swing between the too-large and the too-small, it is a new individual subjectivity within a concept of marriage that is being tested, tried on for size and found wanting.

Chas's first letter is similarly obsessed with space, though, in his case, it is the empty space occasioned by the departure of a wife that he wishes to fill up with his own subjectivity. He has moved his old drafting table and typewriter into the kitchen, over the protests of his daughter, who finds the effect 'unbalanced' (3). 'Here I sit,' he surveys, 'king of the kitchen, in that wasted space between the fridge and the kitchen table' (4). What has been reapportioned is the space of conventional gender relations in heterosexual marriage, with the man's occupation (anxiously figured as the drafting table and typewriter of an unemployed architect) moving into the feminized spaces of the kitchen. The wasted space of the trip from refrigerator to table painfully enacts the process of placing food on a family table – a process often socially figured as wasted time, non-work. Chas's revised cliché, 'king of the kitchen,' anxiously describes this reapportioned space.

Of course, Chas's job as an architect is precisely that – to reapportion spaces – and later in the novel his new housekeeper Sue offers a somewhat New-Age explanation of why Chas's solarium designs are catching on so readily: 'because people feel confined, politically and spiritually, by the spaces society has crammed them into' (131). In that case, Chas's decision to install a solarium in his own home, as a surprise gift to Jock, should occasion some feeling of freedom and progressiveness. The solarium itself, with its renewal of contact between the interior and exterior worlds would seem to promise this. As Chas remarks early on in his stint as king-of-the-kitchen, 'Waiting around is the worst – the walls seem to press closer and closer, and I often think of how you must have sat in this kitchen and waited for the kids to grow up and go to school and then waited around to hear if you'd been accepted for law school. What did you do with yourself all day?' (15). Presumably she spent it traversing that wasted space between the refrigerator and the kitchen table. One person's empty space is another person's life narrative. Similarly, when Chas presents his opened household for Jock to admire, she reads the reapportionment of space, instead, as a denial of the plenitude of the spaces that she has traversed, loved, and imprinted for many years. She refers to the 'little snit' (56) that she gets into over Chas's moving his drafting table into the (her) kitchen, but it is her surprise discovery of the solarium at Christmas that is the big snit of the marriage: she walks into the house, shrieks 'Mon Dieu' and makes a scene about the violation done to her spaces.

As violations of space go, the installation of a solarium in a middle-class North Vancouver home is certainly an upscale one. Although the novel asks us to believe that Jock has been seriously affected by what she has learned working with the commission on the feminization of poverty in Canada, it seems as though an understanding of the comparative weight of violations and oppressions has not been on the curriculum. On the one hand, the solarium snit seems, at times, like a farcical satire on bourgeois values, but readers are also being asked to take the episode seriously as a violation of Jock's space and integrity.

This contradiction arises because Shields and Howard wish to use a relatively minor, even silly, issue of bourgeois material space to signal a debate over substantial issues of property within marriage. These, in turn, echo the property anxieties that I perceive at work in women's artistic collaborations, including this one. Although one might think that the rough division of labour, however misleading, that Shields and Howard agreed to in the planning of their epistolary novel would minimize property anxiety by apportioning responsibility for a character to each writer, this is clearly not the case. As the archival evidence shows, this collaboration was marked by exchange and negotiation, and much of the negotiation involves how one partner's artistic choices necessarily impinge upon the choices of her writing partner. As Shields inquired of Howard in 1984, concerning the dual marital infidelities planned for Chas and Jock, 'But when is "your" infidelity to occur? I must know so I can plan mine' (Thursday n.d. Howard archive, Box 2, file 6). Such negotiations, of course, frustrate the idea that there could ever be a 'yours' and 'mine' in collaboration, but the concepts persist nevertheless, uneasily, in collaborative exchange.

Another way in which the property dynamics of this collaboration were complicated was the decision to write a play based on the novel. Mainly for reasons of time availability, Howard undertook most of the work of this adaptation, though Shields did contribute editorial advice on a draft of the play (Howard archive, Box 8, file 4). Still, when Shields was approached with the idea of a reissue of the novel *A Celibate Season* years later in 1996, she wrote to Blanche Howard to relay the offer from Random House–Vintage to make the volume part of their paperback reissue series of *Shields's* works. Shields promises Howard that this deal is a good one, but she uneasily breaks off from details about it to remark, 'I do think that the play should be yours, though. I've thought a great deal about this, and this is the only way I'd feel right about it' (5 April 1996, Howard archive, Box 2, file 6). So, in Shields's anxious division of the fruits of her collaboration with Blanche Howard, the novel is 'ours' but is in 'my' reissue series, and the play is 'yours.' Or is it?

Whatever the property anxieties of this collaboration, they were not overt enough to make the two collaborators avoid working with each other again. In fact, in the early 90s they began another collaborative novel, which, for reasons I cannot determine, they abandoned. Only twenty-four manuscript pages survive in the Blanche Howard archive: drafts of the Prologue, chapter 1 and chapter 2, and a sketchy plot outline. This manuscript, referred to in the plot outline simply as 'Mystery Story,' gives us further insight into the dynamics of Carol Shields's and Blanche Howard's collaboration. The portion of text that survives deals with a group of academics who are gathered in France to discuss witchcraft and fertility rites. Soon their attention turns to a particular fertility statuette, a 1200-year-old statuette of St Benedict with an erect penis. One academic accuses another of having presented a copy of this statue as the real thing, and all hell, academically speaking, breaks loose at the conference. That is as far as the two collaborators got, though their rough outline shows that they had blocked out the entire novel in a rudimentary way. This time, Shields and Howard did not divide writerly labour by character but, rather, by section of text or chapter. The few pages of manuscript that we have also reveal Shields and Howard moving toward a greater willingness to add bits of text to each other's drafts. For example, in one passage, Howard adds a long, involved clause to the beginning of one of Shields's sentences, something that the collaborators did not tend to do in drafting *A Celibate Season*. Then Shields, in turn, questions one of the words used by Howard in her interpolation. Even these few pages show us a collaborative pair becoming more adventurous with each other's textual property, as though they have come to realize that the notion of individual property claims in collaboration is a chimera. Since their first collaborative effort in which they divided up responsibilities resulted in a collaboration whose property dynamics were more complex than they may have anticipated, with this next text Shields and Howard may have come to feel more comfortable with the notion that, divide the labour though they might, they are present, even as a trace, in each other's words.

This tension between individual and shared performance animates the other collaborative prose text I have chosen to examine,

Sandra Butler and Barbara Rosenblum's *Cancer in Two Voices*. In many ways it is a profoundly different production from the light, bourgeois comedy of Shields and Howard. *Cancer in Two Voices* grows out of the tensions and mutualities of two women in a loving relationship who must negotiate the profoundly isolating experience of one woman's terminal cancer. The very title of the book signals this uneasy juncture of isolation and bivocality in the collaboration. In fact, *Cancer in Two Voices* mirrors the very condition of women's collaboration that particularly attracts my attention in a range of very different-seeming texts: the impossibility of the unproblematically collective.

The conditions of the book's production signal this tension and provide a telling contrast with Howard and Shields's *A Celibate Season*. For example, although the memoir is about the experience of Barbara Rosenblum's breast cancer, the collection opens with, in Sandra Butler's words, the 'first writing that Barbara and I did together, two years before her diagnosis' (i), a short piece on their negotiations of their identities as Jewish lesbians. From the outset, collaboration is established as a firmly entrenched way of negotiating positions, subjectivities, and experiences, not as a temporary authorial holiday from individual careers. And although the introductory piece places some emphasis on the cultural positionings that brought Butler and Rosenblum together, their Jewishness, that observation is tempered by the careful exploration of how different their Jewish backgrounds were. Butler came from a fully assimilated middle-class suburban family that was 'scrubbing to erase all traces of the *shtetl*' (4) and Rosenblum from a working-class immigrant family where stories of Holocaust were part of her daily childhood fare. From the beginning, then, we have an awareness in this memoir of how sameness and difference coexist, rendering problematic or simplistic any idealistic notions of seamless unity in relationship. As Barbara explains:

Sometimes, only sometimes, does my Jewish or lesbian side match her Jewish or lesbian side. More often, it is a mismatch: my lower-class facet faces her maternal side, or my spare, tight conceptual, academic side faces her dramatic, flamboyant emotional side. The same rubbing against, the same reaching out and not connecting, the same as in all other relationships. Is it like coming home? Only sometimes.

But when it is, it is powerful, rich, sustaining, fulfilling. It is a connection of a sort unlike any other. A *mechaye!* (3)

The very format of this piece enacts this dynamic of mismatch and connection: Barbara and Sandy write short paragraphs in response to each other, in a statement-and-response manner. They even negotiate their metaphors; Butler opens the piece by using the metaphor of a mirror, albeit a cloudy one, to describe their relationship, and Rosenblum opens her paragraph with a response and a revision: 'I know she will say it's like a mirror, like looking at yourself in a mirror. It's not that way for me. It's more like two diamonds, each of which is spinning around. Maybe like a *dreydl* or dice, and I don't know which side will be up when it stops moving' (3). This is, again, the recognizable statement-and-response format of many collaborations, and it mirrors, in this case, the material production of the text, the give-and-take of Butler and Rosenblum's compositional process: 'We typed, interrupted, criticized, added, paced, drank coffee, laughed, then grew thoughtful, intense, or joyous with relief when just the right word or image emerged. It was a making of love' (141). This sounds not all that different from the process of Somerville and Ross's joint composition, but with one revealing difference: its description finds its way into the published product rather than resting in the shadowy demi-privacy of letters or journals. It is a mode of composition that, like the lovemaking that Butler and Rosenblum describe, can accommodate difference and disagreement.

Lest this description of process still sound easy or predominantly joyous, a closer look at Butler and Rosenblum's *Cancer in Two Voices* reveals that there are times when the mismatches outnumber or stall the connections or when the pressures of Barbara's disease take their toll on the collaborative work and relationship. The passage I have just quoted above, for instance, sounds unproblematic until one realizes that the textual lovemaking that is described is a replacement for the physical lovemaking that Sandra and Barbara are no longer able to share because of the

ravages of the disease itself and of the massive doses of chemo-
therapy needed to fight it. 'The work we did,' recalls Sandra in the
same section, 'had the focus, the passion, the sense of completion
our lovemaking once had' (141), and Barbara comments, 'We
make love at the typewriter, not in the bedroom,' but there is also
a sense of nostalgia and loss in connection with the sexual parts of
their lives. Sandra writes of how she found Barbara's changing,
larger body exciting, but 'she, however, felt trapped and alienated
in this stranger's body and was unable or unwilling to respond'
(140). The destabilizing celibacy of Carol Shields and Blanche
Howard's *A Celibate Season*, couched as it is in terms of bourgeois
heterosexual marriage, may seem light years away from Butler and
Rosenblum's predicament, but here, too, celibacy as a figure of
individual subjectivity destabilizes, even as it affirms in some
ways, an intimate personal and writing partnership.

Accordingly, this inability to respond in sexual ways finds its
collaborative equivalent in occasional withdrawals from collective
writing. At the stage where Sandra and Barbara are writing about
their changed physical lives, it becomes clear that some writing of
the body must be done alone. As Sandra painfully recounts, 'She
[Barbara] has just begun to write a piece about her changing
relationship to her body and has announced quite firmly that she
wants to write it alone' (139). Though intellectually Sandra knows
this is appropriate, she receives the news as a rejection and yearns
for the old collaborative process: 'Now I sit wishing she would call
to me from her office down the hall and ask me what I would add
to her piece. What is it like for me, her partner? How does it feel
to live with a woman who now has advanced cancer spreading
through her body?' (140). The separate office becomes a figure for
the inevitably separate, ailing body, and Butler must learn and
accept the limits of collectivity and allow Rosenblum her own
office, her own body, and, ultimately, a space for her own suffering
and death.

Again, as in the relationship, withdrawal and acceptance do not
signal the end of or the failure of the collective project. On the
contrary, it gives that collective project a deeper sense of the
dynamics of collaborative writing and living. The same weather-

ing of withdrawal into separate writing identities occurs in Marlatt and Warland's *Two Women in a Birth*, wherein one collaborator says blankly to another, 'You've left' (156) the page, the collaboration. This accommodation of distance is what keeps the collaboration from mimicking the two-becomes-one immersion of self projected in heterosexual Christian marriage, a condition that might be creatively embraced by Howard and Shields but is resisted by Butler and Rosenblum.

In fact, even besides those moments where the collaborative writing most obviously comes to a halt, there are other moments in *Cancer in Two Voices* where the writing is solitary. Sandra, for instance, writes her very first entry (after the pre-diagnosis collaboration on their Jewishness) from an airplane seat, and there is no collaborator seated beside her: 'I am on my way to Winnipeg for a conference. We had, as always, difficulty separating. Her need of me. Mine of distance' (9). Although this may seem an oddly discordant note to sound at the beginning of a collaborative venture, it becomes emblematic of the dynamics of illness and collaboration that inform the rest of the book. *Cancer in Two Voices* bears testimony to the difficulty of separating from lovers, from collaboration, and from life.

In spite of this inevitability of the solitary amidst the collaborative, *Cancer in Two Voices* also consistently pays tribute to connectedness and to collaboration, mainly through the references to the importance of the collaborative project that are sprinkled throughout the text. It is as though we need to be reminded that the presence of discord and the need for occasional solitariness do not tarnish the ultimate value of the collaborative project. When Barbara thinks of the thirst for learning that her disease has inspired in her, she includes her need 'to write – alone and with Sandy. Together we have developed a new form that can accommodate our individual and unique voices into a dialogue' (132). Even when the pain of her deteriorating condition makes that writing, alone or together, impossible for the moment, collective discussions of the project prove sustaining: 'We talked,' Sandy recalls of one night of serious and prolonged pain, 'as we so often do now, about this book, about ways to shape and complete it'

(157). This becomes a way of talking, without seeming to, of Barbara's completion of her life narrative, her closure. Only two weeks before her death, Barbara writes in an open letter to her friends, 'We [Sandy and I] have written together and we continue to write' (165), another act of imaginatively staving off this ultimate closure. Near the end of this final letter to her friends, Barbara leaps beyond that closure through the agency of the collaborative project: in a variation on that old bibliographic tradition, the *envoi*, Barbara writes, 'Now Sandy and I are completing a book that traces the journey of my cancer. It is called *Cancer in Two Voices*. Even though I may not see the bound volume in my lifetime, I know that the book is already useful because published excerpts have received appreciative responses' (166).

The tension that I have been outlining here, between the collective project and the withdrawal into individual writing, is part of a larger tension in the book between what is 'mine' and what is 'ours.' When Barbara first learns that she has cancer, she describes herself as emerging from solitude into community: 'When the doctor told me I had cancer, I was forced to stand alone on a ledge so steep and so scary that I reached out my hand and grabbed the outstretched hands of the women who form my community' (12). This is an aspect of the collaborative dynamic of *Cancer in Two Voices* that is striking in its expansiveness. In addition to the entries exchanged between Sandra Butler and Barbara Rosenblum, the volume contains a series of interspersed letters from Barbara to her community of women friends, outlining the status of her disease and her reflections on her life. This move, in effect, opens up the collaboration beyond the dyadic relationship that typically constitutes the collaborative writing ventures that I examine in this book. It extends collaboration outward and provides, thereby, some relief for the occasionally claustrophobic relationship between reader and writer, lover and lover. It is also, perhaps above all, a political choice. A little over a week after her diagnosis, Barbara and Sandra invite their network of friends and caregivers to their home, where Barbara reminds them, 'I am trying to live self-consciously (and perhaps die self-consciously) in an exemplary manner. Many of my friends will see their future in the way I handle mine' (12).

For all that Barbara is able to see her experience in simultaneously individual and collective terms, there are still moments when she must insist upon her ownership of the disease, much as she has insisted upon writing alone. When she visits her cancer specialist alone, she reflects on the rebuffing of Sandra's assistance that this decision necessarily entails: 'This painful disentangling is necessary for both of us. The truth is that it is not our cancer but mine. I have to find my way alone now' (15). Sandra, for her part, realizes the same thing, but continues to feel guilt at her occasional feelings of relief at living her own life for a few days while she is away facilitating a workshop or attending a conference: 'I worry about how I will negotiate the high wire of self and other. Autonomy and engagement. Commitment and absence. How will her cancer force me to engage with the choices of being both in my life and in hers as well – and still keep my balance?' (17). This perception of the 'high wire of self and other' is, in this instance and at that moment in time, occasioned by the experience of Barbara's cancer. But it is also a condition that predates the crisis of terminal cancer and attaches itself to the crisis of relationship. As Sandra recalls of their lives together before the diagnosis, 'Our fights were mostly about Barbara's alternating need for me and her need of privacy for herself, longing for our connection and feeling overwhelmed by it' (72). It is important to see the continuing engagement of self and other in this book as nonpathological or, to be precise, as partaking in the pathology of relationship rather than in the pathology of cancer per se.

So cancer does not create those alternating needs that Butler and Rosenblum both describe, but it certainly does heighten the pace of the alternations. Both collaborators describe a violent swing in their needs for dependency and independence, and those swings are metaphorically pathologized in Barbara's swings of energy, strength, and mood. As Barbara observes, 'Our needs seem out of sync and out of proportion. Sandy has never seemed more independent, more separate, and I have never been so needy' (33). Ironically, we read only a few pages later of Sandra's rejection of autonomy, even though she had gone to the extent of renting an office for herself so that she could spend a few hours away from Barbara and from the continuing pain of her condition: 'I don't want to be separate now ... I will be separate soon enough ... I excuse myself from autonomy. I need now to yield, to allow the dependence on this woman who has become my life' (48). Self is, at least temporarily, consumed synecdochally by the other, but it is a synecdoche that is fleetingly temporary. Eventually, Sandra comes to realize that this relationship holds within it the potential for obliteration: 'I am more able now to acknowledge some of the ways I collude with Barbara to be larger than her own sized life – so that she as my partner will mirror my identity as someone often seen as larger than life ... I cannot allow myself to use her life to express my own' (64).

Although the ownership issues that I have explored here seem, at present, fairly abstract, they find a more concrete presentation in *Cancer in Two Voices*, so concrete, in fact, that it is unnerving. I am referring to the conflict that arises, late in the book and in Barbara's life, over her disposition of her money. It is made clear that this is, as Barbara so often remarks, 'blood money,' money that she has won from a legal challenge to the medical centre whose doctors misdiagnosed her for over a year. One of the most painfully frank portions of *Cancer in Two Voices* is Sandra Butler's admission of her feelings of jealousy concerning this money and her transparent reading of the money as love, body, presence:

I recognized that I was not going to be 'well taken care of' in the distribution of her assets. Her parents, sister, and political commitments were going to siphon off what could potentially come to me. I had come to think of this as *my* blood money. My trade-off for the loss of my beloved partner. If I wasn't going to have Barbara, I wanted all the money that had come to represent her life. (89)

This is unflattering to be sure, and not fully representative of Sandra's feelings at other times when she does realize that the money 'was hers [Barbara's], to do with as she saw fit'(88). Still, Sandra's determination to include even the unflattering lends to the depth of this collaboration, the sense, as Barbara said early on, that the collaborative text is a collection of different facets rubbing against each other, misaligning, sometimes meeting in mutuality. Sandra is released from these egocentric thoughts by, ironically, placing her ego in a position of agency, asking herself what she would have done in Barbara's place. Tellingly, the questions that she would have to ask herself are the larger questions that place her, once again, 'on the high wire of self and other': 'Wouldn't I have to evaluate individual life against political need? Collective use against private gain?' (90).

Is this where *Cancer in Two Voices* leaves us, uneasily balancing on that high wire, lost in a never-ending, dizzying alternation between self and other, dependency and autonomy? Not quite. In Butler and Rosenblum's book, ritual becomes the site where one may negotiate these powerful urges, this seeming philosophical dilemma. In terms of conventional notions of plot or event, the book has several focal points that are highly ritualized in nature. There is Barbara and Sandra's commitment ceremony, which they undertake in the face of Barbara's ravaging disease, a ceremony they (and especially Sandra) have not felt comfortable committing themselves to until now. There is also, later in Barbara's illness, her series of letters to her nephew Asher, which she finds from her spiritual counsellor Rabbi Kahn have a ritualized meaning as an 'ethical will,' her ritual bath of *mikvah*, readying herself for her death, and, finally, the traditional Hebrew prayers and chants, ending with the no-less ritual wailing of Barbara's grieving mother. It would be a mistake, I think, to read this increasing emphasis on ritual in *Cancer in Two Voices* as a turn toward the conventionally comforting in a time of immense suffering, however understandable that might be. Rather, I read these instances of ritual as negotiated places where Barbara, Sandra, and their communities can express and not resolve the tensions of the high wire of self and other. This is no comfortably conventional return to religion. To begin with, the *shul* that Barbara and Sandra attach themselves to is a mainly gay and lesbian congregation that exists in defiance of more conservative orthodoxies. And, as it turns out, the rabbi's conventional expectations about the kind of ritual Barbara would like to be remembered by arise from the traditions of that congregation more than from the Talmud and Torah: 'Having officiated at the funerals of many gay men and lesbians, he began by suggesting some words by Stephen Spender and the poetry of Adrienne Rich. Barbara cut him off in mid-sentence, saying firmly, "No. That's not what I want ... They [my family] need the ancient words, the prayers, the sounds"' (168). Undertaken as a 'last offering of love to her parents' (168) this seeming recourse to Jewish convention is truly a negotiation of the self and the other. The cantor sings the traditional songs, the black ribbons worn by Barbara's parents are cut nearly in two, as is the custom, to symbolize the breaking of their hearts, but, less conventionally, Sandra mounts the *bema* and speaks of the love she has shared with this woman. And, finally, she comes to understand Barbara's mother's keening as not breaking the sanctity of the ritual but as its truest expression. Ritual in this collective memoir, properly understood, is an analogue for the collaborative spaces I theorize in this book: a space where, contrary to popular notion, self is not lost in relationship with other, but is placed in a liminal space where self both is and is not other.

English-language poets, those who carry such a long tradition of both a collective (epic, oral) past and of individual genius feel the workings of this tension most forcibly. In the next chapter, I turn my attention to their negotiations of the high wire of collaboration.

5

Being Alone Together:
Collaborative Poetry

> negative feminine space
> walking into the diner
> 'are you ladies alone'
>   'no'
>   'we're together'
>   Daphne Marlatt and Betsy Warland, 'Double Negative'

No other contemporary genre that I deal with in this book has been so thoroughly imbued with the ethos of privacy as has poetry. This holds true, of course, for Western literatures, where the Romantic image of the poet as the solitary, possessed visionary in the attic has taken hold of various poetic communities, in spite of earlier examples of public poetry such as the epic, and in spite of the continuing, though diminished or marginalized, presence of shared, oral forms such as folk ballads, native oratory, and song. But in African and in Eastern cultures, too, particularly Japan, where shared poetic authorship has had a long and vigorous history, the Westernizing drive toward the privatization of the poetic voice has had a homogenizing effect. Small wonder, then, that when contemporary poets collaborate, they see themselves as transgressing a readily visualizable Western code: the poet as Thomas Chatterton, young, alone, possessed, self-destructive. As the American poets Miriam May and Jamie Shepherd observe, 'Institutionally at least, collaboration to some extent suggests cheating and sneakiness. So we're not doing "real work"; we're not slaving alone in our little cold garrets suffering to write poetry in isolation' (quoted in Ede and Lunsford n.p.). But the privacy of the lyric, taken so much for granted as a poetic norm in Western contemporary poetry, is, of course, both culturally and historically produced and performed. Recall Kenneth Koch's reminder to Western readers: 'Japanese poets wrote together as naturally as Shelley wrote alone' (193). Such a formulation ironically contests its own use of nature as a universalizing criterion; Japanese poets, that is, naturalized collective writing just as Western communities constructed a norm of isolate art and deemed it natural.

For that matter, collaborative poetry, too, has been performed in any number of ways in any number of cultural settings, and some of these performances raise issues that are of continuing concern to the contemporary practice of collaborative poetry. For instance, Koch points out the distinctly competitive cast of the collaborative dialogue songs of the troubadours:

The Troubadors wrote (really sang) at each other sometimes because of out-and-out hostility, sometimes because of a mere friendly desire to show off; their *tensos* were contests ... (the challenger would cho[o]se the topic of the *tenso*, but the challenged poet could choose the side of the argument he wanted, and he also got to sing *first*, thereby establishing the rhyme scheme that the challenger had to adhere to in his replies – the spirit of the whole thing is roughly 'I'm a better poet than you are. If you don't believe it, let's have a trial in XZ Castle'. (194, emphasis Koch's)

This combative style of collaboration may find little direct contemporary expression, but the competitiveness that Koch satirically sketches in his portrait of the troubadours is by no means erased or transcended by a wiser, more egalitarian, less macho contemporary female collaboration. Like Foucault's author, poetic competition does not merely die; its functions circulate elsewhere, in other channels. The statement-response format of very old collaborative verse, for example, operates most markedly in contemporary women's collaborative poetry, though it operates ideologically in any number of ways.

Like competition, the historically produced criterion of 'seriousness' continues to haunt and to inspire collaboratively produced poetry. As Koch argues, seventeenth-century verse collaborations, like the 'Letter' of Donne and Goodyere and the stanzaic exchanges of Cowley and Crawshaw, Waller and Suckling, had something of the five-finger exercise about them; they form a series of witty metaphysical rejoinders, one poet to another. Still, few scholars consider these poems worthy of canonical status, even though their authors are canonized poets; they are, more frequently, regarded as second-string curiosities. Poetic play, it would seem, may be the product of two poets; poetic seriousness, on the other hand, has traditionally been thought to be the domain of the single poet alone. Contemporary collaborative poets in general engage in an activity that the literary establishment readily codes as eccentric and whimsical. Women collaborators, however, face the added historical weight of an already coded lack of seriousness, as specialists in, to quote Jane Austen's criticism of her *Pride and Prejudice*, the 'light, bright and sparkling.' Again, how women collaborators bear, shift, or throw off this weight in their poetic collaborations varies widely, according to any number of political and cultural factors.

Historically speaking, for poetic collaboration, the Romantic period in Western poetry was a time of crisis, partly because the tensions between privacy and publicity, seriousness and play that I have associated with collaborative poetry came into sustained and public confrontation. The repercussions continue to be felt in both Western poetry and the poetic discourses of other communities that it has touched and colonized. Kenneth Koch labels the period a turning point for collaboration mainly because these poets 'collaborated, not because they wanted to twist each other's thoughts, but because they felt that they were writing out of a "community of feeling" – they "understood" each other, they had common aims and ideals' (195). But what Koch does not mention is the concurrent cult of the private, isolated poet which dominated that same period: the interiorized poet so vividly summed up in Coleridge's 'Kubla Khan.' What happened in the Romantic period was the crossing of communitarian and individualist discourses, a crossing that complicated notions of authorship and texts not only for the Romantics but for those who inherited a now ubiquitous range of aesthetic assumptions which can loosely be termed Romantic. In this light, I find no coincidence in the fact that two of the most prominent theorists of an expanded notion of authorship are, by origin, Romantic poetry scholars: the Keats and Shelley critic Jack Stillinger and the Byron editor and critic, Jerome McGann. In his indictment of traditional textual critical practices, McGann repeatedly emphasizes their ultimately Romantic basis: 'This is a theory of textual criticism founded in a Romantic ideology' (42); 'These ideas [of the autonomous author] are grounded in a Romantic conception of literary production' (8). Familiarity with Romantic authorship may well breed critique or, at least, the awareness that it is one possible configuration among many and not a normative, universal condition.

I, too, focus, though briefly, on the Romantic period and its crisis of authorship discourses, for it introduces us to issues that are still very much alive in the contemporary women's collaborative poetry I discuss in this chapter. The inevitable touchstone is the much-celebrated collaboration of two men: Wordsworth and Coleridge's 1798 *Lyrical Ballads*. It is a collaboration that, in various ways, richly deserves the adjective that Wayne Koestenbaum applies to men's artistic collaborations of the following century: 'anxious.' But the anxiety that preoccupies me here is one of ownership and property. The Wordsworth-Coleridge collaboration carefully and nervously reinforced, even as it challenged in some measure, the notion of literary property. As Wordsworth was eager to point out, there was a strict agreement between the two poets about the division of artistic labour, Coleridge specializing in the supernatural pieces and Wordsworth himself contributing studies of everyday experience and its dialects (361). Indeed, in his note to 'We are Seven,' Wordsworth was particularly scrupulous about parcelling out the responsibility and, hence, ownership of specific poems and lines of poems: 'Much the greatest part of the story' of *The Rime of the Ancient Mariner*, he recalled, 'was Mr. Coleridge's invention; but certain parts I myself suggested, for example, some crime was to be committed ... I also suggested the navigation of the ship by the dead men, but do not recollect that I had anything more to do with the scheme of the poem.' He does, however, go on to claim 'two or three lines at the beginning of the poem' as his own (361). I would place Wordsworth's nervousness in the context of the dynamic historical forces of property and transgression which Michel Foucault discerns in this very period. Building on his argument that texts were only assigned named, 'ordinary' individual authors when their 'discourse was considered transgressive,' Foucault notes that

> it was at the moment when a system of ownership and strict copyright rules was established (toward the end of the eighteenth and beginning of the nineteenth century) that the transgressive properties always intrinsic to the act of writing became the forceful imperative of literature. It is as if the author, at the moment he [*sic*] was accepted into the social order of property which governs our culture, was compensating for his new status by reviving the older bipolar field of discourse [i.e. sacred / profane, lawful / unlawful] in a systematic practice of transgression. (124–5)

So to collaborate at that historical moment in that particular culture was a transgressive response, but, as Foucault argues in his essay 'On Transgression,' transgression itself includes rather than erases or oversteps the law, the line being crossed. In the case of Wordsworth, this argument is largely borne out; co-authoring *The Lyrical Ballads* was a transgression that consolidated, and rather nervously at that, the boundaries of the relatively new textual property ethic.

Contemporary poetic collaborations have sometimes been just as anxious to reinstate ownership. The editorial note prefacing Octavio Paz and Charles Tomlinson's *Airborn / Hijos del Aire* (1981) draws attention to the scrupulous visual division of poetic spoils: 'The passages in italic type are those written in Spanish by Octavio Paz, and translated by Charles Tomlinson. The passages in roman type are those written in English by Charles Tomlinson and translated by Octavio Paz.' This note is, appropriately, concluded by a traditional acknowledgment of a couple of lines from Gongora, 'from E.M. Wilson's translation of the *Soledades*' (8). Both types of property – shares in collaboration and textual citation – must be vigilantly indicated. It is fascinating to see what contemporary women collaborators will do with this question of property rights in collaboration, especially since women's historical relation to property has been, in many cultures, a tenuous one to begin with.

Collaboration also promised, for Wordsworth, a communitarian fusion which would resolve and submerge difference. That it did not, in Wordsworth's view, deliver that promise, is proof of another conflict of analogies: the author as the solitary wanderer and the author as, in Wordsworth's phrase from his 'Preface to *The Lyrical Ballads*,' a 'man speaking to men,' a social being who is supposedly able to communicate on all social levels. Difference and tension in his own attempt to share communication with Samuel Taylor Coleridge, however, led Wordsworth to revert to the language of artistic individualism and solitude when he later described the composition of *The Rime of the Ancient Mariner*: 'As we endeavoured to proceed conjointly ... our respective manners proved so widely different that it would have been quite presumptuous in me to do anything but separate from an undertaking upon which I could only have been a clog' (361). Wordsworth's figure of speech is revealing; an individual who cannot cede individuality can only be a clog in the wheels of another autonomous individual artist. Critics who have followed Wordsworth's lead by proclaiming the collaboration a failure have also followed his lead, of course, in assuming that two collaborators can only succeed when they combine to form one individual author. In this study of contemporary women's collaborations, rifts and differences are no more negatively valued than communitarian visions of transcended individuality are unquestioningly celebrated. Instead, I examine the continuing conflict between communitarian and individualist discourses in these recent collaborative efforts. Easy though it may be for contemporary collaborators and their readers to feel superior to the assumptions about property and community that animated that most canonical of Romantic collaborations, those conflicting discourses, dramatically reconfigured though they may be, persist to this day.

Many contemporary collaborative women poets do, indeed, sense a powerful lyric tradition peering over their shoulders. As

Suniti Namjoshi and Gillian Hanscombe ask in their introduction to their collection *Flesh and Paper* (1986), 'Who, in lyric poems, is addressing whom and in what capacity? And who is overhearing? And who has authority and credentials to comment on what is being said?' ([3]). The questions are strikingly Foucauldian in their concern with subject position; they recall those 'new questions' about texts that Foucault places at the end of 'What Is an Author?' I ask similar questions of contemporary women's collaborative poetry: What are its possible variations of power-property dynamics? To what extent can it subvert the construction of the bourgeois isolated author? What discourses or performances are possible for subjects and under what circumstances?

Some poets who actively look to tradition in search of a collaborative precedent may be drawn to Japanese renga or linked poetry, a case I consider separately because of its specific history and formal criteria. Octavio Paz, a contemporary Western practitioner of the form, describes it as a 'poem composed by several poets, three or four, who write successively stanzas of three and of two lines, without rhyme, but with a fixed syllabic measure' (Paz and Tomlinson 5). Both women and men, of various cultures, have looked to renga as a means of expanding the possibilities of poetic authorship, though that expansion has had many means and motives. Some stress the formal elaborateness of the renga, and seem to expect that contemporary practictioners of the mode will follow suit. Kenneth Koch, for instance, notes that '[t]his linked verse, so highly serious in intention, was composed in an atmosphere of mutu[a]l esteem and emulation,' the verso of the troubadours' *tenso*. He also calls the traditional rules of Japanese renga, which had to do with how often a specific word had to appear, or where a stanza dealing with a particular subject had to appear, 'complicated and beautiful' (195–6), thus revealing his own aesthetic predilections and assumptions. There has been much free play, however, with the rules; the authors of the 'first western renga' (Paz and Tomlinson 5), Octavio Paz, Jacques Roubaud, Edoardo Sanguineti, and Charles Tomlinson, in a Westernizing move, chose to write unrhymed sonnets, and Paz and Tomlinson, in a later shared renga, dispensed with the traditional physical presence of the authors and wrote another set of sonnet renga by mail, *Airborn / Hijos del Aire.*

The Canadian renga collection, *Linked Alive* (1990), composed of five sets of renga by six poets, is dedicated to the renga of Paz, Roubaud, Sanguineti and Tomlinson, but it is also a critical response to that much-celebrated 1969 event. The two poets whose names appear as copyright holders, Ayanna Black and Dore Michelut, initiated the project and enlisted the other poets: two women, Lee Maracle and Anne-Marie Alonzo; and two men, Charles Douglas and Paul Savoie. Black and Michelut wrote the first set of renga, and collaborated, in turn, with one other woman poet and one male poet, so they participated in three renga sets, whereas the other satellite poets engaged in one each. This renga web is set out at the beginning of the collection thus:

ANNE-MARIE ALONZO		PAUL SAVOIE
with		with
DORE MICHELUT	with	AYANNA BLACK
with		with
CHARLES DOUGLAS		LEE MARACLE (n.p.)

These renga do, like the Paz et al. cycle, explore cultural differences among poets, in this case, Caribbean-Canadian (Black), Italo-Canadian (Michelut), indigenous (Maracle), Scottish-Canadian (Douglas), Franco-Manitoban (Savoie) and Egyptian-born franco-phone Québécois (Alonzo), but they implicitly critique that earlier event by crossing gender lines as well. Of course, one other way of highlighting the gendered exclusivity of the Paz et al. project would be to construct an all-woman renga, and for a while Black and Michelut considered doing this. But after what Michelut calls 'considerable debate' (Michelut 106), they invited Douglas and Savoie.

Another way in which *Linked Alive* challenges the earlier at-tempts to transplant Japanese shared verse onto Western soil is by removing many of the formal restrictions. In her lengthy Afterword to the collection, Michelut notes that the poets 'took a "no rules" approach. There were to be no prior formal constraints: we could write poetry, prose, anything that "felt" right … The only requirement was the necessary link: taking an image or the underlying idea that "spoke" from the previous entry, and working to make it personally meaningful' (107). This decision was probably founded on Michelut and Black's readings of Western renga, many of which they found to be mere 'intellectual exercises' (106). As Kenneth Koch confirms, 'Some contemporary collaborations have had rules of composition almost as elaborate [as Japanese shared verse], though these rules have been voluntarily chosen by the poets themselves' (196). The only other rule that the Black, Michelut et al. renga adheres to is a hand-back rule, whereby collaborators may return an entry 'if we found no concept or image that responded "in kind"' (107). When this happened, the rengaists would discuss the situation and wait for the initiating poet to rework and resubmit the fragment. Ironically, this rule was meant to reinforce the no rules approach; as Michelut explains, the 'partner was always free to reject what could not be assimilated' (112). Still, poetic egos have a way of responding to rejection in a personal rather than a collaborative spirit; one of the rengaists, Charles Douglas, 'politely stormed out' (in co-rengaist Michelut's words) when one of his segments was returned, effectively putting an end to the set. Even those rules that are dedicated to fostering an atmosphere of non-compulsion inevitably participate in the discourse of competition and regulation that they seemingly reject. The pressure to respond 'in perfect accord,' as Paz described one of Charles Tomlinson's renga rejoinders (Paz and Tomlinson 6), is not easily dissipated in renga, however iconoclastic the variation.

Linked Alive, like the renga sets of Paz, Roubaud, Sanguineti, and Tomlinson, and like the Western Romantic precedent of Wordsworth and Coleridge, displays many a symptom of the anxiety of textual property. In the printed text, the poets' names appear in the margins, next to their lines, the first name in the right margin, the second in the left, the two names framing the space that both links and separates the two textual properties, thus:

It is death that tames,
Your weeping nourishes.
Outside, the rain burns.   Michelut
Alonzo   pain is in and around me
                    scars offend me
        carry the body as lead do not fall
           or weep (97)

When I first, briefly, wrote about this collection, in an article dealing with mainly Canadian poetic collaborations ('Lesbianizing Authorship'), I was, frankly, put off by this labelling of property. I found the poems proprietary and sometimes brashly competitive – closer in spirit to the troubadours than the Japanese rengaists. But I now read these poems differently, paying more attention to the anxiety of property and to the critical role of the space between the stanzas, the locus of much of the collaborative work of the poems. Can any label contain what goes on in that space between, wherein two poets simultaneously link and separate?

In revising my earlier stance, then, I need to acknowledge the challenges that these renga pose to the traditional constructions of authorship, even if they do reinforce them in other respects. Most generally, of course, the poems challenge, in some measure, the privacy of most Western art. In her afterword, Michelut astutely notes the ironic situation of Western democracies bragging of high literacy rates while providing 'virtually no written social arenas where, by intermingling, we fully determine our individual, public selves. Self creation, for us, has been banished from the social forum and has become exclusively a private endeavour' (113). Lee Maracle, telling the story of how she came to write her renga set, 'A Celebration,' with Ayanna Black, reveals how even a Native writer, deeply imbued with a strong tradition of shared oral forms, has been 'banished from the social forum.' Writing, for her, had always been a 'solitary affair that develops between myself and my typewriter,' but when she began to write with Black, she felt that '[i]t was exhausting in much the same way as it would be to strip and dance for an audience of one' (51). The image is an arresting, disturbing one: what was once thought intimately private has become public, but in a paradoxically intimate (one-to-one) fashion. It suggests the complexity of the conflict between public and private discourses in shared poetry: writing together is at once a social and an intimate act, and therefore it challenges the habitual tendency to demarcate the two that Michelut criticizes in Western democracies. For Maracle, writing renga with Black convinced her that she was not a Chatterton-like 'victim of poetry, but a child of oratory,' a term that signals Maracle's reunion with her own culture's rich tradition of social authorship.

In their commentaries on the renga, the poets repeatedly emphasize this invigorating movement from the private to the social. Michelut recalls that writing her first renga with Black was like taking a leap 'out of my rar[e]fied, internal space, out of the eerie quiet of the library and into the social fracas' (16). When Black, in her turn, remembers the people she and Michelut socialized with during their stay in Mexico when they wrote the renga, a 'playboy professor toting Plato, a teacher-cum-travel-writer from San Antonio ...,' she is not indulging in peripheral nostalgia, for 'we incorporated all this into the writing as we lived it' (18). The social has ceased to act as background to a foregrounded poetic interiority, as Raymond Williams has said it has often done in traditional humanist analysis; it has leaped onto the page.

The face-to-face encounter of two poets in renga certainly accounts for much of this socializing of the artistic, and it is also a common figure in women's collaborative poetry in general. As Anne-Marie Alonzo writes in her poetic Preface to 'From Inside the Pain,' her renga with Michelut, 'To sit down face to face. To confront each other. Confront what / remains alone with us. Pained. Fragile to defend' (91). Black is struck by the same visual configuration of 'writing that is not experienced alone, done behind the "back" of the other, but is done "in front," facing the other person directly' (70). Of course, not all renga makes this socializing face-to-face gesture. Octavio Paz and Charles Tomlinson, writing *Airborn / Hijos del Aire* by letter, engaged in what Tomlinson called a 'postal meditation' (8); how revealing that he should have employed such a traditionally interior and individualized term to counteract the plurality and publicity of the language of postal communication.

For these face-to-face rengaists, however, the physical presence of the meditators disrupts the interiority that is constructed by the humanist tradition of poetry and ushers in some complicated power dynamics: the dynamics of trust. This trust, however, is not a plateau, an achievement of a blissfully secure state of confidence; it is, instead, a constantly renegotiated, sometimes awkwardly choreographed movement, like the Milan Bookstore Collective's notion of entrustment. As Michelut reflects in her Foreword to the first renga with Black, 'I had to trust her. I had no choice. In turn elated and appalled, I became aware that we were bound and struggling to move together as in a three-legged race' (15). This striking comparison does show traces of the Romantic conception of collaboration as two (or more) selves attempting to ape a unitary self. It also highlights the awkwardness and futility of such an endeavour, without diagnosing those conditions as symptoms of collaborative failure.

As Michelut's example of the three-legged race suggests, the dynamics of trust are also the dynamics of responsibility, and collaborative poetry, particularly the face-to-face renga, dramatically reconfigures artistic responsibility. The notions of responsibility which adhere to the traditionally isolated poetic composition – responsibility to one's public, responsibility to a tradition – are necessarily abstract because there are few means of embodying the 'other' to whom or to which one is responsible. In renga, however, responsibility stares the poet in the face; Michelut movingly writes of her renga exchange with Alonzo, who has been confined to a wheelchair since she was fifteen: '*From Inside the Pain* was dangerous. Anne-Marie and I immediately became aware that renga was not fiction, that there was responsibility for the import of what the writing evoked in the life of the other. How much paralysis can you take? her eyes kept asking. At first, I assumed I could take everything, then I told her how much' (89).

This reworking of trust and responsibility is part of the more general revision of writer-reader relationships in collaborative art: the author is also a reader and the first reader is also, to recall Walter Benjamin, a producer (11). Michelut, in her Afterword, explicitly theorizes this revision:

In Western literary traditions, the writer and the reader, although free to write and read, do not have the social space, the task to negotiate a personal agreement ... in public, in writing. Alone, the writer creates, and alone, the reader re-creates a private, hypothetical negotiation of reality ... Both reader and writer find themselves increasingly foretold by a written body, an expanded public object that has become active to such proportions it is felt as a solid insulating wall, between subject and subject. (108–9)

Michelut compares this dynamic to that of traditional psychoanalysis, whereby the analyst is free to interpret the client, but the 'client does not have the authority to penetrate the subjective life of the analyst' (114). For that, analysts turn to other colleagues, other similarly empowered experts.

These, then, are some of the claims for the disruptive or challenging powers of renga, though they are not without their moments of retrenchment. Nevertheless, at times the rengaists may appear to lay claim to an Edenic realm of equality and sharing; as Black recalls the writing of the final stanzas of 'A Celebration' with Maracle, 'our thoughts synchronized' (50). Maracle, in her turn, reinforces Black's notion of an integrative moment, an 'inside look at the soul of Ayanna at the point where our spirits bonded together' (51). These are, for the most part, rhetorical gestures aimed at capturing only some of the dynamics of renga: renga's meetings and not its partings. As is often the case in collections which pair poetry and prose commentary, the poetry tells a more complex story. Take, for example, the very stanza that Black is talking about, the one that concludes 'A Celebration.' It is, as I have argued elsewhere ('Lesbianizing Authorship'), a brilliant reworking of the property laws of this particular renga format, for it resituates the marginal name-tags in the poetic text, as participants in a discourse of singularity and community:

>   Dawn soft glow
>   playfully casting light
>   on the ceremony of dance,
> a song of blessed peace.   Maracle
> Black   We link hands
>   round the rising sun (65).

At the time I wrote about this text, I think I accepted the subversiveness of this act too readily or, at least, in too unqualified a fashion. I felt that the Black-Maracle collaboration, alone, managed to avoid the competitiveness of the form by acknowledging and yet altering the proprietary name tags. The verses, which are usually separated into dyads, are closer together in this instance, as though drawn toward the collaborative centre that resists competitive separation. If I was too quick to criticize the other portions of the collection as too competitive and property-conscious, I was here too ready to exalt an exception. Now I think that these resituated names transgress only in the Foucauldian sense of both crossing and reinscribing a boundary. These lines, at first appearing to betoken a relatively unproblematic 'Celebration' of women's community, a goddess-worship-like linking of 'hands / round the rising sun,' are all the more moving for their incorporation, not erasure, of those socially produced names that signal particularity, difference, and property.

The persistence of difference even in the midst of such an obviously celebratory moment in *Linked Alive* is proof of the polyvalence which characterizes much collaborative writing by women. Though participants, like Michelut in her Afterword, tend to stress the communitarian aspects of the exchange, conflict is just as frequent a guest at the poetic table. 'We fought,' Michelut remembers of her two-week renga composition with Black, 'Then we embraced ... The balance struck between us was at times comforting, at times excruciating, and there were times when only the writing kept us together' (15–16). This mingling of enmity and embrace marks a difference-based notion of community.

At times, the balancing act is more difficult to espy. There is, as I have mentioned, the abrupt conclusion of Michelut and Charles Douglas's renga when the latter 'politely stormed out,' but there is also Black's description of the Black-Michelut renga, which tips that balance in the direction of conflict and competition:

Writing *All the Way* was not without difficulties. Each day, the opening became more difficult and Dore more demanding. She passed my texts back to me, feeling that I was not digging deep enough. Then we would talk ... Tension and resentment mounted and struck a couple of days later. Dore felt we hadn't reached our goal, that we could have done more with the form. I reacted angrily and told her that I had given everything and that she was pushing herself too hard. (18–19)

Like the tell-tale proprietorial names in the margins, this description initially alienated me from the renga, and convinced me that the very form of renga militates against a fully collaborative, shared authorship. Again, I was tending to rank collaboration, as Koestenbaum does in his *Double Talk*, seeing some forms of collaboration as more satisfyingly or fully collaborative. Rereading this account of collaborative conflict now, I am struck by how it coexists with and does not preempt or deny the more communitarian experiences of the renga. Although Black is less overt than Michelut and her attempts to balance conflict and embrace, she does not neglect the embrace of collaboration either. She follows up her account of anger with a simple, self-chastising reminder, 'Fear is only fear when I do not allow myself to live,' and then concludes with a story about Michelut plucking a cicada off her (Black's) shoulder, whispering 'Don't be afraid ... It's my mother.' This incident inspired a further renga exchange. Fear of conflict may similarly inhibit the life of collaborative poetry; like the cicada, conflict may figure as the pestilence of an idealized collaborative community, but if the collaborators brush it away fearfully, they will have to deny its power to strengthen the collaborative relationship.

There are moments in Michelut's Afterword when she openly acknowledges conflict and tension as part of the crucial dynamics of renga. She writes, for instance, that the hand-back rule 'became the crucial practice that supplied the tension which informs the movement in these renga' (107). It certainly supplied the Michelut-Douglas renga with tension, not to say acrimony. A bit later, she comments that renga 'is an art form that posits encounter as a necessary given' (112). Where, one might ask, do the tension and encounter that are part of a reconstituted community leave off and where do the tension and encounter of blatantly competitive machismo begin? And where do the renga of *Linked Alive* figure in this issue of conflict? In neither one category nor the other; in their dealings with what I have called the fusion versus difference issue in contemporary feminism, there are conflicts of both varieties to be found. For instance, drawing on a female-male collaboration for a moment, Michelut acknowledges that her rupture with Douglas was a two-way battle of egos: 'I was impatient with Charles for the openings [of the renga] I needed' (37). Still, rereading and rethinking the renga today, I sense that I overestimated the presence of this conflict at the expense of the conflict of reconstituted community, which I now discern vigorously at work in the women collaborators' poems. As Alonzo writes in her poetic Foreword to 'From Inside the Pain,' 'I am not you nor you me,' a position which allows community members, as political theorist Shane Phelan says, 'to relate to one another without requiring identity [i.e., sameness]' (55).

Renga should be a welcoming textual space for the performance of such notions of reconfigured community. As Michelut writes, the 'rengaists meet on the divided page and retain individual identity by requesting from each other a committed response' (105). In a passage that sounds straight out of John Stuart Mill (perhaps one of the 'parts [of liberalism]' that Phelan says women's communities may find 'we cannot dispense with' [149]) she also notes that the freedom of renga is, therefore, a freedom of horizons rather than a bourgeois individualistic construction: 'One has all the opportunity to make oneself, but only within the other's hope of self' (116).

The cultural diversity of *Linked Alive* foregrounds this complicated dance of desires: to identify across cultures and, at the same time, to respect cultural specificity. In her prose commentaries, Michelut often speaks of cultural difference as something that renga can operate in spite of, thus coding it as difficulty: 'The different cultures in which Anne-Marie [Alonzo] and I live and write in made way for the impelling need to communicate. We drew from whatever language resources we had in common ... We pushed these languages aside to reach and shape what was between us' (89–90). In her Afterword, she concludes, in a similar vein, that 'I am convinced that any two people who share a common language, even in part, can do renga irrespective of differences of education, age and culture' (118). Again, the poetry tells a more complex tale, moving cultural (and other) differences out of a blocking position and into the very fabric of the exchange. When Maracle and Black, for instance, invoke each other's cultures in their own portions of the renga, they are probing for both sympathetic similarity and energizing differences in the histories of First Nations and African-American women of colour:

> Thorns scratch at Sojourner.
> Whose truth
> weaves a new fabric
> across Red-earth woman's path?   Maracle
>
> Black   Branches of Sojourner
>   extend hunger
>   can't be denied, can't stop
>   the drum beat. (56)

Can there be an inspiring Sojourner Truth figure for native women, Maracle asks? Black's response both posits the possibility of many (branches of) Sojourners, an 'extend[ed]' vision of cultural 'hunger,' but 'the drum beat' of First Nations cultural life – a collective cultural statement – is no simple or universalizing translation of the figure of Sojourner Truth. Do First Nations people need the inspiring single leader, she seems to ask, when the collective expression of cultural activity is so unmistakably commanding? This interplay of identity and difference is, appropriately enough, framed by the collaborative poem's self-conscious exploration of the issue of individual and collective agency.

Although cultural difference may appear in this self-conscious way in a collaborative art form that itself highlights the dynamics of fusion and difference, not all differences are, or can be, thus scrupulously meditated; the text will have its unconscious. In *Linked Alive*, as in some other contemporary women's collaborations, the motif of collective poetry as discovery is one such poetic unconscious. Black and Michelut wrote their set in Merida,

Yucatan, Mexico; 'I was in Merida two weeks before Dore finally arrived via Cancun: a six hour bus ride through the heart of the mysterious Mayan civilization,' recalls Black. 'Beyond the city,' she adds, 'are Mayan ruins, an explorer's paradise.' She then makes the tempting metaphorical transference to the poets' explorations: 'I remember momentarily feeling I was an archaeologist going on a dig: my body, the land, digging deeply, into the brush, brushing away unwanted soil to expose the findings, the poetic truth' (17). Although one might argue that such a positioning of the poet as explorer belongs to an Edenic world of innocence, when Black 'was obsessed with thoughts of a collective process of poetry which was totally equal' (17), before her chastening experience of vitalizing conflict and difference, the basic explorationist myth is not subsequently revised or challenged. Black and Michelut, like other contemporary collaborators, find themselves in the problematic position of probing similarity and difference on a ground that is constructed as other or mysterious, but which is already culturally written and contested by indigenous and settler communities. As in so many other respects, collaborative art departs from the constructed centrality of individual authorship, property, or power relations, only to find that centres replicate themselves. How contemporary collaborators respond to that condition will be the concern of the remainder of this chapter.

Poetic collaborations that do not depend, in however emended a form, on a specific tradition like renga, do have more sources of play at their disposal. The sort of play that Lee Maracle and Ayanna Black fashioned out of their labelling and identifying names in *Linked Alive*, for instance, is more possible; various forms of signature may circulate in the work, as objects of analysis and self-conscious meditation. I focus on two of these poetic collaborations: Suniti Namjoshi and Gillian Hanscombe's little-discussed 1986 volume *Flesh and Paper* and the poetic sequences contained in Daphne Marlatt and Betsy Warland's collection *Two Women in a Birth*: 'Double Negative,' originally published as a separate collection in 1988, 'Reading and Writing between the Lines,' and 'Subject to Change.'

One feature that other poetic collaborations tend to share with the renga, though, is a juggling of the conventional writerly and readerly roles. Daphne Marlatt and Betsy Warland choose as an epigraph for their poetic sequence, 'Double Negative,' for instance, these suggestive lines from another Canadian poet, Lola Lemire Tostevin:

> rereading reverses to resist   resists to reverse the   movement
> along the curve of
> return   as the well-turned   phrase turns on herself to retrace her
> steps   reorient   and
> continue in a different voice [72]

The train-like rhythms make the epigraph especially appropriate to a poetic account of two poets' travels by train through Australia. More important, however, the lines apply to the rereading that is collaborative writing. Texts 'return' 'reorient / and continue,' shunting back and forth from producer/reader to reader/producer. For that matter, Marlatt's depiction of the train, in 'Crossing Loop,' the prose dialogue between the poets 'D.' and 'B.,' could also function as a description of collaborative writing/reading: 'the train is constantly starting and stopping, departing and arriving, coming and waiting at crossing loops and in that sense it's cyclical' (108). In an art form that mingles a writing that is traditionally conceived as active with a reading that is typically cast as either passive or, at most, quietly active, collaborative poets are repeatedly drawn to this train-like shunting between acting and waiting. As Suniti Namjoshi and Gillian Hanscombe write in their collection *Flesh and Paper*, when they describe the beginning of a new relationship, 'I knew how we'd listen and wait; I knew / how we'd go on walking towards one another' (16). In the writerly/readerly dynamic of collaborative art, poetic 'walking' and 'waiting' have ceased to be antithetical states.

Though they share renga's challenging of airtight distinctions between writers and readers, many of these contemporary collaborations feature a more expansive repertoire of response formats. Renga tends to encode a dualistic statement-response format, though occasionally rengaists like Ayanna Black and Lee Maracle may pick up threads from the preceding dyad of renga in the next dyad to come. Still, the fact remains that there is a dualistic format at work, whether it structures or provokes anti-structural gestures. Suniti Namjoshi, describing *Flesh and Paper* in her own (individual) selected poetry volume *Because of India* (1989), describes it as a 'dialogue in its very structure' (113), a term which suggests a variety of conversational patterns beyond the simple statement-response format. The term applies very well to other collections of collaborative poetry. Marlatt and Warland, for instance, incorporate revision in their very text, making the sorts of collaborative decisions that earlier collaborators like Somerville and Ross made in the privacy of their attic, before they presented their novels and stories to the public:

> May white and pink studding our
> northern expectation
>   not studding no
>   it does not *stand*
>   our desire
>   moves continuous around
>   surround, this is no
>   horse stable
>   (73; emphasis Marlatt and Warland's).

Dialogue itself is foregrounded, not only the dialogue of two poets but the dialogue between masculine and sexually inclusive languages; it matters less which poet is revising which. Indeed, the issue of language overflows any simple, dualistic notion of suggestion and correction; on the very next page, I see, the poets have repeated the faux pas: 'palm trees stud this route' (74). Although, as Brenda Carr writes, the project of Marlatt and Warland's poetry may be to overthrow the 'mantle of mastering discourse,' or to 're-verse the masculine coding of words' (114, 115), masculine language is not simply revised, wiped out. Beyond all efforts to correct it, it hangs on, tenaciously, a hardy thread in the continuing dialogue of gender and power.

By incorporating a transcript version of a dialogue between two poets in the middle of their sequence 'Double Negative,' Marlatt and Warland tempt readers to disperse this reading of dialogue in the poetic text that surrounds it. This dialogue is one that allows for both agreement ('Exactly!' exclaims 'B.' at one point; 107) and difference ('It wasn't that way for me,' she comments a moment later; 108). In Namjoshi and Hanscombe's *Flesh and Paper*, there is no dialogue section per se, even though, as Namjoshi tells us in *Because of India*, many of the poems in the collection were excerpted from 'the letters between us and woven into an interconnecting text' (112). There is, instead, a brief co-signed introduction that uses the collective pronoun 'we.' In spite of this suggestion of a united collectivity, however, the collection encodes dialogue in a number of ways. One poem is called a 'Postscript' to another poem (10), and another is entitled 'Reply to your poem of the same ...' (13). Another poem title wittily parodies the language of formal meetings: 'Questions arising' (46; it opens, 'Surely there's a fault in the presentation?' as though the preceding poet had just switched off an overhead displaying graphs and tables.) The next poem self-consciously represents the poet's case: 'Oh birds talk back' (47). So too, apparently, do poets.

Although there are some two-part poems in *Flesh and Paper* ('Meru' i and ii [8–9]; 'I invent the movie' i and ii [14–15]), the poems do not generally separate into dyads, as the renga inevitably do. More typically, there are occasional, loose groupings of poems, forming no tight, overall structure, but suggesting, instead, an informal conversation in which propositions are playfully taken up, examined, contested, celebrated ... responded to in any number of ways. In 'Under My Eyes,' for instance, one poet metaphorically transforms herself and her lover into tigers but, in the next poem, the other poet contests this transformation as the women in Renaissance sonnets rarely could: 'All right, call them another species, throw off nouns with a categorical clink' (41). Metaphor, that traditional refuge of the naming, inscribing poet, is here open to contest, for the object of the poetic gaze, in women's collaborative love poetry, has the capacity to metamorphose into a speaking subject.

When more than one speaker is potentially constructed, as they are in these collaborative poems, it would seem that the predominantly Western notion of private artistic expression is decisively ruptured thereby, but these collections actually reveal a wide range of positions on the question of privacy and collective speech. Marlatt and Warland's 'Double Negative,' for example, tends to associate privacy with women's historical confinement to an inhibiting bourgeois domesticity, thus implicitly linking traditionally isolated authorship with historically isolated woman: 'this is what the women know sunk in upholstered couches opening their doors and closing them creates a threshold children cross. this under. this world the private ... the mouth groans sings its fervid blue note, "you you" muffled under the weight of the others the ones who do not sing out loud' (114). The 'fervid blue notes' of lesbian desire are and have been 'muffled' by the 'weight' of heterosexual history. Retrieval of these muffled, private words into the public arena is, therefore, as important a project for these poets as it was for the 'housewife'-turned-researcher who retrieves the turn-of-the-century schoolteacher Annie Richards from historical desuetude in Marlatt's singly authored novel *Ana Historic* (1988). In 'Double Negative,' the poets quote and create the words of Australian women who have been muffled by history, words that attest to the collusion of domestic privacy with patriarchal silencing: '"struck day after day, week after week in the square metal box, with a brood made fractious by heat"' (117). In vivid contrast to the repeated invocation in this collection, 'two women in a birth,' an invocation to the power of the hushed privacy of lesbian desire made public, we have documented here the sorrowful narrative of one woman in a crate.

In Namjoshi and Hanscombe's *Flesh and Paper*, however, privacy exerts a much stronger tug, mainly because the two lesbian speakers wish to claim the privacy that has traditionally been vouchsafed to heterosexual couples. The opening poems highlight the image of two women who are, at once, the speakers and the objects of the speakers' sight meeting on a 'private beach' (33), a space of erotic celebration. Eventually, the poets must seemingly depart from that space to communicate its pleasures to others in the form of a poetry reading (of, presumably, the poetry contained in this collection). As the poets wistfully reflect, 'we must / appear in public,' even though '[w]e basked on a private beach, then slipped through casual seas'; now there are 'watchers' (33). But, upon closer inspection, the beach is always already public, as is, arguably, lesbian sexuality in a heterosexist culture: 'Yes they walked and watched and / wound arms when they weren't thinking about it and / wavered when they did' (13). This encoding of privacy as the paradoxically denied yet impossible, taken together with Marlatt and Warland's critique of privacy as a silencing patriarchal, bourgeois construction, reveals how privacy may be cross-constructed for lesbian sexuality. It is, at once, a coercive silencing force and a luxury denied. Of course, this paradox has animated and complicated lesbian texts as early as Radclyffe Hall's *The Well of Loneliness* (1928), but collaborative poetry, which takes the genre most decisively encoded private and publicizes by multiplying its authorship, enacts that paradox, that very impossibility of privacy, in its mode of production.

Several of these collaborative texts by women are caught on the horns of this dilemma of wanting to be alone and together. When the speakers of *Flesh and Paper* journey to India, for example, the desire for privacy assumes daunting proportions. A seemingly simple act like stopping for a cup of coffee may become a culturally illicit domestic performance:

>   Why
>   make an issue
> over time for coffee? Time
>   together –
> that was the issue. But we were
>   together,
> not face to face, side by side ...
>   And behind the explanations
> the frightening admission:
>   in this kind country
> of exact relationships, there is
>   no word
> for you and me. (57)

Much of *Flesh and Paper* is concerned with the contradictions, interfaces, and ironies of two women performing togetherness privately and publicly: 'face to face' or 'side by side.' But if the private is always already public, this poem asks, then how does one perform 'lesbian' in a culture that controls the lexicon of that which may be publicly expressed? Is one, in that instance, forced into a conceptualization of a privacy that is truly mute?

I don't think so. *Flesh and Paper* and other women's poetic collaborations, like many lesbian and gay texts, often perform publicity parodically, thereby reinvesting the lexicon with fluid, ideologically diverse connotations. For this reason, I have chosen the lines from Marlatt and Warland's 'Double Negative' as the epigraph to this chapter, for they speak eloquently about the performance of simultaneous codes, and the way in which speakers can both speak and subvert given patriarchal codes of privacy and community:

> walking into the diner
> 'are you ladies alone'
>   'no'
>   'we're together' (87)

Another domestic act (like drinking coffee), walking into a diner is immediately coded heterosexual: waiting for male accompaniment. The speakers negate this codification (note the rather grandly isolated 'no'), but they can only explain their transgression in terms that are both assimilable to and subversive of the initial codification: 'we're together.' Indeed, as I argue of women's poetic collaborations in general, revising Marlatt and Warland's lines, collaborators are continually playing with the multifold conditions and ironies of being alone and together, whether they reinstate the lexicon, on the whole, or whether they transgress it in the Foucauldian sense.

As in renga, this collaborative condition of being alone and together is deeply involved in the issue of how to form community without levelling difference: how to be together and yet alone. In collections like 'Double Negative,' there is a continual need for the assertion of this new conceptualization of community; as the poets ostensibly note of the Australian landscape: 'this shared weather does not mean the mixed grey of our coast monumental thighs breasts slide into (islands touching under the water). this is the brilliance of rainless weather everyone discrete a brilliance flesh dryly supports. but they are opening doors and when they glance up water artesian wells in their eyes' (114). Neither does the 'shared weather' of collaboration mean, for Marlatt and Warland, the undifferentiated community that is so vividly suggested in the image of the 'mixed grey' landscape. Nor is it viable to conceptualize the 'discrete' nature of subjects, a condition metaphorically rendered dry and parched. 'Doors,' like the spaces between stanzas of renga, both link and separate, and this polyvalent condition of opening and closing, merging and individuating, is, not surprisingly, metaphorically associated with life-sustaining water. Collaboration, then, offers both aloneness and togetherness to these poets, these 'islands touching under the water.'

A textual extension of this theory of collaborating women as alone and together is allusion, and so it is not surprising that women's collaborative poetry texts should openly expound the view of themselves as islands touching other islands in the sea of textuality. In Namjoshi and Hanscombe's *Flesh and Paper*, for instance, the most explicit reference is to E.M. Forster's *A Passage to India*, but it is a text which signals, appropriately, both community and differentiation. When the poets travel to India, any dream of collaborative erasure of boundaries is decisively ruptured, leaving one poet – the poet of non-Indian origin – grasping for textual means of reestablishing community: '"And the lesbians ..." I try again. Mrs. Moore, alone / in the cave, lost her bearings. But that's a fiction / and the writer was one of us' (57). Lines of community and difference overlap in a bewildering but productive complexity; the poet's attempt to write over her inevitable participation in 'Western Civilization ... Christendom' (56) looks to lesbian community to heal the breach, but the ellipses speak tellingly of the impossibility of such erasure as healing. The aloneness of Forster's Mrs Moore haunts the speaker. Are all cross-cultural conversations, like the earlier, optimistic one between Mrs Moore and Dr Aziz in the temple, merely chimerical fictions of community, doomed to severence? The poet, as she would say, 'tries again' to forge community, this time between gay and lesbian writers; Forster 'was one of us.' But the further the poet moves away from accepting particularity, the more hopeless her attempts to heal through likeness seem. The other poet responds by recognizing inevitable partings: '"We must go," you say gently' (57). In the spirit of revised community, however, these partings may be shared, as the return to the shared pronoun suggests. At the end of the poem, the Indian-born speaker reiterates this acceptance of rupture and offers it, sacrificially, to her lover:

> Come lover,
> they are my kin
> and I their alien,
> share the bloodied bonds with me. (57)

A few poems later, then, in a poem whose title signals a similar acceptance on the part of the Western poet, 'I see what I can,' Mrs Moore makes a less explicit entrance, but she now does so not to signal a levelling *communitas*, but an acceptance of the inevitable blindnesses of difference: 'Untutored, unenlightened, I do not shed my shoes' (60). The poet has returned to the very episode of *A Passage to India* which signals an initial, overly optimistic assumption of shared understanding, the meeting between Aziz and Mrs Moore in the temple, where Mrs Moore instinctively shows respect by removing her shoes, but only because she conceptualizes God as One, as shared: 'God is here' (39). In this passage, the poet writes herself as a Mrs Moore who is already, in the very midst of the temple of community, lost in the isolating differences of the Cave.

Other texts, like Marlatt and Warland's 'Double Negative,' may make allusion a sustained and explicit part of the collaboration in order to suggest the collaborative nature of texts in general. Marlatt and Warland invoke a lesbian community of texts by referring to works like Canadian novelist Jane Rule's ground-breaking 1964 novel *Desert of the Heart* and Nicole Brossard's *Mauve Desert*.

Sometimes the reference takes the form of direct quotation, a merging of writers' words, as is the case when Marlatt and Warland incorporate and welcome Rule's novel into their own writing: 'Jane writing of Evelyn [a character in the novel] first seeing the desert as "empty" ... Jane's protagonist seeing that "The earth's given out ..."' (119). Quotation, of course, is a most immediate way of signalling the interrelationship of texts, but Marlatt and Warland even write Jane Rule writing into their text, to heighten the self-consciousness of this exchange: 'Jane at her table typing "lightening" "large drops" and "The storm bellied over them" as mine gathers around you in this room within a room this text within a text through this "treeless plain" Jane punching out the keys what is woman (in her own fiction?)' (120). Clearly, the desert of 'Double Negative' is also the space of lesbian writing, as all of these collaborators join Marlatt and Warland at their table, composing: 'Jane at her table (in the desert) u at your table (in the desert) Nicole at her table (in the desert) and me at this table (in the desert)' (128). The Australian desert of 'Double Negative,' the Nevadan desert of *Desert of the Heart*, and the Arizona desert of *Mauve Desert* mingle, but their merger is not seamless. In the passage where Marlatt and Warland invoke Rule's novel the tell-tale quotation marks reinscribe the boundaries of textual property. Allusion, like collaboration, or like the desert, may tempt one with dreams of sameness and identity, but difference needs to be acknowledged. Indeed, when Marlatt and Warland refer to Rule's novel in this instance, they do so also to record a difference of opinion between Rule's protagonists, a debate about imperial innocence and experience that, as I will discuss later, animates this collection of poems too: 'Ann seeing "beauty" yet Evelyn doubtful (no place free from this violent taking' (119).

This reminder is a much-needed one, for there are moments in which collaborative collections expose their allusiveness so openly, where the very heterogeneous concept of textual communities can shade into an undifferentiated concept of tradition. In the prose discussion between the two poets of 'Double Negative,' 'D.' and 'B.,' for instance, B. is tempted by her readings of Rule and Brossard to theorize a 'North American lesbian tradition of ex-

ploring the feminine in relation to the desert which is usually seen
as an arena for *male* activities. I find it quite exciting that there's
this female movement into the desert saying "this is mine too and
i relate to it in a different way"' (110; emphasis Marlatt and
Warland's). Of course, this conceptualization runs the risk of
essentializing female difference. As was true of the renga collection
Linked Alive, the poetry tends to tell a more complex story about
the various pulls and resistances of female sharing and individuation, but the strength of the former, essentializing pull is notice-
able even there.

Part of the reason for this strong tug of communal tradition has
to do, fittingly enough, with the model for the very prose dialogue
that D. and B. are engaged in: Hélène Cixous and Catherine
Clément's *La Jeune Née* (trans. *The Newly-Born Woman*). The
influential text in question is Part Three, the transcript of a
conversation between 'H.' and 'C.' Marlatt and Warland, however, have moved their exchange into the middle of their poetic
text, according it an arguably more dynamic positioning. Like
Cixous and Clément, they interpolate comments on their exchange, though, again, they move those textual interventions into
a more dynamic position – contained in square brackets in the
transcript, instead of relegated to footnotes. So they clearly wish
to suggest the exchange as a crucial part of their text; by naming it
'Crossing Loop' they indicate that it is a pause in the midst of a
journey or, to quote Brenda Carr, a 'textual waiting place, a place
of digression where the text loops back on itself, re-reads itself'
(112). Still, some of the idealizing of collaborative exchange which
I discern in the Cixous and Clément text exerts no small pressure
on Marlatt and Warland's poetic exchange, and is expressed in the
longing for tradition that I have already noted.

Like tradition, space is an object of desire in much collaborative
poetry by women, but that desire is a necessarily conflicted one.
That image of two women inhabiting one space, which I identified early in this study as a recurring one in women's collaborative
art, is by no means politically neutral or an unquestioned ideal. In
Marlatt and Warland's 'Double Negative,' for instance, the dou-
bling of two women in a space (train, bed, womb) is frequently

celebrated: 'rolled in the original glow our bodies / in the one berth' (79); 'two women in a birth' (88); 'table cloths folded / over edges of settings / like you and me / in Robyn's bed' (77). Yet shared space can also be confining; one speaker repeatedly seeks a way out of the train: 'you pace the car, interrogate the conductor / "isn't there any way to get out?"' (94); 'i'm restless irritable,' she admits 'still want to get out / pressed like flora under glass' (96). For all that, once the poets are settled in a non-moving room, they still feel constricted:

> and now
> you unzip and hang up
> in a room three times as large
> and suddenly we feel cramped
> in someone else's house (101)

This is not just a case of the perception of space being relative, though it undoubtedly is; that relativity of space is involved in yet another discourse, about the inability to construct or discover a free space. We are back to the debate between Jane Rule's characters, for these two poets have not just quoted that exchange; they have reenacted it.

In *Flesh and Paper*, the complexities of space and place are even more pressing, mainly because of the cultural difference which the two poets both celebrate and agonize over. There is a strong desire not only to find a free space, an alternative tradition as in 'Double Negative' but, more precisely, to find a middle ground. *Flesh and Paper* opens in Australia, one speaker's land of birth, and ends in India, the birthplace of the other speaker. One would expect, therefore, a fairly conventional search for a common ground and, indeed, the collection sometimes voices that desire: 'All right,' one speaker capitulates, after having introduced the opening story with an Australian setting, 'I'll tell you an entirely different story about a different mountain, taller than Everest and unknown to us both, so that, right at the outset, we start up these slopes on equal terms' (10). At times, desire is constructed as Utopia, in its literal sense of no-place: 'when we got back to whatever bed we were sharing then, wherever it was' (22), and the rest of the poem celebrates the intensity of the erotic meeting. When one poet moves toward particularizing place, the other reinforces the Utopian refusal of place:

> The lake where we stood
> has a name, a location;
> it will be any lake,
> you prophesied gracefully; (26)

But no matter how graceful such prophecies, the last sections of the collection, set in India, deconstruct the tripartite schema initially constructed: a no-place of erotic discovery, bound on either side by the particularities of place – Australia and India. 'Because of India,' as one poem title has it (62), the poets discover that 'there is no undiscovered country,' to quote another title, that of the last poem in the collection (64). And India, in this collection, is merely shorthand for difference and the reconstituted sense of community that an acknowledgment of that difference allows.

The struggle of these poets with the fabled meeting ground, whether of a new tradition or between cultures, is entangled with their ways of handling conflict in general. Again, no one strategy emerges but, rather, a range of possible positionings. There are times, for instance, in 'Double Negative' when I wonder if the only conflict that the two speakers are ever going to encounter is that well-worn dilemma of train travellers: 'our seat backwards i had wanted one facing forwards am disappointed you say "it's more relaxing this way" i joke "it should be familiar – it's how i was born"' (113). Jokes aside, there does seem to be some negotiation of space going on here, some thought about how two subjects embark in the same direction without becoming identical. But a joke does resolve the matter and, as for the conflict that I said is permitted in the prose dialogue section, 'Crossing Loop,' ('It wasn't that way for me ...' 108), it is similarly gentle. Not so in *Flesh and Paper*, wherein India marks a schism that challenges any temptation to read collaboration as seamless conjunction – a temptation that the book's cover blurb actively promotes: 'What is unusual in the sequence is the sense of equality and partnership, so that traditional barriers between speaker and listener, poet and audience, dissolve.' What dissolves is precisely this form of idealization. A number of the poems, instead, deal with frank philosophical disagreements. In 'You say that the world,' for instance, one speaker invests belief in the power of men to change; her son, for instance, 'will be different, / raised without a father, the first, perhaps, / of a new species' (39), but the speaker of this poem, though 'slowly – / under your eyes – I change. Try not to see' violence as linked with masculinity, is not fully convinced. And the poetic sequence does not even attempt to resolve this most fundamental of differences.

India, of course, produces a dramatic schism in *Flesh and Paper*, and the poets revealingly draw back into their own individualizing pronouns: the poets now speak of 'my country' (46) and 'yours' (63). As they now acknowledge, in language that betrays the inevitability of place, 'it's our bodies, not our passports, / fit so uncommonly well' (63). For that matter, both poets must come to the disillusioning realization that bodies, no matter how bonded, have passports too. Whereas, in the middle (ground) of the collection, they can imagine an erotic merging ('and sometimes there was the wondering about / who was who'; 22), India gives them the most harrowing moment of separation and withdrawal into cultural signature:

Is that it?
I'm white. I'm Western civilization. I'm Christendom,
their blood running in rivers. I'm capitalist
imperialism, overlording their lords. I'm
barbarism: misplacing, renaming. I'm us, not them. (56)

If a reader were to subscribe to the fetishizing view of collaboration that the book's own blurb advocates, this moment would be especially traumatic, signalling a failure of the collaborative dream. Indeed, readers may go through much of the collection not knowing who's who in any one poem, but such a reading strategy is clearly impossible here. Difference has erupted on the middle ground.

It would be easy to differentiate between these collections in terms of the way they handle difference and conflict, either praising Marlatt and Warland's text for resolving or dissipating it or valorizing Namjoshi and Hanscombe's for confronting it. But such ranking of collaborative strategies is not my concern. What is important, to my mind, is how women's collaborative poetry texts, participants in the discourses of space and place, community and particularity, perform these discourses differently and cannot, therefore, be reduced to any single position on them.

An example of this shared but different discourse of collaborative poetry is the issue that I raised at the end of my discussion of renga, an issue vitally related to the discourses of space and place flowing through these poems. Two people(s) inhabiting one space has been historically problematic, as anyone even passably familiar with the history of the Middle East, for example, can appreciate. Collaboration's negotiation of space, therefore, is accompanied by its fair share of postcolonial complexity. In many collaborative texts that inhabit an other space, the dream of becoming indigenous is a powerful one. As the speakers of Namjoshi and Hanscombe's collection dream as they initially pursue their unknown mountain, their middle ground: 'Observers will say, "look how they are changed. They have become indigenous"' (10). Even at this stage, however, the sceptical poet-listener questions '[a]nd what about the natives?' (10). As is true of the renga in *Linked Alive*, the dream of discovery and, therefore, of a lack of natives, is difficult to eradicate; in a moving, erotic poem, one of the speakers apostrophizes her lover thus:

you oh you
have
discovered me
unsealed my longing
appointed me mighty
named me (18)

Discovery, appointment, and naming are all heartily redolent of imperialist action, and yet, in this poem, the terms appear to be stolen back from that language – reappointed. Still, this poem derives from the section of the book in which the bonding of two women is conceptualized as taking place in no place, in a haven or private beach. The discovery fable must, therefore, undergo revision, no matter how caught up in the experience of awakening it has been. The resounding final poem of the collection makes this clear: 'There is no undiscovered country.' Instead of offering corrective closure, which would be merely another form of appointment and naming, the poem allows desire to speak too:

> But in spite of a hurtful history
> shall we speak of a peopled place
> where women may walk freely
> in the still, breathable air? (64).

The collection, ending with the open door of a question, does not proscribe desire, no matter how complicit that desire may be with imperialist design. To banish desire would be to adopt a simplistic understanding of imperial transaction.

Marlatt and Warland's 'Double Negative' is similarly caught up in the postcolonial complexities of place and space, no matter how explicitly some of the poems critique imperialistic naming practices. Like Ayanna Black, Marlatt and Warland tend to borrow the 'other' terrain as a metaphor for their own bodies, ready for discovery:

> we entered this
> > here
> Robyn threading us deep
> into blue bush aboriginal sacred look/outs
> creviced waterfalls
> our bodies these Blue Mountains ... (76)

As Brenda Carr describes this fundamental analogy in the collection, 'Such a textual connection between two colonized territories – desert and female body – becomes the means for a literal and symbolic gesture, an ecofeminist gesture of double decolonization'

(120). It is an ideologically uneasy elision, however. This poem, for instance, ends with a celebratory ritual, the two poets on the train 'pouring the ten year Pinot Noir / "you have the first sip, lovey"' (78) as they roll across the terrain, probably over many a sacred aboriginal place violently baptized by the Pinot Noir of colonization.

In other poems in the collection, there is more awareness of the insufficiency of such ritual identifications. The two poets, recalling 'a street hawker' mimicking 'dingo talk didgeridoo style,' '"the real thing" for the kids,' acknowledge that all settler speakers hawk the aboriginal: 'we use their words for things, places / and they are different in our mouths' (80–1). But for all the awareness that, as the two poets say, they are 'un/ / original here,' ab/originality remains an object of reverence and desire. At the end of the poem, then, the two poets reassume their habit of overlaying Australian indigenous causes and conditions with their own, in this case, linguistic alienation:

> we can't go back
> not to the roots we know
>
> Indo-European words, dead wood
> sentences tracking
> across the untracked, the
> intractably here (81)

So, for all the critique of the more explicit forms of imperialistic naming, the place signs, for instance,

> mutating like mixed metaphors
> Peterborough, Jamestown, Gladstone, Port Pirie
> anglo overlays ... (86),

there are still a few overlays that the poetry enacts but does not name.

Looked at from this postcolonial perspective, 'Double Negative' truly participates, as I have intimated, in the debate from

Jane Rule's *Desert of the Heart* that Marlatt and Warland interpolate in their own text:

> Jane writing of Evelyn first seeing the desert as 'empty' (negative space) how can this once have been sea bottom – the desert unbelievable, dangerous (what is woman?) but we are not apart from it Jane's protagonist seeing that 'The earth's given out. Men can't get a living from it. They have to get it from each other.' the desert a different economy (her own woman?) yet there's uranium to be mined, sacred aboriginal sites to plunder Ann seeing 'beauty' yet Evelyn doubtful (no place free from this violent taking) (119)

Marlatt and Warland openly repudiate the negating of marginalized spaces as empty. As they write of their experiences in the Australian outback, 'We stood in the middle of nothing and it was full' (121). But, as Michel Foucault has said of subjecthood, how that space is filled, how it can be occupied, is a more absorbingly difficult question than whether it is filled or not. Like other collaborative women poets, Marlatt and Warland have 'filled' the question of subjectivity in various ways, having, in their own instance, been attracted at moments to arguably essentializing generalizations about woman ('the desert a different economy [her own woman?]'), critiques of subjects who take over the speech acts of others, critiques of their own complicity with 'this violent taking,' and unspoken enactments of that complicity. Like Namjoshi and Hanscombe, who end their collection with the acknowledgment that 'there is no undiscovered country,' but who leave open the door of desire and dream, Marlatt and Warland remain, like Jane Rule's Evelyn, 'doubtful' at times, describing a Utopia which is both a no-place ('no place free from this violent taking') and a place which is, itself, desire. Desire, however, since it inevitably works on a ground of contesting desires, is never extricated from the negotiations of power; as Marlatt and Warland's collection attests, when women poets collaborate in an exchange that many would assume neutralizes power, they find, instead, that 'we are not apart from it.'

This discovery of the operations of power within collaboration lies at the heart of two poetic sequences that Daphne Marlatt and Betsy Warland wrote together: 'Reading and Writing between the Lines,' first published the same year as 'Double Negative,' 1988, and 'Subject to Change,' published three years later. These long, interactive poems testify to the evolution of the poets' collaborative methodologies; as one poet writes in 'Subject to Change,' 'up till now when we've collaborated we've each had individual control of our individual pieces so we could shape them according to our own sense of form' (160). And when those methodologies become 'subject to change,' so do the poets' awareness of the power that they have formerly invested in notions of the 'individual,' 'control,' 'shape' and 'form.'

As one would expect from poets like Marlatt and Warland, who use their poetry to meditate explicitly on language, the two poets have difficulty with even the term that their writing relationship is generally known by: 'with its military censure, its damning in the patriot's eyes ... collaboration implies that who we are collaborating with holds all the power, the lines are drawn' ('Reading and Writing' 133). In response to this (admittedly partial) history of the term, Marlatt and Warland at first seek to neutralize its power by eroticizing it; the second poet transforms the word, via the related term 'labour,' to 'labial' (133). The militaristic connotations of the term persist, however; writing in the very next poem in the sequence, one of the poets refers to collaboration as a 'stumbling onto unexpected gaps, holes, wait, explosive devices – this is not enemy territory we're speaking of or in ...' (137). So when a later poem maintains that 'to keep (y)our word, eroticizing collaboration we've moved from treason to trust' (142), I wonder whether the move is complete, or whether there are 'unexpected gaps, holes,' and, yes, 'explosive devices' waiting to spring upon the collaborators.

In both 'Reading and Writing between the Lines' and 'Subject to Change,' those fissures in the erotic collaborative romance that Marlatt and Warland construct do, in fact, explode upon the page. In 'Reading and Writing,' the two poets confront on the page, as they never do in 'Double Negative,' the unspoken rules of their collaboration, what they call its 'dark side': the 'ground rules, how i can revise me but not you' (138) and the 'talking we do that underlies or underlines (between the lines) what gets written on the page' (140). Then there's also the poetic competition that tends to get sidelined, placed in accompanying prose segments in the renga collection *Linked Alive*: '"where are you going with this?" "You didn't go deep enough"' (139). Taken together, these previously unspoken narratives of the collaboration throw into radical question many of the assertions Marlatt and Warland make, even in this poetic sequence, of collaboration's inherent subversion: 'but perhaps it's the very subversion implicit in collaboration that i might see in our favour were we to move between the lines' (133); 'slip(ping) page(es) / like notes in class' (136).

But what finally arrives as what one poet calls the 'axe-split' in the poetic sequence 'Subject to Change' is the property ethic that has been such a prominent part of poetic collaborations. '*where's mind?*' asks one poet about the apparent lack of an organizing principle in this stream of consciousness writing (her contribution highlighted and differentiated by italics), and the other poet responds, hurtfully, 'where's mine?' (156). At this point in 'Subject to Change,' the poets, who have been alternately sharing the page in italicized and non-italicized fonts, separate and inhabit their own pages: 'you've left,' one poet mourns (156). On these separate pages, they clarify their aesthetic differences; one poet prefers to capture the 'back and forth' (158) of collaborative process, whereas the other sees form as a '3rd entity which develops its own process as we continue' (159). Not surprisingly, the second poet sees the textual traces of the first methodology as formless 'mind-blather' (159).

How can such a fundamental difference of perception be reconciled? Should it? In 'Subject to Change' I think it is less reconciled than acknowledged, but it is, interestingly enough, a formal change in the poems' proceeding that signals that acknowledgment. In the closing stages of the sequence, the two poets take to writing letters to each other, returning, in so doing, to the sort of back-and-forth, statement-response format that I see as characteristic of so many contemporary women's poetic collaborations. Marlatt and Warland finally give up on the goal of sharing the page in an egalitarian idealism; for them, writing and exchanging letter-poems is a way to signal that difference is not easily or idealistically transcended in collaboration:

> *so, letters (safe on the other side). you write downstairs on your computer. i type upstairs, we pass the pages back and forth in the kitchen. not the same as sitting at the same table, writing on the same page. we are not the same, not one, sitting side by side, **sam**, together. not is where desire enters ...*
>
> (169; emphasis Marlatt and Warland's)

Like Sandra Butler and Barbara Rosenblum, passing back and forth their shared writings, from room to room, but ever cognizant of their embodied differences, Marlatt and Warland acknowledge that 'we are not the same.' In the dramatic texts that I examine in the next chapter, the temptation to forge a desired collaborative sameness meets the experience of difference, sometimes overwhelming or drowning it out, but sometimes erupting with the same force as the 'axe split' that has left so many collaborative poets alone and together.

6

'It ... Shook Up My Easy Theories': Theatrical Collaboration

I take my title from one of Metis writer Maria Campbell's comments about her difficult collaborative venture with white actress Linda Griffiths because I am aware of how deeply the words resonate for my own project on collaborative writing. Theatrical collaboration does, indeed, shake up many easy theories about collaborative writing and some not-so-easy ones as well. How, for instance, can I isolate and study a form of collaborative writing that I have specifically demarcated as explicit when I address theatre, where the lines between what is explicit collaboration (in the sense of co-signature) and implicit play-making seem so fuzzy, so indistinguishable? There is, of course, a cliché about all theatre, like film, being *inherently* collaborative; as far back as 1966 even a critic who was as firmly wedded to the notion of individual authorship as Samuel Schoenbaum nevertheless drew on this well-worn assumption: 'All plays, furthermore, are in a sense collaborations, shaped from conception to performance by the author's awareness of the resources of actors and theatre, the wishes of impresario or shareholders, and the tastes and capacities of the audience' (149–50). But this conception of collaboration is much closer to the form I've called implicit, a form that is often studied in non-dramatic literature as well, as when Jack Stillinger or Jerome McGann study creative interventions by editors, publishers, and the like: the social production of writing. Amidst all of the workings of collectivity and cooperation in theatre, is there room for a theory of explicit co-signature that can be meaning-

fully distinguishable from the general workings of collective dramaturgy? I think that there can, and so, in spite of the apparent
abundance of collaborative writing in the theatre, I deal, as in my
other chapters, with a relatively small, though revealing, portion
of the total production in a particular genre.

This choice of focus necessitates that I be very specific about
the terms with which I discuss explicit dramatic collaborations. In
the other portions of this study, I have used terms like collective,
cooperative, and collaborative as though they could function syn-
onymously with very little difficulty, and I think that they can
in cultural fields where collective work has appeared to be abnormal, less frequent. That easy synonymy cannot work in regard to
the theatre, where those terms have previously established but
sometimes inconsistent denotations. Practitioners, in particular,
seem, understandably, to have no problems making these terms
fairly elastic. For example, Canadian playwright Margaret Hollingsworth wrote an article for *Canadian Theatre Review* called 'Collaborators' in which the term refers, without explanation or
theoretical elaboration of any kind, to the relationship between a
playwright and a director (though she also refers, in passing, to
collaborations between actors and directors). So in this sense
collaboration appears to refer to cultural workers with distinct
roles establishing a working relationship, not primarily cultural
workers in the same medium or genre. In an article with a title
that promises to set my terminological inquiry straight, 'Defining
Collaboration,' the director of Cleveland's Theatre Labyrinth,
Raymond Bobgan, uses the same term to talk about his theatre's
particular process, and he further coins the term 'direct collaboration' to describe 'working together through the direct interaction
of *doings*' (36, emphasis Bobgan's). This process involves main-
taining a focus on the working space by, for example, not talking
or joking about working materials outside of work (36). Clearly,
this definition is highly specific to the company and to Bobgan's
own theories of direction.

When we turn to academic theorists and critics of theatre, the
project of discerning terms becomes, not surprisingly, more cut
and dried, more careful, less creative. Diane Bessai, in her valuable

book on collective theatre processes in Canada, distinguishes between collective creation and collaboration in a way that tends to associate collaboration with the workings of individual authors. In collective creations, she notes, such as the influential productions of Paul Thompson's Theatre Passe Muraille, 'all participants are *wrights* in the older sense of the word meaning craftsmen or makers' (46, emphasis Bessai's). But when Bessai discusses the play that will form the centrepiece of my own study of collaborative theatre, Maria Campbell and Linda Griffith's *Jessica*, she notes that, since the whole company was, in a later phase of the process, not having as much input as Griffiths, Campbell, and Paul Thompson, the 'work became a collaboration rather than a collective creation' (231). 'Collaboration' here signals the cooperative workings of two or more single author figures, whereas collectivity seems to signal a less hierarchical, more general and shared creative input. The theoretical problem with this distinction is its tendency to locate authorial subversiveness within collectivity rather than collaboration ('Essentially, the collective creators were subversives,' she writes early in her study [14]). This generalization tends to downplay the ideological potential (shifting, never inherent) of collaboration. Since *Jessica*, in Bessai's own estimation, breaks new ground in dramaturgical process, this formulation is clearly not expansive enough to capture the complexity of what happened when Maria Campbell and Linda Griffiths embarked on the long, ideologically complicated journey that was *Jessica*.

Lisbeth Goodman, on the other hand, in her influential and ambitious study, *Contemporary Feminist Theatre* in Britain, distinguishes among collectives, cooperatives, and collaborations in a way that will inform my own study of collaboration, since it recognizes power at work in manifold ways in all three forms of theatrical writing. Collectives, wherein the group shares responsibility for all aspects of production, potentially has the strength, Goodman argues, to 'expand and enrich the emerging "voice" of any given play' because of the collective input from various members, but they also have the potential to be cumbersome because, Goodman argues, the collective form 'does not take into account the particular skills of individuals' (55). Besides, she observes, if one member takes over a great deal of the work in order to make a production deadline, the process can be just as paternalistic as the traditional forms it seeks to displace (55). Cooperatives, on the other hand, 'retained the ideal of the non-paternalistic power base, but allowed for exploitation (in a positive sense) of individual skills, without assigning different levels of worth or status to those skills' (55). This method sounds like a giant step back towards individual authorship in the theatre, and Goodman is clear about some of its institutional impetus. By adopting this working arrangement theatre groups could escape some of the negative associations that the theatre world holds about collectives as directionless or disorganized. Collaborative writing for the theatre, by comparison, refers specifically to a process 'in which two or more writers pool their efforts toward creation of a single script (as opposed to the devised method in which performance takes precedence over the written script)' (107). Goodman's formulation highlights the scripted nature of the collaborative product, and that accords with my own focus, in this study, on women's collaborative writing. But I must also add that devising, cooperative, and collective methods are not necessarily inimical to collaborative production; they may form particular stages on the collaborative journey. In Linda Griffiths and Maria Campbell's account of their collaboration *The Book of Jessica*, for instance, devising and collective strategies taken from Paul Thompson's method were a major foundational part of the project. The project became collaborative in the scripted sense of the term when the entire written text, both play and post-mortem, came together in *The Book of Jessica*. It is that text, particularly the collaborative commentary, problematic as it is in the distribution of its authorial powers, that forms the focus of my analysis.

Because I see collective, cooperative, and collaborative ways of doing theatre as having distinct emphases but overlapping processes, I preface my study of two collaborative plays with some observations about a wide range of women's collectives, cooperatives, and devisings. These various instances of women working together in the theatre have much to offer my study of specific collaborative relationships in the area of theoretical assumptions and problematics. An initial point to remember is that much theatrical writing is, in contrast with my own focus, unconcerned with scripts and publication. Writing, far from being a normative expression, is a choice, one that harbours any number of ideological, cultural implications. Women's collective performance art, for instance, highlights the intensely scripted nature of the dramas that I will analyse; these performances, by contrast, are events whose creativity lies in the moment or experience rather than in any written script. Jeanie Forte, in her study of 'Women's Performance Art,' argues that this field, which has gained the reputation as a haven for self-obsessed individual exhibitionists can be remarkably collective in its impulses: 'While the history of performance art as a whole might be especially vulnerable to this critique [of "individualism"], women's performance art in particular has promoted both collaborative and collective performance, generating numerous performance groups with specific political interventionist goals' (266). One example is informative and irresistible. The American performance group called The Waitresses moved from a more stereotypically individualist or 'exhibitionist' statement to a much more collective staging of one of their routines. Initially, in 'Ready to Order' one performer from the group wore a waitress uniform with numerous breasts sewn on its front and approached unsuspecting Los Angeles diner customers to ask them what they wanted. In a later staging, however, the group as a whole marched through LA 'in waitress uniforms, playing kitchen-utensil instruments' (253). Forte provides the expected academic reading of this event, one that stresses the group rather than the individual statement being placed on order: 'Apart from the obvious content regarding the exploitation of women in underpaid labour, these performances evoke an awareness of Woman as a sign, blatantly portraying the master/slave relationship inherent in her exploitation' (253).

Cabaret or comedy is another, less script-obsessed theatrical form which has fostered collaborative and collective efforts. Lisbeth Goodman notes a number of these groups in Britain: Parker and Klein, French and Saunders, the group Lip Service (Maggie Fox and Sue Ryding). Such groups form a response to a predominantly male tradition of comedy groups, from Flanders and Swan and Beyond the Fringe to the largely male-dominated Monty Python, in whose early sketches women serve mainly as big-breasted walk-ons. In fact, some women's comedy troupes have argued that because this tradition is so entrenched in Britain, it leaves women's comedy groups little cultural space. As Alex Dallas of the group Sensible Footwear remarked: 'In Britain, a feminist theatre company is seen as being a bit of a ghetto ... whereas in Canada [to which they immigrated in the mid 90s] we're embraced for being women performers and welcomed because we're feminist. In Britain the old-fashioned view seems to be that we can't really be funny because we're women' (Le Rougetel 26). It is revealing to note, though, that Sensible Footwear, like some of the theatre collectives that Goodman studies, has moved away from a strictly collective process of composition: 'Over time, the way in which they develop their scripts has become more individualistic. The process of creating a show used to be a collective agony of writing each word, perfecting each line as a group. Today, they collaborate on themes and ideas and write the sketches individually, coming together to polish the humour and rehearse the lines' (Le Rougetel 26). So the pressures of operating in a thoroughly collective, idealistically egalitarian fashion have given way here, too, to a more cooperative *modus vivendi.*

This is not necessarily the path that collectives need take, however. In her article on 'The Rhetorical and Political Foundations of Women's Collaborative Theatre,' Judith Zivanovic draws on her extensive experience of women's theatre collectives and concludes that many 'are a collective without a designated leader, engaging in largely non-traditional presentations' (211). Her own conception of collaboration is so broad that it does tend to take in activities that Goodman would call cooperative or collaborative or devising (in the example of British playwright Megan Terry's method 'in which the company collaborates to form a final script written by herself'[212]). Still, the point holds: collective theatre need not break down, ultimately, into a collection of single authors, though the many pressures and the continuing function of authorial power in other avenues in theatrical collaborations can cause some companies or collaborative playwrights, particularly those who may have entered into collaboration with idealistic expectations of the dissipation of authorial power, to reexamine and alter their procedures. Such a realization would appear to confirm Foucault's analysis of the persistence of authorial power functions.

Still, women's theatre groups have unquestionably been drawn to experimenting with collective authorship, particularly in countries where there is a rich collective theatre tradition in general. Judith Zivanovic argues that women, in particular, have found theatrical collaboration attractive 'because of the special rhetorical capacity of theatre' and because they have decided that traditional (determined as male-dominated) theatre has not fulfilled their artistic needs (210). In reference to the former reason, Zivanovic explains that 'theatre has the special capacity to speak, in a collective voice, of collective, human concerns' (210). Whether her observation is theoretically valid is one question, but what is important, for my purposes here, is that some women have believed that theatre does have this capacity and have often organized themselves accordingly. Other critics cite reasons why a particular nation may find collective theatre sympathetic; Diane Bessai argues that in Canada, for instance: 'collective creation became the solution to a lack of written Canadian material. Of course, there were other good reasons for collective creations. The presence of imported fare and personnel in Canadian theatres reinforced the aversion to the tyranny of the text – a trend initiated by the counter-culture, with its dedication to the creativity of the actor' (27). So whether the oppressive force be colonialism or patriarchy, collective theatre has consistently been theorized as a way out of existing structures for groups who feel themselves culturally disenfranchised.

For this reason, collective theatre movements have been characterized by the same idealism that I have discerned at work in other collaborative texts. British playwright Caryl Churchill, for instance, describes her work with the theatre collective Monstrous Regiment in testimonial-like terms. This working relationship was basically one of devising a text. Churchill would engage in discussions with Monstrous Regiment and would then go off and produce a play text, bring it back to the group, hear feedback, and incorporate suggestions. This proceeding is, of course, capable of all sorts of explorations of difference, but in Churchill's case, at least as she has described it, the experience was entirely rosy and characterized by a heady sense of shared purpose:

I left the meeting exhilarated. My previous work had been completely solitary – I never discussed my ideas while I was writing or showed anyone anything earlier than a final polished draft ... I felt briefly shy and daunted, wondering if I would be acceptable, then happy and stimulated by the discovery of shared ideas and the enormous energy and feeling of possibilities in the still new company ... Though I still wanted to write alone sometimes, my attitude to myself, my work and others had been basically and permanently changed. (129, 131)

This may well have been an accurate portrait of Churchill's experience with collective theatre, but it is an experience that has tended to become generalized and established as a horizon of expectations for when women sit down to do cultural work together. Judith Zivanovic tends to reinforce this ideal picture of women's theatre collectives, though not without a certain amount of internal tension in her argument. Though she declares that her experience of these companies suggests that they were born of a 'desire to share skills and ideas without engaging in a power struggle,' and though the balance of her article accepts this horizon of expectation as reasonable and attainable, in the closing paragraphs of her article, she makes brief but revealing mention of difference and dissension: 'A collective and largely leaderless method of making decisions in all matters, including the script and style of production, is a time-consuming and frequently frustrating and chaotic form of decision-making, yet when it works, there is something immensely satisfying about this process-orientation' (217). The reference to frustration and time-consumption comes as something of a surprise, and it is quickly swallowed up, transcended by the somewhat mystic joys of collaboration 'when it works.'

Again, as in other genres, most notably in criticism and theory, such idealism is usually formed as a response to material, institutional pressures operating on creative women, so that I find my sceptical, theoretical criticisms of the idealistic stance modified by some sympathy. There are many references to the very concrete material advantages lost to women (and men) who choose to write collaboratively (or collectively, or cooperatively) for the stage. Lisbeth Goodman describes these in some detail, in reference to British theatre; critics, she maintains, would tend to denigrate 'collectively written plays as "weak" due to what they perceived as overt politics superseding artistic form' (54). And, as a member of the collective Trouble and Strife wrote to Goodman, because they tend to adhere strictly to collective writing practices, 'This is a problem we have come up against with publishers as well. They are reluctant to accept that a play is written by a company' (102). Judith Zivanovic confirms this situation: she finds that groups sometimes leave the drafting of a final script to a single author because, among other reasons, 'publishers are not very interested in publishing the group efforts – they want a discernible, preferably recognizable, name' (213). Funding agencies, too, are often put off by collective theatrical authorship and so, Goodman reveals, a number of British women's theatre companies have either shifted to a management-style board or have needed to bring a single author on board to write plays with or for them in the light of drastic cuts to the arts in Britain in the 1980s and 90s. Sometimes these changes appear blatantly strategic or cosmetic, seeking to hide collective work beneath a veneer of acceptable conservative-style management and single authorship. As a marketing officer for one of these groups wrote to Goodman, 'The name no longer reflects the truth about the company – we are no longer a co-operative, but have a small fixed management structure' (67). This would be humorous if it weren't so obviously painful: collective authorship meets market-driven arts funding and learns to wield neo-conservative jargon in self-defence.

There are other factors besides financing that keep the mystique of the single author active in contemporary women's collaborative and collective theatre. Intellectually, there is still a strong impetus to retain single author constructions, whether it proceeds from a critical conservatism or from a voice-centred individualizing liberal feminism. Even a critic who has done as much to research and publicize the workings of women's theatre collectives as Lisbeth Goodman is nevertheless wary of Barthes's theory of the death of the author. Although she notes that the concept of the death of the author does have 'important implications for theories of spectatorship, which inform the study of feminist theatre,' she pulls back, as does Nancy K. Miller, into a feminist version of romantic author theory. She concludes, rather surprisingly, that 'feminist studies should, by definition, respect the views and intentions of authors' (20). Perhaps the British academy's noted history of conservatism on this topic is partly the reason, but so wary is Goodman of treading on the concept of a woman's voice that she warns against the application of theory itself to performance; though it has many 'potential benefits. It tends, in fact, to be a dangerous process' (21). This goes far beyond Miller's uneasiness and her argument that this particular theoretical construct is merely inappropriate to women's writing.

Though other critics may take a less conservative stance on authorship theory, many simply tend to fall back into criticism of the theatrical *auteur* by force of habit and publishing convention. Diane Bessai charts the enormous influence that collective theatre has had in Canada; according to her, Canadian theatre 'owes more to collective creation than has been acknowledged before' (15). Still, she organizes her book on this phenomenon so as to reinforce the distinctions between collective 'wrights' and collective-influenced playwrights. Part One focuses on one of the most influential of these collectives, Paul Thompson's Theatre Passe Muraille, and Part Two profiles particular playwrights who have, so to speak, cut their individual authorial teeth at collectives. While this makes for an absorbing study of the pervasiveness of collective theatrical processes that Canadian audiences might otherwise think of as individually created, it also has the side-effect of reinforcing the notion of canonized authors: Rick Salutin, John Gray, Linda Griffiths. This can have an effect on how collaborative pieces like *Jessica* are treated: Bessai's discussion of this play is part of – one might say, consumed by – the section of Part Two devoted to Linda Griffiths, even though Bessai makes comments in this section about what Maria Campbell accomplished in that play. A British equivalent of this phenomenon is Lisbeth Goodman's treatment of Caryl Churchill's career, which she divides into three stages: 'solitary writing'; a 'period of collaboration'; and a period that saw the the production of some of her most successful plays, 'independent, often commissioned' (94). And although the intention probably is, once more, to bring collaboration into a discussion of what otherwise might be understood unproblematically as a single creative genius in the theatre, this handling has the effect of making theatrical collaboration appear as the poor cousin to individual accomplishment. In the pages that follow, I seek another way of describing and understanding women's collaborative theatre, not as an impure subset of an individual playwright's *oeuvre*, but as independent acts, perhaps fraught with tension, perhaps not, of a writing together that both is, and exceeds, the product of two creativities.

The collaboration of British playwrights Cordelia Ditton and Maggie Ford produced two plays, *About Face* (1985), based on the bitter 1984–5 coal-miners' strike and *The Day the Sheep Turned Pink* (1986), a satirical comedy about the nuclear age. Lisbeth Goodman points to the 'crucial role of comedy' (108) in their work, noting that many women's theatrical collaborations have their origins in stand-up comedy and cabaret. Still, she argues, it's difficult for women in Britain to take the next step from comedy routines and cabaret to comic drama: 'While collaborative comedy teams are not uncommon, collaborative comedy which is written and staged as theatre, rather than as cabaret or stand-up, is relatively rare' (109). Again, funding issues appear to be at the heart of this difficulty; as Goodman argues, the fact that Ditton and Ford's collaborative playwriting stopped in 1986 after *The Day the Sheep Turned Pink* is 'indicative of the destructive effects of funding shortages, particularly on small-scale alternative work, which ... does not correspond to the categories and criteria of the funding bodies' (109).

About Face, the play I will concentrate on here, is a one-woman show, performed by Cordelia Ditton and she also did the preliminary research, not simply in libraries but in the homes of coal miners and in soup kitchens, in a way reminiscent of Canadian Paul Thompson's method of sending actors out into communities that they are ultimately going to represent on stage. The staging credits were further subdivided in that Maggie Ford served as director. But the writing was done together. In a published discussion, Ford and Ditton talk about their process, those '[h]ours staring at blank pages waiting for a decent interval to elapse before making the next tea or coffee' (37). But in spite of the standard temporary writers' blocks, the picture they paint of their collaboration is almost as rosy as Caryl Churchill's account of her work with Monstrous Regiment. They began with a central aim – to represent the coal-miners' strike primarily through the eyes of women – and it seems as though that fundamental resolve carried them through whatever further artistic quandaries they faced. There are two factors to keep in mind, however. First of all, Ditton and Ford have similar cultural and theatrical backgrounds, so the hard work of cross-cultural collaboration that Maria Campbell and Linda Griffiths had to undertake was not at issue for them. Second, they entered the project not only with a division of production roles in mind, but with another built-in difference or asymmetry: it was Cordelia Ditton who had done the preliminary research and Maggie Ford who received this material at second hand. As Ford thoughtfully considered: 'In a way my not being involved with all this proved to be an advantage – there was so much material which you had become deeply involved with but which I approached from a totally fresh perspective. I could talk about parts of the work which had made a particular impact on me' (36). There is, of course, no inherent power dynamic in any method of work. In another situation this asymmetry of close-up researcher and distanced director could spell collaborative trouble, but in this case the level of asymmetry seems to have relieved the pressure of collaborators to be in synch, together on every aspect of production.

It is appropriate that *About Face* explores precisely this problematic: women's solidarity. The play opens with Bet, a miner's wife, reflecting:

Once upon a very hard time a woman were stood alone in her kitchen looking at an empty cupboard. There was nothing in cupboard, nothing in fridge. Suddenly she found herself walking out through door, down path and onto road. And when she looked up she saw to her surprise that all the other women in street were all walking down their paths and onto road, all carrying empty pots. Not only that, it were happening all over country. (15)

As Bet starts to narrate the women's occupation of the welfare hall, which they turned into a soup kitchen, she is joined by other women characters: Eileen, Jane, Sheila. They are, of course, all played by Ditton, in a visual representation of women's solidarity. But though the coal-miners' wives are depicted as being in common cause, the play is careful not to generalize a women's solidarity untouched by issues of class difference, for example. Tina, the television reporter, finally gets clearance to cover the women's occupation of the hall (under the derogatory category of 'human interest') and she immediately starts to stage the women, to represent them, asking them to slide into their sleeping bags even though it's the afternoon, to heighten the domesticity of the scene by showing them buttering bread, and she even grabs one of the babies to film, presumably to heighten the human interest of the story. Bet and the others refuse this condescending representation of their political action as a simple extension of wifedom:

This were ridiculous! I weren't doing that. And Jane were furious. Well her baby were only tiny.
And buttering bread. That's what that Tina wanted us all doing in't end. We never did butter bread during whole sit-in!
It were stupid. She just wanted us to act. She might as well have said, 'These women are sitting in hall buttering bread.'
Honestly, I'll never believe another thing I see on't telly. I'll always think, 'Well they weren't doing that.' (22)

Ditton and Ford do not extend this same analysis of difference to the miners' wives themselves, however, probably because of the play's implicit call on working women to unite, born of its obvious grounding in activist drama.

The ending of *About Face* would lead directly to the collaborative playwrights' next project, *The Day the Sheep Turned Pink*. As Bet prepares to leave the stage, she reveals that she has received a letter from one of the other women, Eileen, who is now trying to stop the construction of the new nuclear plant at Dounreay in Scotland. Eileen's words are still hanging in the air: 'They're starting up a whole new lot of nuclear power stations in the next few years, wasted billions on them. Maybe *that's* got something to do with more pits suddenly becoming "uneconomic"?' (33, emphasis Ditton and Ford's). Cordelia Ditton's research, like Eileen's social activism, carries over from one project to the next; as she commented in her discussion with Maggie Ford, 'You cannot look at the coal strike without looking at nuclear power policy, they're inextricably linked' (36). That's exactly what this pair of collaborative writers proceeded to do, until funding exigencies made it impossible for them to pursue their joint authorship profitably.

Not all obstacles to collaborative playwrighting proceed from institutional or bureaucratic power imposed from outside. When Metis storyteller Maria Campbell and white improvisional actor Linda Griffiths joined forces to produce a play based on and extending Campbell's memoirs *Halfbreed* (1970), little did the two women foresee the difficult road that lay ahead of them as cross-cultural collaborators caught up in issues of appropriation of indigenous materials. Campbell originally approached Paul Thompson of Theatre Passe Muraille because she wanted to learn something about his method of community-based theatre that she could use to serve her own community's needs. But gradually she was persuaded by Thompson to enter into a collaborative relationship with Griffiths because Thompson claimed that he couldn't teach Campbell his methods; she had to experience them firsthand. Before she knew it, Campbell was watching Griffiths improvise a character based on Campbell, using stories and reminiscences that Campbell had told her. These are the makings of conflict, feelings of betrayal and appropriation and, not too surprisingly, the collaborative relationship became acrimonious and strained, Campbell feeling emptied out of her stories, used, and Griffiths feeling as though she could do no right as a white actress playing a native role. Because their journey was fraught with such conflicted aims and desires, they decided, at Campbell's instigation, to publish an account of their experiences along with the play *Jessica*. This long account (over 100 pages) is mainly composed of Griffith's first-person narrative, interspersed with excerpts from taped conversations that she and Maria Campbell held on various occasions, subjecting their collaboration to a relentlessly candid post-mortem. Because this is one of the most extensive accounts of cross-cultural women's collaboration, and because the volume attracted and continues to attract a great deal of critical attention in Canada, it forms the focus of my analysis of women's theatrical collaborations. In both the documentation of the troubled collaboration and in the criticism that has grown up around it in the academic community, I find certain by now recognizable assumptions about collaborative process being drawn upon, assumed, or frustrated, and those assumptions have every-thing to do with how power circulates in a cross-cultural ex-change.

First of all, I want to linger over the growing critical commen-tary on *The Book of Jessica* in Canada, because it signals the various ways in which the joint authorship of *The Book of Jessica* has been constructed and understood. Many of the critics argue that out of the collaborative venture a single author emerges to exert control: Linda Griffiths. Jennifer Andrews comments that 'Griffiths liter-ally frames the playscript by writing her introduction to the text using the personal pronoun "I"' (298). There is no doubt that Andrews sees this as an attempted imposition of authorial power over a collaboration that had turned out to be more complicated, more unwieldy, than Griffiths had bargained for: 'In the case of Linda Griffiths, the opportunity to posit power through a fic-tional frame of her own creation becomes central to the published version of *Jessica*' (309). In this respect, Andrews is following the example of Helen Hoy, who argues that the whole production of *Jessica* and its later incarnation as *The Book of Jessica* is one large appropriative power-grab by Griffiths. Noting that the *Book* breaks with tradition by listing Linda Griffiths anti-alphabetically before Maria Campbell, and enumerating the ways in which Griffiths structures and frames the text through not only the introduction but also the seemingly objective chronology, Hoy concludes that 'this story can now finally only be read as Griffiths' (26). Both critics note, to this end, the evolution of the credits on the play – those institutional markers of ownership – from its first production in Saskatoon in 1981, 'Written by: Maria Campbell, Linda Griffiths, Paul Thompson' (artistic director of the already-discussed Canadian collective Theatre Passe Muraille) to its rewritten (by Griffiths) form at Theatre Passe Muraille in Toronto and at the Great Canadian Theatre Company in 1986: 'Linda Griffiths, in collaboration with Maria Campbell' (Andrews 298, Hoy 26). This would appear to offer incontrovertible proof that the play slowly became the property of a single author, Linda Griffiths.

Still, critics of this collaboration do not feel comfortable with this reading of *The Book of Jessica* as a terminus for their arguments. For the most part, they wish to balance their critique of Griffiths's appropriation with a postcolonial argument that Campbell fights back, resists and reasserts her control over the text and the collaboration. Helen Hoy does this most dramatically, by staging her critical argument as a three-act play (or three 'takes' as she says), in which, first, Griffiths appropriates; colonializing institutions such as theatrical contracts aid and abet the appropriation; and, finally, Maria Campbell takes back the book by resisting and naming the appropriation, calling both Griffiths and Thompson to account. The turn-around is complete; by 'Take 3' Hoy can assert, '*The Book of Jessica* is Maria Campbell's book' (34). Jennifer Andrews takes the same journey from appropriation to postcolonial resistance by the end of her article, concluding that 'it is Campbell's voice, though mediated in *The Book of Jessica*, that breaks the frames imposed by Griffiths and Thompson on the playscript of *Jessica*,' though she reaches this conclusion through a postmodernist twist: 'She [Campbell] successfully posits power in the hands of the reader by undercutting the absolute authority of Griffiths's perspective' (309). Another critic, Kathleen Venema, essentially agrees, though she lays the blame particularly on the dramaturgical methods that Griffiths absorbed during her time at Paul Thompson's Theatre Passe Muraille: '*The Book of Jessica* can be read as the record of the way Griffiths's theatrical and enormously appropriate theory of the "theory of the subject" was critically and fundamentally disrupted by Maria Campbell, the uniquely, inimitably, and persistently *present* "othered subject"' (35, emphasis Venema's). Susanna Egan takes a different route to a similar conclusion, arguing that what 'inspires and guides this text despite the final editorial control of the white co-author' is a 'native aesthetic' that 'challenges all these boundaries as boundaries, transforming the conflictual boundaries of the original situation into a continuous and, I will suggest, a healing circle' (10). Like Venema and Hoy, she maintains that the text 'reasserts a Native voice in a situation we might commonly describe as appropriative' (12). Her article's title deliberately locates authorial control in Maria Campbell's hands: '*The Book of Jessica*: The Healing Circle of a Woman's Autobiography.' But what of the other woman? Are critics of *The Book of Jessica*, particularly WASP critics, tempted to jettison and repress the embarrassing presence of the appropriative white woman by reconfiguring Maria Campbell as a single author?

Of the critics writing on this complex issue Jeanne Perreault, alone, seems to recognize agency in Maria Campbell's participation in the project from the very first. Though she says that she 'largely' shares Hoy's view that *The Book of Jessica* is, in the final analysis, Griffiths's alone, she still reminds her readers that Campbell instigated the further project of writing an account of the collaboration and that, by setting 'Her signature alongside Griffiths's,' she in effect attests that 'the words of Campbell [in the taped discussions incorporated into Griffiths's introduction] are accurately transcribed' (15). Perreault does make it clear, though, that, in a sense, Campbell hands over the assignment of completing the book to Griffiths, since she senses that Griffiths needs to heal, and so this view is quite different from the scenario of Griffiths wresting editorial and authorial power from a victimized Campbell. Still, after describing what she sees as Campbell handing over the writing to Griffiths, Perreault, too, assumes that the writing is essentially Griffiths's, and she devotes the rest of her article to an absorbing reading of 'Linda Griffiths's Raced Subjectivity in *The Book of Jessica*': how Griffiths writes her whiteness. While that is one of the stories told in *The Book of Jessica*, one that needs to be listened to, meditated upon, and analysed as Perreault does, it by no means functions synecdochally as the entire story, any more than Campbell's story does.

Why is it that the criticism of *The Book of Jessica* seems to replicate the property dispute that lies at the heart of that text: the theft of stories by white artists? Are white women critics, in particular, likely to use Linda Griffiths as a repository for their own feelings of white shame, just as Griffiths, catching sight of white people at a graduation that she attends with Campbell thinks, 'I saw the other white people and I didn't want to be one of them' (22)? To be sure, there is much in Griffiths's participation in this project that is shameful. The taped exchange that shows her wilfully overriding Maria Campbell's insistence that she not divulge certain sacred ritual practices is perhaps the most obvious:

There were drums and rattles, stones too, something in the very centre, and long. ...
MARIA: I don't believe you're doing this! We went through all this at the rehearsals. We talked about why you weren't supposed to describe this, turn it into journalism. ...
[two pages later ...]
'Then Eagle came in, the chanting rose again. ...
MARIA: Linda!
LINDA: Just let me do this part. (27, 29)

Still, I wonder if critics' moves to relocate authorial control within Maria Campbell *solus* don't move us further away from taking a hard look at the exchange that is *The Book of Jessica*. It may be that the assumption that collaboration is going to be a meeting of equals appears to be so patently contradicted by appropriative aspects of this text that critics have difficulty regarding it as a collaboration at all, or else they suspect that to view it as one would be to make a claim for some sort of basic egalitarianism in the text. But within the framework of collaboration as a sometimes uneasy negotiation of undeniable authorial power functions that I have adopted for this study, the exchange that is *The Book of Jessica* takes its place without theoretical apology. It is a collaboration in which both authors participated, to some degree, in a utopian vision of what collaboration could effect, only to have that idealism harshly corrected by the power and the pain that can be unleashed in cross-cultural collaboration in a country haunted by its imperialisms.

Critics have not been slow to point to Griffiths's naivete in this regard. They point to her initial confidence in her ability to 'get' Campbell's voice and character in her preparatory improvisations, her unquestioned belief in theatre as a safe aesthetic space: 'Theatre was already blessed, it didn't need more blessings to protect it from being theatre' (41). But critics are slower to point out that Maria Campbell, too, entered into the project with a certain amount of untried idealism, though her expectations of the collaboration come closer to a model of reciprocity rather than of untheorized equality. When Linda Griffiths likens *Jessica* to a 'sacred ... treaty,' Maria Campbell responds that their collaboration could never be a treaty because a 'treaty has to be two equals, two people sitting down and respecting what the other one has to offer, and two people doing it together, negotiating' (82). It is difficult to see how Campbell's collaboration with a white improviser, forged under the sign of Thompson's cultural authority, could ever have fulfilled these expectations, though the reciprocity that Campbell calls for engages a politics of difference more thoroughly than a simple wish for collaborative equality; as she explains to Griffiths on another occasion: 'You can't lay something out, and then say, "Well, I can't do that because it might hurt some people." You can do it. But don't lay rules on me that you can't follow yourself ... Don't ask me to do something that you're not prepared to do, and if you're not prepared to do it, then understand why I'm nervous about working with you' (88). Partners to the treaty bring different offerings. The treaty does not, for Campbell, involve one participant 'getting,' 'sibylling,' reproduc-

ing another; there must, instead, be reciprocity in working processes so that the 'theatrical transformation' spoken of in the subti-
tle of *The Book of Jessica* will be a mutually instructive one. As
Campbell recalls to Griffiths, 'Someone once said, "When the
student is ready, the teacher is there, so the teacher can learn."
Does that make sense? ... it does to me' (89). In pedagogical terms,
Campbell calls for a collaboration that is not the simple reproduction of the teacher's material by the student.

Though this collaboration of Campbell and Griffiths appears
to chart entirely new waters by examining its cross-cultural dynamics in such relentless detail, in many ways it shares conditions
of other artistic collaborations that I have examined in this book.
For many collaborators, the fact of face-to-face collaboration is
particularly daunting, as it is in renga collaboration. Theatrical
work makes this face-to-face work a necessary condition, and the
sort of improvisatory collective method that Paul Thompson es-
poused heightens the impact of this encounter. The *Jessica* process
differed from many devising methods, where a writer would encounter a collective face-to-face and then retreat into solitary
authorship to write a script. Speaking of her past work and her
project of sibylling people's psyches, Griffiths points out that, in
those cases, the '"subject" was never in the room, never a part of
the process until *Jessica*' (14). Both she and Campbell recall with
shudders the effect of Griffiths standing up to do her improvisation of the character based on Campbell with Campbell sitting in
front of her. Griffiths felt exposed; Campbell felt betrayed, taken.
Similarly, in the renga exchanges in *Linked Alive*, participants
speak a great deal about self-exposure, about the vulnerability of
opening yourself up. But in renga the expectation is that exposure
will be reciprocal. When Anne-Marie Alonzo writes deeply about
her life in a wheelchair, for instance, her collaborator Dore Michelut
is, in turn, challenged to look within herself: 'Anne-Marie de-
manded that I voice, that I recognize, that I "see" her paralysis
exactly for what it was. To do this, I went as close as I have been to
the sense of death since the death of my mother' (89). Campbell
makes similar demands of Griffiths, asking her repeatedly why she
doesn't look into her own culture and history. In the creative

mimicry that is improvisational theatre, however, Griffiths felt constrained to imitate Campbell rather than respond to her.

Another feature of *The Book of Jessica* that recalls other contemporary collaborations is its occasional use of the statement-response format. This format readily suggests the critical arguments about Campbell resisting or taking back the text, since Campbell frequently figures as the respondent. Her words interrupt Griffiths's characterization of her as 'Metis writer, activist, teacher, catalyst ...' to place that discourse within a particular institutional setting: 'What a bunch of garbage. I'm a community worker. A mom. "Metis writer" – I should have a giant typewriter? "Activist"? – I should be throwing Molotov cocktails? It just sounds so ... so much like a white professor introducing me at a convention of anthropologists' (18). And then there is the dramatic instance that I have already mentioned of Campbell interrupting Griffiths's narrative of a ceremony to protest her appropriation of it in print. Although Campbell is going to figure as respondent more frequently in a text where Griffiths is doing the framing, there are also instances where Griffiths inserts a response. After Campbell's humorous (in retrospect) story about trying to hit Griffiths with her cowboy boots, Griffiths interjects, 'That's all part of the fun of it, but there's a tantrum I have to have, the one I never had, not out loud,' and she then adds an excerpt where she is speaking about feeling undervalued and never right (14). So to an extent it is true that, as Susanna Egan argues, this text 'replay[s] uninformed assumptions, renegotiate[s] misunderstandings, play[s] back to each other what each has heard' (18). But it may be going too far to argue, on this basis, that the 'relationship between the two women in the text refuses the oppositional and works instead toward a mutual recognition' (14). It may be more accurate to say that the text engages the oppositional and thus works toward a mutual recognition that is, I think, posited as a horizon but never achieved.

I have already shown how criticism of *The Book of Jessica* tends to restage questions of property on the level of authorial control. On the issue of property itself as it figures in the exchange section of *The Book of Jessica*, there tends to be critical consensus that the text stages a contrast between white appropriativeness and native rejection of ownership rules. This position lies uneasily with these critics' assertions that, after all, Maria Campbell, in a sense, recovers ownership of this text. But looking more closely at the exchange on this question between Campbell and Griffiths, one realizes that the contrast seems a bit less stark than has been suggested. Obviously there is the arrival, mid-text, of the print-based contract drawn up by Thompson and approved by Griffiths. It is a clearly ungiving piece of legal documentation that would give Griffiths first right of refusal on the Jessica part in perpetuity, an amazingly blatant artistic and cultural property-grab that has been denounced as such by critics like Hoy and Venema. This intervention signals another, associated textual interruption: the arrival upon the scene of Paul Thompson himself, and the revelation of another uneasily triangulated collaboration. But what of other manifestations of the property issue in the text? Are they so deeply riven by opposition as the contract eventually and irrevocably makes them? Clearly, there is no shortage of places in the text where Griffiths makes her property values clear. Critics like Hoy, especially, have enumerated these, though Jeanne Perreault argues of Griffiths's much-criticized image of the treasure chest ('Then I saw your culture, and it was like a treasure chest opening up.' 85) that it is, in retrospect, 'self-conscious, that she indeed recognizes the greed and neediness of this reaction' (25). Moments of self-recognition notwithstanding, however, Griffiths simultaneously and persistently shows herself as needy in this appropriative way:

LINDA: ... And then there's still something that hurts.
MARIA: What do you think it is?
LINDA: That I can never own it. (*Book of Jessica* 90)

Maria Campbell's counter-statement appears, at first, to be starkly oppositional: 'our culture isn't one of ownership' (91). On that basis, it would be easy to construct a dualism, but as her statement proceeds, it becomes clear that the issue is more complicated. Ownership does exist in Campbell's culture, but it exists differently:

Sure, we have traditional copyrights on songs, stories composed by people, and there's a different kind of copyright on the songs and stories that are sacred, it's all oral and those copyrights are respected, and no one would dream of breaking that. But when outsiders come in and are included in the sharing of these things, they think it's alright to claim them because no one said, 'You can't,' or because there's no contract. But the very sharing of those things is a contract, and there has to be respect for the sharing. (91)

As Helen Hoy points out, Campbell changes the terms in which ownership is discussed, shifting the focus to 'respect and a sense of the sacred' (33). Campbell does even more: she locates 'property' as an unstable site of ethical meaning for her, a site that is arguably associated with her sometimes uneasy negotiation of 'white' and 'Indian' in her Metis subjectivity. In a revealing anecdote, Campbell recalls having to choose her most valued possession to take to a 'give-away' and parting unwillingly with some beautiful red cloth for a dress. She admits that even though 'I give lots of stuff away,' 'every once in a while ... and I have to work on that almost everyday ... I'm really quite stingy ... God I hate to admit that' (111). Rather than setting herself virtuously apart from the ownership values that she critiques, Campbell reveals her occasional, uneasy complicity with them; as she remarks in passing in her discussion of property ethics in her culture, 'It's bloody hard to live that [ideal of giving away] outside, in a society that takes and takes' (91). Property, then, is no easy matter in *The Book of Jessica*; it is, like so much else in this book, a site of cross- and intra-cultural struggle.

The collaboration itself becomes one part of this already disputed concept; *The Book of Jessica* charts the process of Campbell and Griffiths coming to terms with what their association means for them, how it can be understood. At times, both of them seem attracted to the notion of collaboration as incorporation. 'I breathed her in without thinking,' admits Griffiths at one point (24), though the face-to-face format of this collaboration, as I have said, ultimately resists her attempted acts of consumption. 'I couldn't

get your body. I couldn't get your voice,' she tells Campbell (33).
But Griffiths is not alone in the temptation to see collaboration as
physical union. Drawing on an eerily corporeal metaphor, Campbell
likens their shared project of transformation to bodily fusion:
'Linda, we're stuck to each other like Siamese twins' (64). True,
the metaphor figures the joining of two entities rather than the
incorporation of one entity by the other, and that distinction
is revealing of the different expectations that Campbell has of
the collaboration, as a meeting of discrete agents. But the figure
suggests, nevertheless, an uneasy duplication, even though the concept of reciprocity that has been fundamental to Campbell's understanding of this collaboration remains part of the picture. As
she explains her metaphor to Griffiths, 'If you don't talk, do
something about it [the personal matters that Griffiths says she is
holding back] then I can't do anything about my stuff' (64).

Out of this reciprocity can come a view of collaboration that
can withstand the temptations of naive notions of unity or incorporation. Campbell tries to scuttle the whole attempt to see her
collaboration with Griffiths in the prevailing property terms, asking, 'But in *Jessica* who created the story? I didn't create it myself
and you didn't either. We have to stop thinking "you and me"'
(91). One way that *The Book of Jessica* enacts this paradigm shift is
by bringing one of, in Campbell's words, 'the other people in the
room' (91) into their collaborative space: Paul Thompson. Critics
have been understandably puzzled by this third collaborator's
uneasy entrance on the scene unconventionally late in the dramatic action. Venema calls it the 'most unsettling of *The Book*'s
variously unsettling elements' (42), and Andrews sees his intervention as a reminder of the power that other members of a
creative ensemble hold in the production of a work of dramatic
art. It is, indeed, an unsettling reminder of how power is dispersed, not located only in the collaborative duet identified as
authors of this text. But it is something else – strategically funny.
Like whatever laughter there is in the exchange portion of *The
Book of Jessica*, it is a laughter tinged with pain, but it plays a large
role in the process of getting beyond the 'you and me' of Campbell
and Griffiths's collaboration. Since the discussion has turned to

Thompson's accountability for the rifts and anxieties that attended the creation of *Jessica*, the two collaborative playwrights, as it were, bring him on stage. This is in direct violation of Thompson's own aesthetic practice, as his first comment reveals: 'That's not going to work. I've said it before – my place is not on stage' (107). This speech is wonderfully satirical, with its joining of a classic director's power-speech, 'That's not going to work,' with his disingenuous assertion of marginality. Indeed, he is situated as the 'VOICE FROM THE MIDDLE OF THE ROOM,' Godlike in his invisible-seeming power. Metaphorically, he is linked to the contract which is, Campbell says and Griffiths agrees, 'right there in the middle of the whole thing' (104) and the fact that 'we just skirt around him [Thompson]' is characterized as 'like a lie in the middle' (104). When Griffiths and Campbell place him in the middle of their collaborative space, refusing to let him 'get off that easily,' they are, for this time only, dramatically rendered together 'MARIA AND LINDA' instead of being separated, halved as they usually are in the transcript segments 'MARIA' (versus) 'LINDA.' True, the voice does take them up on their offer, with a vengeance, pouring out almost two-and-a-half pages of authoritative dramaturgical discourse, ending with the humorous proclamation, 'The process works.' The final manifesto gains its comic power from the previous discussions in *The Book of Jessica* of Thompson's tendency to mystify the 'process,' to claim that it cannot be taught but it can be absorbed in practice.

Venema, in her interesting argument, moves Thompson back into the centre of the discussion too, mainly to blame him and the colonizing tendencies of his process, and there may be a good deal of truth in this critique. Still, it needs to be balanced with an acknowledgment that Campbell, in turn, wanted something from him: 'skills and tools to help make change' (16). She characterizes their initial agreement as an 'exchange,' though later, of course, she was to see it as a robbery. Instead, Thompson brought Campbell into the centre of his cultural space and asked her to 'give my bag of goodness knows what' to Griffiths. Bringing Thompson back into the centre of the space that is this strange, conflicted collaboration serves a dramatically apposite turn, but it is something that

Campbell and Griffiths do together. This coup de théâtre makes it impossible to see Campbell as purely a victim of Griffiths's collaboration-as-consumption, who, in reviewer Monica Pastor's harsh terms, 'gave out, gave in and gave up' (36).

If there is any characteristic of their collaboration that both Linda Griffiths and Maria Campbell both celebrate and bemoan throughout this text, it is this capacity (or is it inability?) to 'give up' on this exchange. In fact, it frames the text of their shared exchange: 'Open it all up again?' Griffiths asks at the beginning of *The Book of Jessica*, and Maria Campbell closes the exchange section with a corresponding double-take on her own persistence: 'I don't know if I'll ever stop being angry with you, but I want to adopt you [*laughing*] ... What am I saying? I must be out of my mind' (112). Against all the odds, no one gave up on this collaboration.

Theatre has proven an uneasy and therefore revealing site in which to study the workings of women's literary collaborations. It has challenged all the theories about what collaboration is or should be. Is it about equality? About sharing artistic property? Or is it about exchange and reciprocity? Seemingly dominated by the notion of the single creative genius (its European avatar, of course, Shakespeare), theatre is a cultural form that has nevertheless contradicted that author conception so thoroughly and creatively in practice throughout its history. Theatre is, from the standpoint of authorial theory, a schizophrenic art, and at the heart of this schizophrenia I find the sorts of power exchanges that have so absorbed my attention in this study, set out in all their permutations as the dynamic performances that they are.

Epilogue: 'Giving Each Other the Gears, We Are Still Engaged'

Although I have characterized theatre as schizophrenic in its relation to collaboration, I sense that the institution that is even more internally riven in its responses to collective cultural work is the one that I work in: the university. For this reason, I prefer to conclude on a pedagogical and institutional note, thinking about responses to collaboration that I have witnessed as a scholar and teacher in a Canadian university. At several points in this study I have described the suspicion with which North American humanities divisions of universities regard collaborative work, in the form of negative tenure and promotion decisions and collegial distrust of research that gets characterized as time-consuming and less serious. But 'collaborative' is currently just as trendy a label as 'interdisciplinary' in academic circles, particularly in government-sponsored academic grant councils. In Canada, the Social Sciences and Humanities Research Council explicitly promotes collaborative research. A current search on their website for the word 'collaborative' yields eighty-one hits. One of their richest grant programs is the Major Collaborative Research Initiatives or MCRI grant, which, to quote their program document, is designed to 'strengthen Canadian research capacity in the humanities and social sciences, by promoting high quality, innovative, collaborative research, and unique student training opportunities in a collaborative research environment.' It is as though the policy drafters are looking for any available place to showcase that hot term, 'collaborative.' In fact, the document goes on to make the following definitive statement about the objectives of the MCRI grants: to 'promote collaborative research as *the* central mode of research activity' (www.sshrc.ca, emphasis mine. Updated 05/25/2001 accessed by me 05/31/2001.) Grants of up to $500,000 per year are available. With such support potentially offered to scholars in the humanities, why are local institutional bodies such as departmental and faculty tenure and promotions committees so slow to welcome and reward collaborative work? How does this schizophrenia affect the way I work as a scholar and a teacher, and how can it be remedied?

Even a scholar as sympathetic to collaborative work as I am still inherits some of the contradictions and tensions surrounding collaboration in an institution that recognizes and rewards scholarly merit on an individual basis. I, in turn, am responsible for making judgments about the merits of scholars in training, like graduate students, and this produces some ironies that are worth pondering. For example, after I had completed a draft of this manuscript, I taught a new graduate course on contemporary women's collaborative literature. In fact, I deliberately delayed introducing this course until I could ensure that I would complete a draft of this book, because I have always felt uneasy about teaching topics that I am currently writing about to graduate students. What if I were to unconsciously reflect my students' work in my own writing? How could I be sure, if a parallel were to arise between my own work and a graduate colleague's, that I had not crossed the line that I've been analysing in this book – the line between 'mine' and 'yours'? One aspect of graduate teaching that I particularly enjoy is that feeling of sitting in a group of colleagues and fellow experts and listening to what they have to say. But my own feeling of collegiality is always informed, however silently, by the indisputable differences in power that structure the university. One of the readings for a session was an article of mine on women's collaboration and space. Since the article hadn't yet been published, I looked forward to receiving critiques from my group of fellow experts. Knowing that it would be a challenging prospect for graduate students to criticize the work of the scholar who is handing out the final grades for the course, I introduced this issue at the beginning of the session. As a result, we had a fascinating discussion about collaboration and institutional power – but I still did not get much feedback. We had done an excellent job of diagnosing the problem, but none of us knew exactly how to solve it. Clearly, the property anxieties that I have discerned at work in many of these texts – critical or literary – are my anxieties and my students' anxieties too, as denizens of an academic world that is predicated on individual accomplishment and a well-defined professional power structure.

Most of the major assignments for the course were – ironically – to be carried out individually. I was frank with myself about the individualistic, competitive nature of the graduate school that I knew, both as graduate student and as instructor. Individual grades are objects of paramount concern to most of these students; they largely determine all-important external scholarship funding, for one thing and, of course, they are reproduced as part of job applications, whether in the academy or in other employment situations. But I could not conceive of a course on collaborative writing that did not entail some hands-on experience of what it can mean to work with other human beings on an intellectual task. And so I asked them to sign up for what I called collaborative discussion-starters. In this exercise, two or three students would work together on their own time to devise some way to introduce one of the readings under discussion for a particular day, and they would carry out this task of stimulating further discussion for approximately fifteen minutes at the beginning of the class. Each student would need to work on a total of three collaborative discussion-starters throughout the whole year. By the end of the course, students would write a ten-page paper analysing the collaborative experiences they'd had, framing those reflections in terms of the theoretical and critical discussions we had shared all year. What, I wondered, would happen when the individualistic, competitive ethic of graduate school meets the need to work collaboratively with one's peers?

The collaborative discussion-starters were nothing short of revelations for me. First of all, I was amazed by the creativity and dedication shown by students for whom this course was but one of their many responsibilities and sources of academic stress. Students promoted discussion by presenting letters that they had exchanged (in imitation of Shields and Howard's epistolary method), collaborating on comic strips (a popular culture form that also negotiates the individual ['frame'] and the collective ['strip']). They did powerpoint presentations showing themselves in the process of coming to terms with the texts, cut-and-paste collaborative paragraphs that the seminar group was challenged to piece together into a whole. In short, they worked with wit, creativity, and style, truly dramatizing the many routes that collaborators may take in quest of their goals.

The short reflective papers were more revealing still. They took me behind the scenes of the collaborative text, showing me the tensions, fusions, challenges, frustrations, and burgeoning friendships that animated these diverse experiences of collaboration. They showed me, with great subtlety and insight, how power, variously perceived, may operate even in work undertaken by peers, colleagues in roughly the same institutional situation. Who talked and who wrote during brainstorming sessions? Who perceived himself or herself to have done more work than other colleagues? Who worried about contributing less (however such amounts might be defined) to the group? How did personal dynamics inform work on a professional task? I was led to believe, as a result of witnessing both the collaborative discussion-starters and the individual post-collaboration musings, that this bifocality was valuable, and that individual musings on the collaborative process were not a stepping away from collaboration but an integral part of it.

Two contributions of those reflection papers particularly stand out in my memory, and I offer them here as a way of retrospectively commenting on and setting in perspective my own project on women's collaborative writing. First, the issue of responsibility – the ethics of working collaboratively – was one that I had introduced in the course, mainly through the teaching of renga and the inter-cultural collaboration of Maria Campbell and Linda Griffiths. Still, seminar participants had seized upon this issue with great energy, and I found that a number of them reverted to it in subsequent discussions. I was not surprised, then, to hear it return in the reflection papers, though I was impressed by the way in which these collaborators had thought deeply about the ethical implications of many aspects of their own collaborations.

The second prominent feature of these meditative pieces is actually an outgrowth of the first: participants' concerns with the role of technology in their collaborations, and its potential to blunt those ethical dimensions of collaboration that are brought to the fore in face-to-face collaborations such as renga or theatrical collaboration of the sort typified by *Jessica*: face-to-face improvisation by one woman of another woman's stories. Email communication, in particular, became a focus of a number of these reflection papers, with participants sometimes reaching back to our earlier discussions of collaboration and hypertext (electronic texts such as email and web-based documents). Many seminarists had been sceptical, at the time, of claims made by critics such as George P. Landow for hypertext as a form of authorship that had been reconfigured as collaborative. In their own occasional reliance upon the convenience of email for some of their collaborative brainstorming, many of them found a focus for their discontent, preferring the challenges, contact, and even the difficulties and awkwardness of personal, face-to-face collaborative experiences. Reading their meditations, I was impressed by their ability to bring issues of responsibility and ethics into their own critical practice, and I was also moved to consider the deeper implications of a generation of young academics, with immeasurably more technical savvy than my generation could lay claim to, feeling a need to ask difficult questions about a technology that, as its promoters often tell us, has the capacity to make collaborators of us all. This study has not been concerned to as great a degree with the ethics of particular technologies of collaboration, and my students' responses signal, to my mind, some very important directions for further research.

The other academic issue that must be addressed is the persistent split that I have described between granting bodies' support of collaboration and humanities divisions' continuing difficulties in recognizing collaborative scholarship. Institutions should undertake a thorough review of their tenure and promotion documents in the light of changing notions of research. Would there be anything so very strange or unfair in judging, for instance, that two scholars who write a book together have each, in effect, written the equivalent of a book if by writing a book we mean not simply the production of the literal object, bound by hard or soft covers, but the undertaking of a major, sustained scholarly work? Will this open the floodgates to scholars jumping on the collaborative bandwagon, to find an easier route to academic recognition? Any reader of this present study would soon be disabused of the notion that collaboration represents the easy way out. And if such a reform results in a greater amount of collaborative work being undertaken by young scholars, then that is an argument in its favour, particularly for women, who often find their experience of university structures alienating and isolating.

My project has grown out of a persistent concern that women, in particular, not jump to the conclusion that collective work needs to be seen as productive only when it proceeds on the basis of agreement and likeness of opinion. This misunderstanding has perhaps been fostered by exposure to decision making on the basis of competition and put-down debating style. On the other hand, collective work – of whatever sort – that gets tied up in differences and chasms between women's experiences and positions leaves a somewhat bitter taste in my mouth; it seems to replicate a bourgeois sense of aloof individuality and gets mired in an egotistical fascination with the particularity and incommensurability of individual experience. Collaborative writing by women has provided me with a framework within which to think about women's collective practices in general and the two extremes that I have sketched rather starkly here. Reading texts by women writing together has convinced me that neither the vanguard nor the islands-in-the-stream approach to women's collective projects is satisfying or theoretically defensible. I have, at times, worried that I have seemed to deny the joys of writing together in favour of the sorrows. Ultimately, however, I have come to feel that the fault lines that run through women's collaborations make them all the more compelling.

Works Cited

Alexander, Christine, ed. *An Edition of the Early Writings of Charlotte Bronte*. Vol. 2, *The Rise of Angria, 1833–1835*. Oxford: Basil Blackwell, 1991.

Alm, Mary. 'The Role of Talk in the Writing Process of Intimate Collaboration.' Peck and Mink 123–40.

Anderson, Marjorie. 'Interview with Carol Shields.' *Prairie Fire* 16:1 (1995): 139–50.

Andrews, Jennifer. 'Framing *The Book of Jessica*: Transformation and the Collaborative Process in Canadian Theatre.' *English Studies in Canada* 22:3 (1996): 297–313.

Andrews, Melodie. '"Educate, Organize, and Agitate": A Historical Overview of Feminist Collaboration in Great Britain and America, 1640–1930.' Peck and Mink 11–29.

Ashton-Jones, Evelyn, and Dene Kay Thomas. 'Composition, Collaboration, and Women's Ways of Knowing: A Conversation with Mary Belenky.' In *Women Writing Culture*. Ed. Gary A. Olson and Elizabeth Hirsh. Albany: SUNY P, 1995.

Aswell, E. Duncan. 'James's Treatment of Artistic Collaboration.' *Criticism* 8 (1966): 180–95.

Atwood, Margaret. *Second Words: Selected Critical Prose*. 1982. Boston: Beacon, 1984.

Barthes, Roland. 'The Death of the Author.' *Image, Music, Text: Essays Selected and Translated*. Trans. Stephen Heath. Glasgow: Fontana, 1977.

Battersby, Christine. *Gender and Genius*. Bloomington: Indiana UP, 1989.

Benjamin, Walter. 'The Author as Producer.' *Reflections: Essays, Aphorisms, Autobiographical Writings*. Trans. Edmund Jephcott, ed. Peter Demetz. New York: Harcourt Brace Jovanovich, 1978.

Bessai, Diane. *The Canadian Dramatist*. Vol. 2, *Playwrights of Collective Creation*. Toronto: Simon and Pierre, 1997.

Boardman, Kathleen. 'Autobiography as Collaboration: *The Book of Jessica*.' *Textual Studies in Canada* 4 (1994): 28–39.

Bobgan, Raymond. 'Defining Collaboration: On Attention and Collaboration.' *Canadian Theatre Review* 88 (1996): 35–7.

Bono, Paola, and Sandra Kemp, eds. *Italian Feminist Thought: A Reader*. Oxford: Basil Blackwell, 1991.

Boyce Davies, Carol. 'Collaboration and the Ordering Imperative in Life Story Production.' In *De/Colonising the Subject*. Ed. Sidonie Smith and Julia Watson. Minneapolis: U of Minnesota P, 1992.

Burke, Sean, ed. *Authorship: From Plato to the Postmoderns: A Reader*. Edinburgh: Edinburgh UP, 1995.

– The *Death and Return of the Author: Criticism and Subjectivity in Barthes, Foucault and Derrida*. Edinburgh: Edinburgh UP, 1992.

Butler, Sandra, and Barbara Rosenblum. *Cancer in Two Voices*. San Francisco: Spinsters, 1991.

Cafferty, Helen, and Jeanette Clausen. 'What's Feminist about It? Reflections on Collaboration in Editing and Writing.' Peck and Mink 81–98.

Canton, Jeffrey. Review of Carol Shields's *The Republic of Love* and Carol Shields and Blanche Howard's *A Celibate Season*. *Paragraph* 14:2 (1992): 32.

Carr, Brenda. 'Collaboration in the Feminine: Daphne Marlatt / Betsy Warland's "Re-versed Writing" in *Double Negative*.' *Tessera* 9 (1990): 111–22.

Carson, Neil. 'Collaborative Playwriting: The Chettle, Dekker, Heywood Syndicate.' *Theatre Research International* 14:1 (1989): 13–23.

Chadwick, Whitney, and Isabelle de Courtivron, eds. *Significant Others: Creativity and Intimate Partnership*. London: Thames and Hudson, 1993.

Chitham, Edward. *The Poems of Anne Bronte: A New Text and Commentary*. London: Macmillan, 1979.

Churchill, Caryl. *Plays: One*. London: Methuen, 1985.

Cixous, Hélène, and Catherine Clément. *The Newly-Born Woman*. Trans. Betsy Wing. Intro. Sandra Gilbert. Theory and History of Literature Series, vol. 24. Manchester: Manchester UP, 1986.

Collis, Maurice. *Somerville and Ross: A Biography*. London: Faber and Faber, 1968.

Cronin, John. *Somerville and Ross*. Lewisburg: Bucknell UP, 1972.

Curley, Thomas M. 'Johnson's Secret Collaboration.' In *The Unknown Samuel Johnson*. Ed. John J. Burke Jr and Donald Kay. Madison: U of Wisconsin P, 1983.

Derrida, Jacques. *Of Grammatology*. Trans. Gayatri Chakravorty Spivak. Baltimore: Johns Hopkins UP, 1976.

Dever, Maryanne. '"No Mine and Thine but Ours": Finding "M. Barnard Eldershaw."' Laird, ed. Vol. 14, 65–75.

Diotima. *Il pensiero della differenza sessuale*. Milan: La Tartaruga, 1987.

Ditton, Cordelia, and Maggie Ford. *About Face*. *Plays by Women*. Vol. 6. Ed. Mary Remnant. London: Methuen, 1987.

Docherty, Thomas. *On Modern Authority: The Theory and Condition of Writing 1500 to the Present Day*. Sussex: Harvester / St Martin's, 1987.

DuBois, Ellen Carol, et al. *Feminist Scholarship: Kindling in the Groves of Academe*. Urbana: U of Illinois P, 1985.

Dyer, Richard. 'Believing in Fairies: The Author and the Homosexual.' In *Inside/Out: Lesbian Theories, Gay Theories*. Ed. Diana Fuss. New York: Routledge, 1991.

Ede, Lisa, and Andrea Lunsford. *Singular Texts/Plural Authors: Perspectives on Collaborative Writing*. Carbondale: Southern Illinois UP, 1990.

Egan, Susanna. '*The Book of Jessica*: The Healing Circle of a Woman's Autobiography.' *Canadian Literature* 144 (1995): 10–26.

Elbrecht, Joyce, and Lydia Fakundiny. 'Scenes from a Collaboration: Or Becoming Jael B. Juba.' Laird, ed. Vol 13, 241–57.

Faderman, Lillian. *Surpassing the Love of Men: Romantic Friendship and Love between Women from the Renaissance to the Present*. 1981. London: Women's Press, 1985.

Field, Michael. British Library Manuscripts 45851–3, 46777, 46779.

– *Dedicated: An Early Work of Michael Field*. London: G. Bell and Sons, 1914.

- *A Selection from the Poems of Michael Field*. London: The Poetry Bookshop, 1923.
- *Works and Days: From the Journal of Michael Field*. Ed. T. and D.C. Sturge Moore. London: John Murray, 1933.

Forster, E.M. *A Passage to India*. 1924. Harmondsworth: Penguin, 1985.

Forte, Jeanie. 'Women's Performance Art: Feminism and Postmodernism.' In *Performing Feminisms: Feminist Critical Theory and Theatre*. Ed. Sue-Ellen Case. Baltimore: Johns Hopkins UP, 1990.

Foucault, Michel. 'What Is an Author?' In *Language, Counter-Memory, Practice: Selected Essays and Interviews*. Ed. Donald F. Bouchard. Trans. Donald F. Bouchard and Sherry Simon. Ithaca: Cornell UP, 1977.

Frey, Charles H. 'Collaborating with Shakespeare: After the Final Play.' Frey, ed. 31–44.

Frey, Charles H., ed. *Shakespeare, Fletcher and 'The Two Noble Kinsmen.'* Columbia: U of Missouri P, 1989.

Gere, Anne Ruggles. 'Common Properties of Pleasure: Texts in Nineteenth-Century Women's Clubs.' Woodmansee and Jaszi 383–99.

- 'Gendered Literacy in Black and White: Turn-of-the-Century African-American and European-American Club Women's Printed Texts.' *Signs* 21:3 (1996): 643–78.

Gilbert, Sandra M., and Susan Gubar. 'Forward into the Past: The Female Affiliation Complex.' In *Historical Studies and Literary Criticism*. Ed. Jerome McGann. Madison: U of Wisconsin P, 1985.

- *The Madwoman in the Attic: The Woman Writer and the Nineteenth-Century Literary Imagination*. New Haven: Yale UP, 1979.

Godard, Barbara, ed. *Collaboration in the Feminine: Writings on Women and Culture from 'Tessera.'* Toronto: Second Story, 1994.

Goodman, Lisbeth. *Contemporary Feminist Theatre: To Each Her Own*. London: Routledge, 1993.

Griffin, Dustin. 'Augustan Collaboration.' *Essays in Criticism* 37:1 (1987): 1–10.

Griffiths, Linda, and Maria Campbell. *The Book of Jessica: A Theatrical Transformation*. Toronto: Coach House P, 1989.

Gruppo insegnanti di Milano. *Liberta femminile nel '600.* Milan: Gruppo insegnanti di milano, 1992.

Gruppo pedagogica della differenza sessuale. *Educare nella differenza.* Ed. Anna Maria Piussi. Turin: Rosenberg and Sellier, 1989.

Hedrick, Donald K. '"Be Rough with Me": The Collaborative Arenas of *The Two Noble Kinsmen.*' Frey, ed. 45–77.

Herd, David. 'Collaboration and the Avant-Garde.' *Critical Review* 35 (1995): 36–63.

Hinds, Leonard. 'Literary and Political Collaboration: The Prefatory Letter of Madeleine de Scudery's *Artamene, ou le Grand Cyrus.*' *Papers on Seventeenth-Century Literature* 23:45 (1996): 491–500.

Hollingsworth, Margaret. 'Collaborators.' *Canadian Theatre Review* 69 (1991): 15–19.

Hollis, Hilda. 'Between the Scylla of Essentialism and the Charybdis of Deconstruction: Margaret Atwood's *True Stories.*' In *Various Atwoods: Essays on the Later Poems, Short Fiction and Novels.* Ed. Lorraine M. York. Toronto: Anansi, 1995.

Howard, Blanche. 'Collaborating with Carol.' *Prairie Fire* 16:1 (1995): 71–8.

Hoy, Helen. '"When you admit you're a thief, then you can be honorable": Native/Non-Native Collaboration in *The Book of Jessica.*' *Canadian Literature* 136 (1993): 24–39.

Hutcheon, Linda, and Michael Hutcheon. '"All Concord's Born of Contraries": Marital Methodologies.' Laird, ed. Vol. 14. 59–64.

Ingham, David, and Kathleen Barnett. 'Mightier than the Phone.' *NeWest Review* 18:1 (1992): 30– 1.

James, Henry. 'Collaboration.' In *The Complete Tales of Henry James.* Vol. 8, *1891–2.* Ed. Leon Edel. London: Rupert Hart-Davis, 1963.

Jaszi, Peter. 'On the Author Effect: Contemporary Copyright and Collective Creativity.' Woodmansee and Jaszi 29–56.

Johnson, Brian. 'Necessary Illusions: Foucault's Author Function in Carol Shields's *Swann.*' *Prairie Fire* 16:1 (1995): 56–70.

Kaplan, Carey, and Ellen Cronan Rose. *The Canon and the Common Reader.* Knoxville: U of Tennessee P, 1990.

– 'Strange Bedfellows: Feminist Collaboration.' *Signs* 18 (1993): 547–61.

Kaplan, Cora. *Sea Changes: Culture and Feminism.* London: Verso, 1986.

Koch, Kenneth. 'A Note on This Issue.' *Locus Solus* 2 (1961): 193–7.

Koestenbaum, Wayne. *Double Talk: The Erotics of Male Literary Collaboration.* New York: Routledge, 1989.

Laird, Holly, ed. Forum on Collaborations. *Tulsa Studies in Women's Literature.* Vols 13 & 14 (1994, 1995).

– 'Preface.' Laird, ed. Vol. 14, 11–18.

Landow, George P. *Hypertext: The Convergence of Contemporary Critical Theory and Technology.* Baltimore: Johns Hopkins UP, 1992.

Leonardi, Susan J., and Rebecca A. Pope. 'Screaming Divas: Collaboration as Feminist Practice.' Laird, ed. Vol. 13, 259–70.

LeRougetel, Amanda. 'Wear Your Politics: Try on Sensible Footwear.' *Herizons* 8:2 (1994): 24–6.

Lewis, Gifford, ed. *The Selected Letters of Somerville and Ross.* Foreword Molly Keane. London: Faber and Faber, 1989.

– *Somerville and Ross: The World of the Irish R.M.* Harmondsworth: Viking, 1985.

Limbert, Claudia A., and John H. O'Neill. 'Composite Authorship: Katherine Philips and an Antimarital Satire.' *Papers of the Bibliographical Society of America* 87:4 (1993): 487– 502.

Locus Solus 2. A Special Issue of Collaborations (1961).

Macherey, Pierre. 'Creation and Production.' Burke, ed. 230–2.

Major Collaborative Research Initiatives (MCRI) 25 May 2001. Social Sciences and Humanities/Research Council of Canada. 31 May 2001. <http://www.sshrc.ca/english/programinfo/grantsguide/mcri.htm>.

Mannocchi, Phyllis F. 'Vernon Lee and Kit Anstruther-Thomson: A Study of Love and Collaboration between Romantic Friends.' *Women's Studies* 12 (1986): 129–48.

Marlatt, Daphne, and Betsy Warland. *Two Women in a Birth.* Toronto: Guernica, 1994.

Masten, Jeffrey. 'Beaumont and/or Fletcher: Collaboration and the Interpretation of Renaissance Drama.' *ELH* 59 (1992): 337–56.

– 'My Two Dads: Collaboration and the Reproduction of Beaumont and Fletcher.' In *Queering the Renaissance.* Ed. Jonathan Goldberg. Durham: Duke UP, 1994.

– 'Playwrighting: Authorship and Collaboration.' *A New History of Early English Drama.* New York: Columbia UP, 1997.

McGann, Jerome. *A Critique of Modern Textual Criticism.* Chicago: U of Chicago P, 1983.

Michelut, Dore, et al. *Linked Alive.* Laval: Editions trois, 1990.

Milan Women's Bookstore Collective. *Sexual Difference: A Theory of Social-Symbolic Practice.* 1987. Trans. Patricia Cicogna and Teresa de Lauretis. Intro. Teresa de Lauretis. Bloomington: Indiana UP, 1990.

Miller, Nancy K. 'Changing the Subject: Authorship, Writing, and the Reader.' In *Feminist Studies / Critical Studies.* Ed. Teresa de Lauretis. Bloomington: Indiana UP, 1986.

Moriarty, David J. '"Michael Field" (Edith Cooper and Katherine Bradley) and Their Male Critics.' In *Nineteenth-Century Women Writers of the English-Speaking World.* Ed. Rhoda B. Nathan. New York: Greenwood, 1986.

Morrison, Blake. 'A Canon of One's Own.' *Independent on Sunday* 18 Dec. 1994: 4–7.

Namjoshi, Suniti. *Because of India: Selected Poems and Fables.* London: Only Women P, 1989.

Namjoshi, Suniti, and Gillian Hanscombe. *Flesh and Paper.* Charlotte-town: Ragweed, 1986.

Nesbitt, Paula D. and Linda E. Thomas. 'Beyond Feminism: An Intercultural Challenge for Transforming the Academy.' Peck and Mink 31–49.

O'Meara, Anne, and Nancy R. MacKenzie. 'Reflections on Scholarly Collaboration.' Peck and Mink 209–26.

Pastor, Monica. Review of *The Book of Jessica. Performing Arts in Canada* 26:1 (1990): 36–8.

Paz, Octavio, and Charles Tomlinson. *Airborn / Hijos del Aire.* London: Anvil Press Poetry, 1981.

Pease, Donald E. 'Author.' Burke, ed. 263–76.

Peck, Elizabeth G., and JoAnna Stephens Mink, eds. *Common Ground: Feminist Collaboration in the Academy.* Albany: SUNY P, 1998.

Perreault, Jeanne. 'Writing Whiteness: Linda Griffiths's Raced Subjectivity in *The Book of Jessica.' Essays on Canadian Writing* 60 (1996): 14–31.

Phelan, Shane. *Identity Politics: Lesbian Feminism and the Limits of Community*. Philadelphia: Temple UP, 1989.

Piternik, Anne B. 'Author! Author!' *Scholarly Publishing* 23:2 (1992): 77–93.

– 'Author Problems in a Collaborative Research Project.' *Scholarly Publishing* 25:1 (1993): 21–37.

Powell, Violet. *The Irish Cousins: The Books and Background of Somerville and Ross*. London: Heinemann, 1970.

Ratchford, Fannie Elizabeth. *The Brontes' Web of Childhood*. New York: Columbia UP, 1941.

Rich, Adrienne. *The Dream of a Common Language: Poems, 1974–1977*. New York: Norton, 1978.

Robinson, Hilary. *Somerville and Ross: A Critical Appreciation*. New York: Gill and Macmillan/ St Martin's, 1980.

Sattler, Traudel. Personal interview. 20 March, 1995.

Schlau, Stacey, and Electa Arenal. '*Escribiendo yo, escribienda ella, escribiendo nosotras*: On Co-Laboring.' Laird, ed. Vol. 14, 39–49.

Schoenbaum, Samuel. *Internal Evidence and Elizabethan Dramatic Authorship: An Essay in Literary History and Method*. London: Edward Arnold, 1966.

Shapiro, Laura. 'Gilbert and Gubar.' *Ms.* 14 (1986): 59–60, 62, 103, 106.

Shields, Carol, and Blanche Howard. *A Celibate Season*. Regina: Coteau, 1991.

Sicker, Philip. '*Pale Fire* and *Lyrical Ballads*: The Dynamics of Collaboration.' *Papers on Language and Literature* 28:3 (1992): 305–18.

Simon, Linda. *The Biography of Alice B. Toklas*. Garden City, NY: Doubleday, 1977.

Singley, Carol J., and Susan Elizabeth Sweeney. 'In League with Each Other: The Theory and Practice of Feminist Collaboration.' Peck and Mink 63–79.

Somerville, Edith Oenone, and Martin Ross. *The Real Charlotte*. 1894. Intro. Molly Keane. London: The Hogarth P, 1988.

– *Some Experiences of an Irish R.M. and Further Experiences of an Irish R.M.* 1944. Intro. Edith Somerville. London: Dent, 1982.

Stillinger, Jack. *Multiple Authorship and the Myth of Solitary Genius*. New York: Oxford UP, 1991.

Brontes (Charlotte, Emily, Anne, Branwell), 63
Brossard, Nicole, 144–5
Browning, Elizabeth Barrett, 72
Browning, Robert, 71, 73–4, 75, 77, 78–9, 80, 81
Burke, Sean, 26, 64–5
Butler, Sandra, and Barbara Rosenblum, 97, 110–18, 156

Cafferty, Helen, and Jeanette Clausen, 19, 48
Campbell, Maria, and Linda Griffiths, 3, 157, 159, 160, 167, 168, 170–82, 186
Cancer in Two Voices (Butler and Rosenblum), 97, 110–18
Canton, Jeffrey, 101
Carr, Brenda, 138, 146, 151–2
Carson, Neil, 65
Cavarero, Adriana, 44
Celibate Season, A (Shields and Howard), 96–110, 112
Chadwick, Whitney, and Isabelle de Courtivron, 17, 62–3, 76
Chitham, Edward, 63
Chodorow, Nancy, 6, 20
Churchill, Caryl, 163–4, 167, 168
Cixous, Hélène, and Catherine Clément, 5, 16, 30–1, 41–3, 146
Clausen, Jeanette. *See* Cafferty, Helen, and Jeanette Clausen
Clément, Catherine. *See* Cixous, Hélène, and Catherine Clément
coalition collaborations (Laird), 47–8, 53, 59, 60

Coe, Richard M., 15
Coghill, Nevill, 86, 88
Coleridge, Samuel Taylor. *See* Wordsworth, William, and Samuel Taylor Coleridge
collaboration: and allusion, 143–6; in autobiography, 95–6; and bibliographical practice, 27, 75–6, 92, 98; cross-cultural, 134–5, 168, 171–82; defined, 4–5, 158–60; discouragement of in the university, 14, 40, 53, 55–6, 59–60, 183–5, 187–8; ethics of, 186–7; face-to-face encounter in, 129–30, 176, 187; and friendship, 10, 47, 54; fusion theory of, 7, 21, 38, 42, 60, 134; history of women's, 62–94; idealization of, 6, 7, 9, 15, 18–20, 38, 40, 52–3, 54, 58, 146, 165; and Italian feminism, 43–7; and lesbianism, 51–2, 60, 62, 69, 90–1, 92–3, 140–2, 144–5; materialist approaches to, 23–4, 25, 28; in maths and sciences, 39–40; and pedagogy, 44, 184–7; and poststructuralist theory, 8, 25–8, 30, 32–6; pronoun use in, 54, 73–4, 149; property issues in, 7–8, 48, 58–9, 69–70, 95, 108–9, 116–17, 122–4, 131–2, 150–1, 155, 177–9, 184–5; statement-response format of, 30, 111, 120, 137–8, 139, 155, 177; technol-

Stone, Albert E. 'Collaboration in Contemporary Autobiography.' *Revue française d'études americaines* 7:14 (1982): 151–65.
– 'Two Recreate One: The Act of Collaboration in Recent Black Autobiography.' *Autobiographical Occasions and Original Acts: Versions of American Identity from Henry Adams to Nate Shaw*. Philadelphia: U of Pennsylvania P, 1982.
Venema, Kathleen. '"Who Reads Plays Anyway?": The Theory of Drama and the Practice of Rupture in *The Book of "Jessica."* Open Letter 9:4 (1995): 32–43.
Walker, Cheryl. 'Feminist Literary Criticism and the Author.' *Critical Inquiry* 16 (1990): 551–71.
White, Daniel E. 'The "Joineriana": Anna Barbauld, the Aikin Family Circle, and the Dissenting Public Sphere.' *Eighteenth-Century Studies* 32:4 (1999): 511–33.
Williams, James S. 'The Beast of a Closet: The Sexual Differences of Literary Collaboration in the Work of Marguerite Duras and Yann Andrea.' *Modern Language Review* 87:3 (1992): 576–84.
Williams, Raymond. *Marxism and Literature*. Oxford: Oxford UP, 1977.
Winkelman, Carol L. 'Electronic Literacy, Critical Pedagogy, and Collaboration: A Case for Cyborg Writing.' *Computers and the Humanities* 29:6 (1995): 431–48.
Woodmansee, Martha. 'Genius and the Copyright.' In *The Author, Art and the Market: Rereading the History of Aesthetics*. New York: Columbia UP, 1994.
Woodmansee, Martha, and Peter Jaszi, eds. *The Construction of Authorship: Textual Appropriation in Law and Literature*. Durham: Duke UP, 1994.
Woolf, Virginia. *A Room of One's Own*. 1929. London: Hogarth P, 1974.
Wordsworth, William. *The Poetical Works of William Wordsworth*. Vol. 1. Ed. E. de Selincourt 1940. Oxford: Clarendon, 1952.
York, Lorraine M. 'Lesbianizing Authorship.' *Essays on Canadian Writing* 54 (1994): 153–67.
Zivanovic, Judith. 'The Rhetorical and Political Foundations of Women's Collaborative Theatre.' *Women in Theatre*. Ed. James Redmond. Themes in Drama Series. Cambridge: Cambridge UP, 1989.

Index

About Face (Ditton and Ford), 167–70

Addison, Joseph, and Richard Steele, 67

Alexander, Christine, 63

Alm, Mary, 7, 40

Anderson, Marjorie, 98, 99

Andrews, Jennifer, 171, 172

Andrews, Melodie, 6

Anstruther-Thomson, Kit. *See* Lee, Vernon, and Kit Anstruther-Thomson

Arenal, Electa. *See* Schlau, Stacey, and Electa Arenal

Ashbery, John, 12, 23

Ashton-Jones, Evelyn, and Dene Kay Thomas, 6

Aswell, E. Duncan, 9, 13

Atwood, Margaret, 28

Austen, Jane, 63, 121

Autobiography of Alice B. Toklas, The (Stein), 64

Bakhtin, Mikhail, 17, 54–5

Barbauld, Anna Letitia, 68

Barnard, Marjorie, and Flora Eldershaw [pseud. M. Barnard Eldershaw], 91–3

Barthes, Roland, 8, 22, 26, 35, 36, 61, 99, 166

Battersby, Christine, 79

Beaumont, Francis, and John Fletcher, 11, 12, 27, 74, 81

Belenky, Mary, 6

Benjamin, Walter, 30, 130

Bentley, G.E., 65, 66

Berenson, Bernard, 93

Bessai, Diane, 158–9, 163, 166–7

Beyond the Fringe, 162

Bloom, Harold, 12–13

Bobgan, Raymond, 158

Bono, Paola, and Sandra Kemp, 43, 44, 45

Book of Jessica, The (Campbell and Griffiths), 3, 170–82

Boyce Davies, Carol, 96

Bradley, Katherine, and Edith Cooper [pseud. Michael Field], 4, 5, 17, 69, 70–85, 87, 88, 90, 92, 93, 94, 97, 105

ogy and, 187; tendency to
separate individual contribu-
tions to, 7–8, 14, 74–7, 89–91,
92
collectives, 159–60, 162–4,
165, 170, 172, 173. *See also*
Marxist-Feminist Literature
Collective; Milan Women's
Bookstore Collective
Collis, Maurice, 87, 88, 89, 90
Cooper, Edith. *See* Bradley,
Katherine, and Edith Cooper
copyright law, 65, 76–7, 179
Cronin, John, 86, 89–90
Curley, Thomas M., 67

*Day the Sheep Turned Pink,
The* (Ditton and Ford), 167,
170
'Death of the Author, The'
(Barthes), 8, 22, 26, 35, 99
de Lauretis, Teresa, 16, 45
Demau group, 45
Derrida, Jacques, 8, 26, 33–4
Dever, Maryanne, 91–3
Diotima group, 44
Ditton, Cordelia, and Maggie
Ford, 167–70
Docherty, Thomas, 29
'Double Negative' (Marlatt and
Warland), 119, 137, 138–9,
140, 142–3, 144–7, 148,
151–3, 154
DuBois, Ellen Carol, et al., 61
Dyer, Richard, 34–5

Eagleton, Terry, 58

Early Modern collaboration,
11–12, 13, 27, 65–7, 74
Ede, Lisa, and Andrea Lunsford,
15, 17–18, 54–6, 59, 65, 87,
95, 120
Egan, Susanna, 173, 177
eighteenth-century collaboration,
67–8
Elbrecht, Joyce, and Lydia
Fakundiny, 7–8, 21
Eldershaw, Flora. *See* Barnard,
Marjorie, and Flora Eldershaw
Eldershaw, M. Barnard. *See*
Barnard, Marjorie, and Flora
Eldershaw
Ellis, Havelock, 75
entrustment, 46, 52, 130

Faderman, Lillian, 75, 93
Fakundiny, Lydia. *See* Elbrecht,
Joyce, and Lydia Fakundiny
Field, Michael. *See* Bradley,
Katherine, and Edith Cooper
Fielding, Sarah, 68
Flanders and Swan, 161
Flesh and Paper (Namjoshi and
Hanscombe), 91, 104, 125,
136, 137, 138, 139, 140–2,
143–4, 147–8, 148–9
Ford, Maggie. *See* Ditton,
Cordelia, and Maggie Ford
Forster, E.M., 143–4
Forte, Jeanie, 161
Foucault, Michel, 8, 22, 24, 26,
27, 28, 31–2, 35, 36, 37, 65,
66, 68, 70, 90, 99, 120, 123,
125, 153, 163

French and Saunders, 161
Frey, Charles H., 12, 77

Gere, Anne Ruggles, 56
Gerrard, E.D., 17
Gilbert, Sandra M., 16
Gilbert, Sandra M., and Susan
    Gubar, 20–1, 38, 40, 47–51,
    54, 57, 59
Gilligan, Carol, 6, 20
Giovanni, Nikki, 20
Gondal sagas (Brontes), 63
Goodman, Lisbeth, 159–60, 161,
    162, 165, 166, 167
Gray, J.M., 73–4, 77, 78
Griffin, Dustin, 67–8
Griffiths, Linda. See Campbell,
    Maria, and Linda Griffiths
Gruppo insegnanti di Milano, 44,
    56
Gruppo pedagogia della
    differenze sessuale, 44
Gubar, Susan. See Gilbert, Sandra
    M., and Susan Gubar

Halfbreed (Campbell), 170
Hall, Radclyffe, 141
Hanscombe, Gillian, 99. See
    Namjoshi, Suniti, and Gillian
    Hanscombe
Happenstance (Shields), 98
Hedrick, Donald K., 66
Herd, David, 12, 16, 25
Hinds, Leonard, 67
Hollingsworth, Margaret, 158
Hollis, Hilda, 32
Howard, Blanche. See Shields,
    Carol, and Blanche Howard

Hoy, Helen, 171–2, 173, 178, 179
Hutcheon, Linda, and Michael
    Hutcheon, 39
hypertext, 24–5, 187

Ingham, David, and Kathleen
    Barnett, 101
Irigaray, Luce, 59

James, Henry, 9–10, 13, 27
Japanese collaborative poetry, 15,
    119, 120, 125, 127
Jaszi, Peter, 76
Jessica (Campbell and Griffiths),
    159, 166, 171, 176, 187
Johnson, Brian, 99
Johnson, Samuel, and Sir Robert
    Chambers, 67–8

Kaplan, Carey, and Ellen Cronan
    Rose, 3, 51–4, 57, 77, 87
Kaplan, Cora, 56–8
Keane, Molly, 89
Kermode, Frank, 58
Knapp, Steven, and Walter Benn
    Michaels, 35
Koch, Kenneth, 12, 120–1, 125,
    127
Koestenbaum, Wayne, 3, 4, 10,
    16–17, 32–3, 62, 69, 97, 122,
    133
Kraus, Charlotte, 15

Laing, Alexander, 72
Laird, Holly, 18, 47, 53, 75, 98
Landow, George P., 14, 25, 187
Larry's Party (Shields), 98
Leavis, F.R., 58

Lee, Vernon, and Kit Anstruther-Thomson, 91, 93

Leonardi, Susan J., and Rebecca A. Pope, 16–17, 21, 59–60

LeRougetel, Amanda, 162

Lewis, Gifford, 86, 87, 88, 89, 90–1

Linked Alive (Michelut et al.), 126–38, 146, 150, 155, 176

Lip Service, 161–2

Lunsford, Andrea. *See* Ede, Lisa, and Andrea Lunsford

Lyrical Ballads (Wordsworth and Coleridge), 122–3, 124

Macherey, Pierre, 79

MacKenzie, Nancy R. *See* O'Meara, Anne, and Nancy R. MacKenzie

Madwoman in the Attic, The (Gilbert and Gubar), 48–9

Mannocchi, Phyllis F., 93

Marlatt, Daphne, and Betsy Warland, 5, 7, 29, 41, 42, 43, 113, 119, 136, 137, 138–9, 140, 141, 142–3, 144–7, 148, 150, 151–6

Martin, Violet [pseud. Martin Ross]. *See* Somerville, Edith, and Violet Martin

Marxist-Feminist Literature Collective, 56–8

Masten, Jeffrey, 11–12, 13, 16, 27–8, 36, 65, 66, 69, 74, 75–6, 81, 92

Mathews, Harry, 12

May, Miriam, and Jamie Shepherd, 119

McGann, Jerome, 23, 25, 27, 28, 29, 32, 75, 122, 157

Meredith, George, 74–5

Michelut, Dore, et al., 126–38, 176

Milan Women's Bookstore Collective, 16, 43, 44, 45–7, 51, 57, 130

Miller, Nancy K., 33–4, 35–6, 166

Mink, JoAnna Stephens. *See* Peck, Elizabeth G.

Mitford, Nancy, 14

Modernist collaboration, 91–3

Monstrous Regiment, 163–4, 168

Monty Python, 162

Moore, George, 75

Moriarty, David J., 83–4

Morrison, Blake, 13

Muraro, Luisa, 44

Nabokov, Vladimir, 13, 14

Namjoshi, Suniti, and Gillian Hanscombe, 91, 104, 125, 136, 137, 138, 139, 140–2, 143–4, 147–9, 150–1, 153

Nesbitt, Paula D., and Linda E. Thomas, 19, 20, 40

No Man's Land (Gilbert and Gubar), 48

O'Meara, Anne, and Nancy R. MacKenzie, 5

O'Neill, John, and Claudia Limbert, 67

Parker and Klein, 161

Pastor, Monica, 182

Paz, Octavio, and Charles
Tomlinson, 123–4, 125–6,
127; and Jacques Roubaud,
Edoardo Sanguineti, and
Charles Tomlinson, 125, 127,
129
Pease, Donald E., 65–6, 69
Peck, Elizabeth G., and JoAnna
Stephens Mink, 18, 19, 20, 40,
48
Perreault, Jeanne, 173–4, 178
Phelan, Shane, 134
Phillips, Katherine, 67
Piternik, Anne B., 39
Pope, Rebecca A. See Leonardi,
Susan J., and Rebecca A. Pope
Powell, Violet, 90

Ratchford, Fannie, 63
'Reading and Writing between
the Lines' (Marlatt and
Warland), 154–5
renga, 125–6, 137–8, 139, 146,
150, 155, 176, 187
Robinson, Hilary, 87, 89, 90
Romantic collaboration, 68–70,
121–3, 124
Rose, Ellen Cronan. See Kaplan,
Carey, and Ellen Cronan Rose
Rosenblum, Barbara. See Butler,
Sandra, and Barbara
Rosenblum
Rule, Jane, 144–5, 147, 152–3

Sackville-West, Vita. See Virginia
Woolf
Sattler, Traudel, 46

Schlau, Stacey, and Electa Arenal,
19
Schoenbaum, Samuel, 11, 12, 13,
157
Schuyler, James, 12, 23
Scudery, Madame de, 67, 68
Sensible Footwear, 162
Sexual Difference: A Theory of
Social-Symbolic Practice (Milan
Women's Bookstore Collec-
tive), 45–7
Shakespeare, William, 12, 13, 64,
66, 77, 80–1, 182
Shapiro, Laura, 38, 48, 49, 50
Shields, Carol, and Blanche
Howard, 96–110, 112, 113, 186
Sicker, Philip, 13–14
Simon, Linda, 64
Singley, Carol J., and Susan
Elizabeth Sweeney, 18–19, 20,
40
Singular Texts / Plural Authors
(Ede and Lunsford), 15,
17–18, 54–6, 65, 87
Social Sciences and Humanities
Research Council of Canada,
183–4
Somerville, Edith, and Violet
Martin [pseud. Martin Ross],
17, 29, 56, 69, 85–91, 92, 93,
94, 97, 98, 102, 111, 138
Sottosopra (Milan Women's
Bookstore Collective), 44
Spivak, Gayatri, 34
Stedman, Edmund, 72–3
Stein, Gertrude, and Alice B.
Toklas, 64, 91

Stillinger, Jack, 21–3, 27, 122, 157
Stone, Albert E., 95–6
Stone Diaries, The (Shields), 98–9, 102
Sturge Moore, T., and D. C., 73, 75, 76
Sturgeon, Mary, 75
'Subject to Change' (Marlatt and Warland), 5–6, 154–6
Swann: A Mystery (Shields), 98, 99
Sweeney, Susan Elizabeth. *See* Singley, Carol J., and Susan Elizabeth Sweeney

Terry, Megan, 162
Theatre Passe Muraille, 166, 170, 172, 173
Thirteen Hands (Shields), 99
Thomas, Linda E. *See* Nesbit, Paula D., and Linda E. Thomas
Thompson, Paul, 166, 168, 170, 172, 173, 175, 176, 178, 180–1
Tomlinson, Charles. *See* Paz, Octavio, and Charles Tomlinson
Tostevin, Lola Lemire, 137
Trouble and Strife, 165
Two Noble Kinsmen, The (Shakespeare), 66, 77

Two Women in a Birth (Marlatt and Warland), 7, 29, 113, 136–7, 138–9, 140, 142–3, 144–7, 148, 151–6

Valverde, Mariana, 34
Venema, Kathleen, 172–3, 178, 180, 181

'Waitresses, The' 161
Walker, Cheryl, 32, 35–6
Warland, Betsy. *See* Marlatt, Daphne, and Betsy Warland
'What Is an Author?' (Foucault), 26, 28, 31–2, 35, 70, 90, 99, 123, 125
White, Daniel E., 68
Williams, James S., 64
Williams, Raymond, 23–4, 28, 31, 32, 100, 129
Wilson, Edmund, 13, 14
Winkelman, Carol, 25
Woodmansee, Martha, 65, 69
Woolf, Virginia, 3, 10, 15, 50; and Vita Sackville-West, 63
Wordsworth, William, and Samuel Taylor Coleridge, 13–14, 122–3, 124; and Dorothy Wordsworth, 62

Zivanovic, Judith, 162, 163, 164, 165

Stone, Albert E. 'Collaboration in Contemporary Autobiography.' *Revue française d'études americaines* 7:14 (1982): 151–65.

– 'Two Recreate One: The Act of Collaboration in Recent Black Auto-biography.' *Autobiographical Occasions and Original Acts: Versions of American Identity from Henry Adams to Nate Shaw*. Philadephia: U of Pennsylvania P, 1982.

Venema, Kathleen. '"Who Reads Plays Anyway?": The Theory of Drama and the Practice of Rupture in *The Book of "Jessica."' Open Letter* 9:4 (1995): 32–43.

Walker, Cheryl. 'Feminist Literary Criticism and the Author.' *Critical Inquiry* 16 (1990): 551–71.

White, Daniel E. 'The "Joineriana": Anna Barbauld, the Aikin Family Circle, and the Dissenting Public Sphere.' *Eighteenth-Century Studies* 32:4 (1999): 511–33.

Williams, James S. 'The Beast of a Closet: The Sexual Differences of Literary Collaboration in the Work of Marguerite Duras and Yann Andrea.' *Modern Language Review* 87:3 (1992): 576–84.

Williams, Raymond. *Marxism and Literature*. Oxford: Oxford UP, 1977.

Winkelman, Carol L. 'Electronic Literacy, Critical Pedagogy, and Collaboration: A Case for Cyborg Writing.' *Computers and the Humanities* 29:6 (1995): 431–48.

Woodmansee, Martha. 'Genius and the Copyright.' In *The Author, Art and the Market: Rereading the History of Aesthetics*. New York: Columbia UP, 1994.

Woodmansee, Martha, and Peter Jaszi, eds. *The Construction of Authorship: Textual Appropriation in Law and Literature*. Durham: Duke UP, 1994.

Woolf, Virginia. *A Room of One's Own*. 1929. London: Hogarth P, 1974.

Wordsworth, William. *The Poetical Works of William Wordsworth*. Vol. 1. Ed. E. de Selincourt 1940. Oxford: Clarendon, 1952.

York, Lorraine M. 'Lesbianizing Authorship.' *Essays on Canadian Writing* 54 (1994): 153–67.

Zivanovic, Judith. 'The Rhetorical and Political Foundations of Women's Collaborative Theatre.' *Women in Theatre*. Ed. James Redmond. Themes in Drama Series. Cambridge: Cambridge UP, 1989.

Index

About Face (Ditton and Ford),
167–70

Addison, Joseph, and Richard
Steele, 67

Alexander, Christine, 63

Alm, Mary, 7, 40

Anderson, Marjorie, 98, 99

Andrews, Jennifer, 171, 172

Andrews, Melodie, 6

Anstruther-Thomson, Kit. *See*
Lee, Vernon, and Kit
Anstruther-Thomson

Arenal, Electa. *See* Schlau, Stacey,
and Electa Arenal

Ashbery, John, 12, 23

Ashton-Jones, Evelyn, and Dene
Kay Thomas, 6

Aswell, E. Duncan, 9, 13

Atwood, Margaret, 28

Austen, Jane, 63, 121

*Autobiography of Alice B. Toklas,
The* (Stein), 64

Bakhtin, Mikhail, 17, 54–5

Barbauld, Anna Letitia, 68

Barnard, Marjorie, and Flora

Eldershaw [pseud. M. Barnard
Eldershaw], 91–3

Barthes, Roland, 8, 22, 26, 35,
36, 61, 99, 166

Battersby, Christine, 79

Beaumont, Francis, and John
Fletcher, 11, 12, 27, 74, 81

Belenky, Mary, 6

Benjamin, Walter, 30, 130

Bentley, G.E., 65, 66

Berenson, Bernard, 93

Bessai, Diane, 158–9, 163,
166–7

Beyond the Fringe, 162

Bloom, Harold, 12–13

Bobgan, Raymond, 158

Bono, Paola, and Sandra Kemp,
43, 44, 45

Book of Jessica, The (Campbell and
Griffiths), 3, 170–82

Boyce Davies, Carol, 96

Bradley, Katherine, and Edith
Cooper [pseud. Michael
Field], 4, 5, 17, 69, 70–85,
87, 88, 90, 92, 93, 94, 97,
105

Brontes (Charlotte, Emily, Anne,
    Branwell), 63
Brossard, Nicole, 144–5
Browning, Elizabeth Barrett, 72
Browning, Robert, 71, 73–4, 75,
    77, 78–9, 80, 81
Burke, Sean, 26, 64–5
Butler, Sandra, and Barbara
    Rosenblum, 97, 110–18, 156

Cafferty, Helen, and Jeanette
    Clausen, 19, 48
Campbell, Maria, and Linda
    Griffiths, 3, 157, 159, 160,
    167, 168, 170–82, 186
Cancer in Two Voices (Butler and
    Rosenblum), 97, 110–18
Canton, Jeffrey, 101
Carr, Brenda, 138, 146, 151–2
Carson, Neil, 65
Cavarero, Adriana, 44
Celibate Season, A (Shields and
    Howard), 96–110, 112
Chadwick, Whitney, and Isabelle
    de Courtivron, 17, 62–3, 76
Chitham, Edward, 63
Chodorow, Nancy, 6, 20
Churchill, Caryl, 163–4, 167, 168
Cixous, Hélène, and Catherine
    Clément, 5, 16, 30–1, 41–3,
    146
Clausen, Jeanette. *See* Cafferty,
    Helen, and Jeanette Clausen
Clément, Catherine. *See* Cixous,
    Hélène, and Catherine Clément
coalition collaborations (Laird),
    47–8, 53, 59, 60

Coe, Richard M., 15
Coghill, Nevill, 86, 88
Coleridge, Samuel Taylor. *See*
    Wordsworth, William, and
    Samuel Taylor Coleridge
collaboration: and allusion,
    143–6; in autobiography,
    95–6; and bibliographical
    practice, 27, 75–6, 92, 98;
    cross-cultural, 134–5, 168,
    171–82; defined, 4–5, 158–60;
    discouragement of in the
    university, 14, 40, 53, 55–6,
    59–60, 183–5, 187–8; ethics
    of, 186–7; face-to-face encoun-
    ter in, 129–30, 176, 187; and
    friendship, 10, 47, 54; fusion
    theory of, 7, 21, 38, 42, 60,
    134; history of women's, 62–
    94; idealization of, 6, 7, 9, 15,
    18–20, 38, 40, 52–3, 54, 58,
    146, 165; and Italian femi-
    nism, 43–7; and lesbianism,
    51–2, 60, 62, 69, 90–1, 92–3,
    140–2, 144–5; materialist
    approaches to, 23–4, 25, 28; in
    maths and sciences, 39–40;
    and pedagogy, 44, 184–7; and
    poststructuralist theory, 8,
    25–8, 30, 32–6; pronoun use
    in, 54, 73–4, 149; property
    issues in, 7–8, 48, 58–9,
    69–70, 95, 108–9, 116–17,
    122–4, 131–2, 150–1, 155,
    177–9, 184–5; statement-
    response format of, 30, 111, 120,
    137–8, 139, 155, 177; technol-

ogy and, 187; tendency to separate individual contributions to, 7–8, 14, 74–7, 89–91, 92

collectives, 159–60, 162–4, 165, 170, 172, 173. *See also* Marxist-Feminist Literature Collective; Milan Women's Bookstore Collective

Collis, Maurice, 87, 88, 89, 90

Cooper, Edith. *See* Bradley, Katherine, and Edith Cooper

copyright law, 65, 76–7, 179

Cronin, John, 86, 89–90

Curley, Thomas M., 67

Day the Sheep Turned Pink, The (Ditton and Ford), 167, 170

'Death of the Author, The' (Barthes), 8, 22, 26, 35, 99

de Lauretis, Teresa, 16, 45

Demau group, 45

Derrida, Jacques, 8, 26, 33–4

Dever, Maryanne, 91–3

Diotima group, 44

Ditton, Cordelia, and Maggie Ford, 167–70

Docherty, Thomas, 29

'Double Negative' (Marlatt and Warland), 119, 137, 138–9, 140, 142–3, 144–7, 148, 151–3, 154

DuBois, Ellen Carol, et al., 61

Dyer, Richard, 34–5

Eagleton, Terry, 58

Early Modern collaboration, 11–12, 13, 27, 65–7, 74

Ede, Lisa, and Andrea Lunsford, 15, 17–18, 54–6, 59, 65, 87, 95, 120

Egan, Susanna, 173, 177

eighteenth-century collaboration, 67–8

Elbrecht, Joyce, and Lydia Fakundiny, 7–8, 21

Eldershaw, Flora. *See* Barnard, Marjorie, and Flora Eldershaw

Eldershaw, M. Barnard. *See* Barnard, Marjorie, and Flora Eldershaw

Ellis, Havelock, 75

entrustment, 46, 52, 130

Faderman, Lillian, 75, 93

Fakundiny, Lydia. *See* Elbrecht, Joyce, and Lydia Fakundiny

Field, Michael. *See* Bradley, Katherine, and Edith Cooper

Fielding, Sarah, 68

Flanders and Swan, 161

Flesh and Paper (Namjoshi and Hanscombe), 91, 104, 125, 136, 137, 138, 139, 140–2, 143–4, 147–8, 148–9

Ford, Maggie. *See* Ditton, Cordelia, and Maggie Ford

Forster, E.M., 143–4

Forte, Jeanie, 161

Foucault, Michel, 8, 22, 24, 26, 27, 28, 31–2, 35, 36, 37, 65, 66, 68, 70, 90, 99, 120, 123, 125, 153, 163

French and Saunders, 161
Frey, Charles H., 12, 77

Gere, Anne Ruggles, 56
Gerrard, E.D., 17
Gilbert, Sandra M., 16
Gilbert, Sandra M., and Susan
 Gubar, 20–1, 38, 40, 47–51,
 54, 57, 59
Gilligan, Carol, 6, 20
Giovanni, Nikki, 20
Gondal sagas (Brontes), 63
Goodman, Lisbeth, 159–60, 161,
 162, 165, 166, 167
Gray, J.M., 73–4, 77, 78
Griffin, Dustin, 67–8
Griffiths, Linda. *See* Campbell,
 Maria, and Linda Griffiths
Gruppo insegnanti di Milano, 44,
 56
Gruppo pedagogia della
 differenze sessuale, 44
Gubar, Susan. *See* Gilbert, Sandra
 M., and Susan Gubar

Halfbreed (Campbell), 170
Hall, Radclyffe, 141
Hanscombe, Gillian, 99. *See*
 Namjoshi, Suniti, and Gillian
 Hanscombe
Happenstance (Shields), 98
Hedrick, Donald K., 66
Herd, David, 12, 16, 25
Hinds, Leonard, 67
Hollingsworth, Margaret, 158
Hollis, Hilda, 32
Howard, Blanche. *See* Shields,
 Carol, and Blanche Howard

Hoy, Helen, 171–2, 173, 178, 179
Hutcheon, Linda, and Michael
 Hutcheon, 39
hypertext, 24–5, 187

Ingham, David, and Kathleen
 Barnett, 101
Irigaray, Luce, 59

James, Henry, 9–10, 13, 27
Japanese collaborative poetry, 15,
 119, 120, 125, 127
Jaszi, Peter, 76
Jessica (Campbell and Griffiths),
 159, 166, 171, 176, 187
Johnson, Brian, 99
Johnson, Samuel, and Sir Robert
 Chambers, 67–8

Kaplan, Carey, and Ellen Cronan
 Rose, 3, 51–4, 57, 77, 87
Kaplan, Cora, 56–8
Keane, Molly, 89
Kermode, Frank, 58
Knapp, Steven, and Walter Benn
 Michaels, 35
Koch, Kenneth, 12, 120–1, 125,
 127
Koestenbaum, Wayne, 3, 4, 10,
 16–17, 32–3, 62, 69, 97, 122,
 133
Kraus, Charlotte, 15

Laing, Alexander, 72
Laird, Holly, 18, 47, 53, 75, 98
Landow, George P., 14, 25, 187
Larry's Party (Shields), 98
Leavis, F.R., 58

Lee, Vernon, and Kit Anstruther-Thomson, 91, 93
Leonardi, Susan J., and Rebecca A. Pope, 16–17, 21, 59–60
LeRougetel, Amanda, 162
Lewis, Gifford, 86, 87, 88, 89, 90–1
Linked Alive (Michelut et al.), 126–38, 146, 150, 155, 176
Lip Service, 161–2
Lunsford, Andrea. *See* Ede, Lisa, and Andrea Lunsford
Lyrical Ballads (Wordsworth and Coleridge), 122–3, 124

Macherey, Pierre, 79
MacKenzie, Nancy R. *See* O'Meara, Anne, and Nancy R. MacKenzie
Madwoman in the Attic, The (Gilbert and Gubar), 48–9
Mannocchi, Phyllis F., 93
Marlatt, Daphne, and Betsy Warland, 5, 7, 29, 41, 42, 43, 113, 119, 136, 137, 138–9, 140, 141, 142–3, 144–7, 148, 150, 151–6
Martin, Violet [pseud. Martin Ross]. *See* Somerville, Edith, and Violet Martin
Marxist-Feminist Literature Collective, 56–8
Masten, Jeffrey, 11–12, 13, 16, 27–8, 36, 65, 66, 69, 74, 75–6, 81, 92
Mathews, Harry, 12
May, Miriam, and Jamie Shepherd, 119

McGann, Jerome, 23, 25, 27, 28, 29, 32, 75, 122, 157
Meredith, George, 74–5
Michelut, Dore, et al., 126–38, 176
Milan Women's Bookstore Collective, 16, 43, 44, 45–7, 51, 57, 130
Miller, Nancy K., 33–4, 35–6, 166
Mink, JoAnna Stephens. *See* Peck, Elizabeth G.
Mitford, Nancy, 14
Modernist collaboration, 91–3
Monstrous Regiment, 163–4, 168
Monty Python, 162
Moore, George, 75
Moriarty, David J., 83–4
Morrison, Blake, 13
Muraro, Luisa, 44

Nabokov, Vladimir, 13, 14
Namjoshi, Suniti, and Gillian Hanscombe, 91, 104, 125, 136, 137, 138, 139, 140–2, 143–4, 147–9, 150–1, 153
Nesbitt, Paula D., and Linda E. Thomas, 19, 20, 40
No Man's Land (Gilbert and Gubar), 48

O'Meara, Anne, and Nancy R. MacKenzie, 5
O'Neill, John, and Claudia Limbert, 67

Parker and Klein, 161
Pastor, Monica, 182

Paz, Octavio, and Charles
Tomlinson, 123–4, 125–6,
127; and Jacques Roubaud,
Edoardo Sanguineti, and
Charles Tomlinson, 125, 127,
129
Pease, Donald E., 65–6, 69
Peck, Elizabeth G., and JoAnna
Stephens Mink, 18, 19, 20, 40,
48
Perreault, Jeanne, 173–4, 178
Phelan, Shane, 134
Phillips, Katherine, 67
Piternik, Anne B., 39
Pope, Rebecca A. *See* Leonardi,
Susan J., and Rebecca A. Pope
Powell, Violet, 90

Ratchford, Fannie, 63
'Reading and Writing between
the Lines' (Marlatt and
Warland), 154–5
renga, 125–6, 137–8, 139, 146,
150, 155, 176, 187
Robinson, Hilary, 87, 89, 90
Romantic collaboration, 68–70,
121–3, 124
Rose, Ellen Cronan. *See* Kaplan,
Carey, and Ellen Cronan Rose
Rosenblum, Barbara. *See* Butler,
Sandra, and Barbara
Rosenblum
Rule, Jane, 144–5, 147, 152–3

Sackville-West, Vita. *See* Virginia
Woolf
Sattler, Traudel, 46

Schlau, Stacey, and Electa Arenal,
19
Schoenbaum, Samuel, 11, 12, 13,
157
Schuyler, James, 12, 23
Scudery, Madame de, 67, 68
Sensible Footwear, 162
*Sexual Difference: A Theory of
Social-Symbolic Practice* (Milan
Women's Bookstore Collec-
tive), 45–7
Shakespeare, William, 12, 13, 64,
66, 77, 80–1, 182
Shapiro, Laura, 38, 48, 49, 50
Shields, Carol, and Blanche
Howard, 96–110, 112, 113, 186
Sicker, Philip, 13–14
Simon, Linda, 64
Singley, Carol J., and Susan
Elizabeth Sweeney, 18–19, 20,
40
Singular Texts / Plural Authors
(Ede and Lunsford), 15,
17–18, 54–6, 65, 87
Social Sciences and Humanities
Research Council of Canada,
183–4
Somerville, Edith, and Violet
Martin [pseud. Martin Ross],
17, 29, 56, 69, 85–91, 92, 93,
94, 97, 98, 102, 111, 138
Sottosopra (Milan Women's
Bookstore Collective), 44
Spivak, Gayatri, 34
Stedman, Edmund, 72–3
Stein, Gertrude, and Alice B.
Toklas, 64, 91

Stillinger, Jack, 21–3, 27, 122, 157

Stone, Albert E., 95–6

Stone Diaries, The (Shields), 98–9, 102

Sturge Moore, T., and D. C., 73, 75, 76

Sturgeon, Mary, 75

'Subject to Change' (Marlatt and Warland), 5–6, 154–6

Swann: A Mystery (Shields), 98, 99

Sweeney, Susan Elizabeth. *See* Singley, Carol J., and Susan Elizabeth Sweeney

Terry, Megan, 162

Theatre Passe Muraille, 166, 170, 172, 173

Thirteen Hands (Shields), 99

Thomas, Linda E. *See* Nesbit, Paula D., and Linda E. Thomas

Thompson, Paul, 166, 168, 170, 172, 173, 175, 176, 178, 180–1

Tomlinson, Charles. *See* Paz, Octavio, and Charles Tomlinson

Tostevin, Lola Lemire, 137

Trouble and Strife, 165

Two Noble Kinsmen, The (Shakespeare), 66, 77

Two Women in a Birth (Marlatt and Warland), 7, 29, 113, 136–7, 138–9, 140, 142–3, 144–7, 148, 151–6

Valverde, Mariana, 34

Venema, Kathleen, 172–3, 178, 180, 181

'Waitresses, The' 161

Walker, Cheryl, 32, 35–6

Warland, Betsy. *See* Marlatt, Daphne, and Betsy Warland

'What Is an Author?' (Foucault), 26, 28, 31–2, 35, 70, 90, 99, 123, 125

White, Daniel E., 68

Williams, James S., 64

Williams, Raymond, 23–4, 28, 31, 32, 100, 129

Wilson, Edmund, 13, 14

Winkelman, Carol, 25

Woodmansee, Martha, 65, 69

Woolf, Virginia, 3, 10, 15, 50; and Vita Sackville-West, 63

Wordsworth, William, and Samuel Taylor Coleridge, 13–14, 122–3, 124; and Dorothy Wordsworth, 62

Zivanovic, Judith, 162, 163, 164, 165